Gleeson White

Ballades and Rondeaus

Gleeson White

Ballades and Rondeaus

ISBN/EAN: 9783744785242

Printed in Europe, USA, Canada, Australia, Japan

Cover: Foto ©Thomas Meinert / pixelio.de

More available books at **www.hansebooks.com**

BALLADES AND RON-
DEAUS, CHANTS
ROYAL, SESTINAS, VIL-
LANELLES, &c., SELECTED
BY GLEESON WHITE.

LONDON:

WALTER SCOTT, LIMITED,

PATERNOSTER SQUARE.

NEW YORK: 3 EAST FOURTEENTH STREET.

To

Robert Louis Stevenson.

THE crowning pleasure in the compilation of this book is the permission to dedicate it to you, and this token of personal admiration is not without special fitness, since you were among the earliest to experiment in these French rhythms, and to introduce CHARLES D'ORLÉANS *and* FRANÇOIS VILLON *to the majority of English readers.*

" Those old French ways of verse making that have been coming into fashion of late. Surely they say a pretty thing more prettily for their quaint old-fashioned liberty! That TRIOLET *—how deliciously impertinent it is! is it not? . . . The variety of dainty modes wherein by shape and sound a very pretty something is carved out of nothing at all. Their fantastic surprises, the ring of their bell-like returns upon themselves, their music of triangle and cymbal. In some of them poetry seems to approach the nearest possible to bird-song—to unconscious seeming through most unconscious art, imitating the carelessness and impromptu of forms as old as the existence of birds, and as new as every fresh individual joy in each new generation, growing their own feathers, and singing their own song, yet always the feathers of their kind, and the song of their kind."*—

"Home Again."—GEORGE MACDONALD.

INDEX.

RONDELS.

RONDEAUS.

THE SICILIAN OCTAVE.

ROUNDELS.

SESTINAS.

TRIOLETS.

VILLANELLES.

VIRELAI.

VIRELAI NOUVEAU.

BURLESQUES, ETC.

PREFACE.

THIS anthology is chosen entirely from poems written in the traditional fixed forms of the *ballade, chant royal, kyrielle, rondel, rondeau, rondeau redoublé, sestina, triolet, villanelle,* and *virelai,* with the addition of the *pantoum.* That such a choice is the result of circumstances it is needless to point out, since only those that had found favour with English writers were available for the purpose. So far as I know, this collection is the first of its sort, although Mr. W. Davenport Adams' *Latter Day Lyrics* included a section chosen on the same lines. Having, in company, no doubt, with many others, a genuine regard for the group Mr. Adams included there, I had long hoped to see a more ample compilation of later work in this school ; but notwithstanding the steady increase in the number of poems written in the forms systematically arranged herein, the ground remained unoccupied, until the appearance of this book ; which may fairly claim to be the first in the field, since no other volume has devoted its whole space to them, save in the rarer cases, where an author has published a collection of original poems cast in one mould, notably Mr. Swinburne's *Century of Roundels* and Mr. Andrew Lang's *Ballades in Blue China.*

In Mr. Adams' volume another valuable feature was the *Note on some Foreign forms of Verse* by Mr. Austin Dobson, which many years since introduced to me the laws of the various forms and created my special interest in them. It is no derogation to the charming group in the former volume to say of the present collection, that it far exceeds its predecessor in number and variety, for now there is a wide field to choose from, whereas Mr. Adams was then limited to a selection from the small number extant.

The rules which Mr. Austin Dobson was the first to formulate in English are made the basis (side by side with the treatises of M. de Gramont, M. de Banville, and other authorities) of the following chapter on the rules of the various forms. Lest a name so intimately associated with the introduction of the old French metrical shapes in English poetry should appear to be brought in to add weight to my own attempt, and the reputation of a master invoked for the work of one who at furthest can but style himself an apprentice, I must ask that this necessary tribute to Mr. Dobson's labours be taken only as an apology for so freely using his material, and that his ready help is by no means to be regarded in the faintest way as an imprimatur of any statements in this prefatory matter, save those quoted avowedly and directly from his writings.

It may be best to name at once the authorities who have been consulted in the preparation of the introductory chapter. These include the French treatises of De Banville, De Gramont, and Jullienne, Mr. Saintsbury's *Short History of French Literature*, Mr. Hueffers' *Troubadours*, an article by Mr. Gosse in the *Cornhill Magazine*, July 1877, *Les Villanelles* by M. Joseph Boulmier, *The Rhymester* of Mr. Brander Matthews, and many occasional papers on the various forms that have appeared in English and American periodicals. To arrange in one chapter the materials gathered from these and other sources is all that I have attempted. If at times the need to crowd enough matter for a volume into the limits of a few pages results in a want of lucidity, I must plead the necessity imposed by limited space. To those who, by their kindly permission, have allowed their poems to be quoted here, the thanks that I can offer are as hearty as the expression of my gratitude is brief. The somewhat onerous task of obtaining consent from about two hundred authors has been turned to a pleasure, by the evidence of interest taken in this, the first collection of the later growth of this branch of poetic art. Nor did the help cease with the loan of the poems ; in many instances a correspondence followed that brought to light fresh material, both for the body of the book and the introductory chapter, and rendered assistance not easy to over-value. If any writer is quoted without direct permission, it was through no want of effort to trace him, excepting in the case of a very few that reached me in the shape of newspaper cuttings, wholly devoid of any clue to the locality of the writer. To Mr. Austin Dobson my best thanks are due. From Mr. Andrew Lang and Mr. Edmund Gosse I have also appropriated material, acknowledged as often as practicable ; also to my friend, Mr. A. G. Wright, for invaluable help during the rather monotonous task of hunting up and copying at the reading-room of the British Museum ; and to Mr. William Sharp, whose critical advice and generous encouragement throughout have left a debt of gratitude beyond payment.

In a society paper, *The London*, a brilliant series of these poems appeared during 1877-8. After a selection was made for this volume, it was discovered that they were all by *one* author, Mr. W. E. Henley, who most generously permitted the whole of those chosen to appear, and to be for the first time publicly attributed to him. The poems themselves need no apology, but in the face of so many from his pen, it is only right to explain the reason for the inclusion of so large a number.

From America Mr. Brander Matthews and Mr. Clinton Scollard have shown sympathy with the collection, not only by permitting their works to be cited, but also by calling my attention to poems by authors almost unknown in England ; while all those writers who in the new world are using the old shapes with a peculiar freshness and vigour, gave ready assent to the demand.

To Messrs. Cassell & Co., for allowing poems that appeared in *Cassell's Family Magazine* (those by Miss Ada Louise Martin and Mr. G. Weatherley) ; to Messrs. Longman, for liberty to quote freely from the many graceful examples that appeared in *Longman's Magazine ;* to Messrs. Kegan Paul, Trench, & Co., for endorsing Mr. Andrew Lang's permission to include specimens from *Rhymes à la Mode* and *Ballades in Blue China*, the utmost thanks are due for the courtesy shown ; also to the proprietors of the *Century Magazine*, where so many of the American poems (many since collected by the authors in their own volumes) first appeared ; and to Messrs Harper for permission to use Mr. Coleman's *Sestina*, and Mr.

Graham R. Tomson's *Ballade of the Bourne,* which first appeared in their popular monthly. The poems that are cited by the courtesy of Mr. John Payne appear respectively in *Songs of Life and Death* (W. H. Allen & Co.), *New Poems* (ditto), and *Poems by François Villon* (Reeves & Turner), now out of print.

Having named so many who have lent aid, it is but fair to exonerate them from any blame for errors that, no doubt, in spite of the utmost care, may have crept in. In view of a later edition, I should be glad to be informed of any additional data of the use of the forms in English verse, which, if quoted, would add to the value of the collection, or to have any erroneous statements corrected.

Notwithstanding the many shortcomings of my own share in the production of this volume, I cannot doubt but that the charm of the poems themselves will endear it to readers; and as a lover of the "Gallic bonds," I venture to hope it may do some little towards their complete naturalisation in our tongue.

GLEESON WHITE.

August 1887.

NOTES
ON THE EARLY USE OF THE VARIOUS FORMS.

SOME NOTES ON THE EARLY USE OF THE VARIOUS FORMS, AND RULES FOR THEIR CONSTRUCTION.

IN the limited space available, it is hardly possible to give more than a very crude sketch of the origin of these forms; but some reference to early Provençal literature is inevitable, since the nucleus of not a few of them can be traced among the intricate rhyming of the Troubadours. Yet it would be beyond the purpose to go minutely into the enticing history of that remarkable period, nor is it needful to raise disputed questions regarding the origin of each particular fashion. The number of books on Provençal subjects is great, the mere enumeration of the names of those in the library of the British Museum would fill several pages. The language itself has a fascination which allures many to disaster, for as Mr. Hueffer points out, it "looks at first sight so like the Latin and more familiar Romance languages that it offers special temptations" to guess at its meaning, with very doubtful success.

The term Provençal is usually applied to a dialect more correctly known as "the Langue d'Oc, which, with the Langue d'Oil, forms the two divisions of the Romance language spoken in the country we now know as France;" but Mr. Saintsbury remarks that, strictly speaking, the Langue d'Oc should not be called "French" at all, since it is hardly more akin to the Langue d'Oil than it is to Spanish and Italian, and that those who spoke it applied the term " French " to northern speech, calling their own Limousin, or Provençal, or Auvergnat. The limits where it prevailed extended far beyond Provence itself. Authorities differ with regard to the exact boundaries. It will suffice for the present purpose to take those Mr. Hueffer adopts—namely, the district within a boundary formed by a line drawn from the mouth of the Gironde to that of the Saone, in the north, while the southern limit includes parts of Spain, such as Aragon, Valencia, Catalonia, and the Balearic Islands.

Herr Karl Bartsch, the eminent historian of Provençal literature, divides it into three periods:—the first, to the end of the eleventh century; the second, which is the one that marks the most flourishing time of the poetry of the Troubadours, extending over the twelfth and thirteenth; and the third period—of its decadence—in the fourteenth and fifteenth centuries. To this may be added the attempt to revive it in our own day, by the school of the so-called *Félibres,* including Mistral, Aubanel, Alphonse Daudet, and others, who have worked vigorously, and with no mean success, to produce a modern literature in the old dialect, worthy of its former dignity. In this preface it is impossible to mention any part of the prose of this marvellous literature, which sprang almost suddenly into a gigantic growth, that has been a fruitful theme for wonder and admiration ever since, and left its influence widely felt. The point that is to the purpose here, concerns the invention by the Provençal poets of many set forms of verse, some few of which are still written, but most so altered and renewed by later use, that their original character is well-nigh obscured. The forms included in this book are often erroneously attributed *en masse* to the *jongleurs* of Provence, yet few assumptions are less true. Altered by the Trouvères, the fifteenth century poets, the Ronsardists, and later writers, it is safer to assign to the Troubadours only the germs which evolved gradually into their now matured forms. To linger over the extraordinary period is a temptation hard to dismiss; the very name still has a flavour of romance, and brings a curious medley of images to the mind when it is heard, many perhaps as far from the actual Provençal Troubadour as *Nanki-Poo* in the "*Mikado*" is from the wandering minstrel of the court of King Thibaut. Of the Troubadours who have come down to fame, four hundred and sixty are recorded by name, besides two hundred and fifty-one pieces that have survived without evidence of their authors. King Richard I. (our own Cœur de Lion), Guillem de Cabestanh, Peire Vidal, Bertran de Born, The Monk of Montaudon, and many others, have biographical sketches of exceeding interest allotted to them in Mr. Hueffer's "The Troubadours." A halo of romance has gathered round their names, and thrown a glamour over the record of their lives; to read their history is to be transported to a region where all topics but love and song are deemed unimportant trifles, unless the old chroniclers are singularly untruthful in their state-ments. We know now-a-days many a young poet's crushed life appears only in his verses, and outside those he appears but an average Philistine to vulgar eyes. Perhaps the "land of the nightingale and rose" was not so idyllic as its historians paint it; but with every deduction, there yet remains evidence of an exceptional importance attached to the arts, more especially to that of song. To those who wrote, or rather sang, witty impromptus (made often, we can but fancy, with much labour beforehand), or produced dainty conceits in elaborate rhymes and rhythms, when sound came perilously near triumphing over sense, a welcome was extended, as widespread and far more personal in its application than even that accorded to our modern substitute for the troubadour—the popular novelist. The doings of the Courts of Love, set down in sober chronicles, are hardly less fantastic than Mr. Gilbert's ingenious operas. Matters of the most sentimental and amorous character were debated in public, with all the earnestness of a question of state. That their poetry was singularly limited in its character there is little doubt, but Mr. Hueffer declares that it had its serious side, often lost sight of, and that no small portion was devoted to stately and dignified subjects. Mr. Lowell, on the other hand, in an essay on Chaucer in *My Study Windows*, says—

"'Their poetry is purely lyric in its most narrow sense, that is, the expression of personal and momentary moods. To the fancy of the critics who take their cue from tradition, Provence is a morning sky of early summer, out of which innumerable larks rain a faint melody (the sweeter because rather half divined than heard too distinctly) over an earth where the dew never dries and the flowers never fade. But when we open Raynouard it is like opening the door of an aviary. We are deafened and confused by a hundred minstrels singing the same song at once, and more than suspect the flowers they welcome are made of French cambric, spangled with dew-drops of prevaricating glass."

The forms in which the Provençal poets wrote were chiefly these :—The oldest was called *vers*, and consisted of octosyllabic lines arranged in stanzas ; from this grew the *canzo*, with interlaced rhymes—later on with the distinctive feature still prominent in French, but unknown in English poetry, the rhymes *masculine* and *feminine*. The *canzo* was used entirely for subjects of love and gallantry, but the *sirvente*, composed of short stanzas, simply rhyming, and corresponding one to the other, was employed for political and social subjects, sometimes treated seriously, at others satirically. The *tenso* was a curious trial of skill in impromptu versification. Two antagonists met and agreed that the one should reply on the opposite side to any argument the first might select. The opening stanza, chosen at will by the speaker, was imitated in the reply, both in observance of its rhyme and rhythm, the same rhyme-sound being often kept throughout the whole poem. It must not be forgotten that the Langue d'Oc was singularly fertile in rhymes, so that the feat was less arduous than it would be in other tongues. The *alba*, a farewell at morning, and the *serena*, or evening song, the *pastorella*, devoted, as its name implies, to pastoral subjects, appear to govern the themes of the verses rather than the form. There is record, however, of the *breu-doble* (double short), invented by Guirant Riquier, a little form with three rhymes, two of which are repeated twice in three four-lined stanzas, and given once in a concluding couplet, while the third finished each quatrain. The *retroensa* is noticeable for its refrain of more than one line. The sonnet has ceased to be claimed as a Provençal invention, yet it must be noted, as at one time its origin there was a favourite theory. The *ballade*, "a song serving to accompany the dance," must not be confused with the later ballade; and lastly, the greatest in most respects, the *sestina*, which, as it occurs among the poems noticed technically later on, need not be further mentioned here.

" The artificial verse-forms of Provence include some as peculiar and arbitrary as ever issued from the brain of Persian poet—verse-forms by the side of which the metrical glitter of *ballade, chant royal, rondeau, rondel, triolet, virelai* and *villanelle* must pale," says a writer in the *Westminster Review* (October 1878), and instances the *tenso* and the *sestina* in proof of his assertion. Mr. Hueffer also treats the *chant royal* as mere child's play beside the intricate feats displayed by the Troubadours. The above short list shows many examples of forms using the refrain and some other features preserved in Northern poetry ; but the debt owed by the North to the Troubadours is far less, according to later writers, than that assigned to Provençal influence some few years ago. Mr. Saintsbury says that " poems called *rondeaux* and *ballades*, of loose construction and undecided form, began to make their appearance at the end of the twelfth and beginning of the thirteenth century," but the forms as we know them owe their present shape to their reformation in Northern France, culminating in the poems of Charles d'Orléans and François Villon. In this revival, the *lai* and *pastourelle* kept their Provençal titles, but were made much more exact in form, and never attained the widespread celebrity of the newer shapes, which are to all intents and purposes the models for the forms in this volume, save the *sestina*, which is practically an Italian, and the *pantoum*, an Eastern form.

There is no space here to notice more than the names of a few of even the most prominent of the poets who succeeded the Provençal singers in their use of these forms. There are thousands of ballades in MSS. in the Royal French Library, by known and unknown writers. Eustache Deschamps (1328-1415), a friend of Chaucer's, " has left no less than 1175 ballades. Rondeaus, virelais, etc., also proceeded in great numbers from his pen ; also an important *Art of Poetry*, a treatise rendered at once necessary and popular by the fashion of artificial rhyming."* Some of the earliest ballades and rondel-triolets bear the name of Jehan Froissart (1337-1410), the chronicler. Messire Guy de la Tremouille, according to Mr. Gosse, is supposed to have

* See Saintsbury's *Short History of French Literature*, p. 103.

been the first to devise the elaborate rules of construction of the ballade, which have been in force ever since. He was guard of the Oriflamme in 1383, and died in 1398; but Deschamps is more often credited with the honour. That he cultivated the form we know, besides writing an "Art of making Chansons, Ballades, Virelais, and Rondels," which is a valuable relic of his time. Jehannot de Lescurel, "of whom absolutely nothing is known, has left sixteen ballades, fifteen rondeaus (not in regular form), and other pieces, said to be 'of singular grace, lightness, and elegance.'"

Guillaume de Machault (1284-1377) was also a voluminous writer. One of his poems, a *chanson balladée*, is printed in Mr. Saintsbury's *Short History of French Literature*, which contains also a *Ballade* by Alain Chartier (1390-1458), the hero of the famous story of the kiss of Queen Margaret of Scotland, and other specimens of this period, in a succinct and trustworthy account of the growth of French poetry, surpassed by no book in our own language.

Charles d'Orléans (1391-1466), noticed among the English writers, is specially honoured as the master of the rondel; while François Villon (1431-1485) stands out as the "prince of all ballade-makers." For brief, but splendid sketches of these two, Mr. R. L. Stevenson's *Familiar Studies of Men and Books* should be consulted, while for more prosaic description there is no lack of data. Since the revival of interest in Villon, France has done tardy but unstinted honour to her most famous poet, as it is the fashion just now to style him, but there is a doubt whether the praise given is not in danger of being exaggerated. Yet, making all allowances, there is vital humanity in his wondrous writings, that now, after four hundred years, read as living and modern in their presentation of life, as though they were by a realist of our own day. In Villon, student, poet, housebreaker, we find the forerunner of the Zola of to-day—one who, in so eminently an artificial form as the ballade, cast aside all conventional restraints, and sang of what he saw and knew, It is much to be regretted that space forbids more translations of his poems to be included in this collection. For those who wish to tackle him in his old, and by no means easy, French, a good edition is published for a franc, in the *Collection Jannet-Picard (Paris).* Mr. Payne has translated the whole of his authentic works into English in a volume, at present out of print, which contains also a very graphic and full biography of this remarkable man. Space forbids insertion of the sketch of his life prepared for this chapter. Born in 1431, student 1448, B.A. in 1452, writing his *Lesser Testament* in 1446, his *Greater Testament* in 1461 ; in those few years he contrived to win more fame, and, to speak truly, more infamy, than a whole generation of lesser poets. He was condemned to die—he wrote his marvellous *Ballade of the Gibbet* while lying under sentence of death—but escaped. Where he died is unknown, the date of his *Greater Testament* being the last record of Master François Villon of Paris.

In 1493 appeared *L'art et science de rhéthorique pour faire rigmes et ballades*, by Henry de Croï—an invaluable treatise on French Poetics. The works of Pierre Gringoire (1478-1544) must be named, if only for the fact of De Banville's splendid ballade in his comedy " Gringoire," founded on an incident in the poet's life. By Mr. Lang's permission a translation is quoted in the body of this volume. Mr. John Payne also englished it, in the *Dublin University Magazine*, 1879. The works of Clement Marot (1497-1544) demand special note, since his *ballades* and *chants royaux* are now accepted as the ideal models for imitation.

In his *Art Poëtique*, 1555, Thomas Sibilet reviews

many of the former writers, and gives the rules of the poetry then in force. Immediately after this date came another change; with the famous school of Ronsard (1524-1585) and the *Pléiade*, as they are styled, one of whom, however, Du Bellay, was eager to abolish the *ballade* and *chant royal* in favour of the *sonnet.* The members of this group produced some notable work in strict forms. Among the Ronsardists we find Grévin the dramatist, who wrote some graceful poems which he called *Villanesques*—a modified form of the *Villanelle*—and Jean Passerat (1534-1602) who is specially noteworthy, since in his hand the *Villanelle* crystallised into its present shape, Joseph Boulmier, in the last revival, making this form his special study, and writing all his verses after Passerat's model given elsewhere in this volume.

The rondeau was revived in great splendour in the middle of the seventeenth century. Foremost among the brilliant group is Voiture (1598-1648), the acknowledged master of this form. Only thirty of his rondeaus are left, but each one of these is a masterpiece, and may be studied for all the subtle devices and dainty inventions that the form has yet yielded. Benserade (1612-1691) and Sarrasin were also famous for rondeau-making, the former translating the whole of Ovid's *Metamorphoses* into rondeaus, which were sumptuously printed at the King's Press at a cost of 10,000 francs. When Voiture died in 1648, it is curious to note that Sarrasin wrote a " pompous funereal poem—possibly the most funny serious elegy ever composed—in which, among other strange mourners, he makes the 'poor little triolet,' all in tears, trot by the side of the dead poet," who, according to Mr. Gosse, from whom the above paragraph is quoted, had never written one in his life. Sarrasin also left a curious specimen of the *Glose*, written on the famous Sonnet "de IOB" by Benserade.   In

1649 Gérard de Saint Amant wrote a volume of sixty-four triolets. From the seventeenth to the nineteenth century no important examples occur. About thirty years ago De Banville revived these old shapes, and initiated a movement that Daudet, Glatigny, Boulmier, and a host of others have helped forward, so that now modern French literature is flooded with examples of the forms—the ballade, rondeau, and triolet being the most widely used.

Having imperfectly followed the growth of the forms in France, it will be interesting to give a few notes of the various attempts made to acclimatise some in England. Although no effort previous to 1873 warrants us in claiming an English pedigree for them, yet it is curious to see how often the attempt was made to write them in our own tongue. The sonnet gradually grew into use, until it became as little an exotic as the potato, to employ an uncouth simile ; the ballade and rondeau—hardly more formal in their rules, and with susceptibilities of infinite grace and beauty—failed to be even residents amongst us, much less naturalised subjects, sharing the rights and duties of citizens. Chaucer is believed to have used these forms, as in "The Legend of Good Women" he says, speaking of himself—

> " Many a himpne for your holy daies
>   That highten balades, roundels, virelaies."

His " Balade de Vilage sauns Peynture," however, does not correspond with the accepted form. Mr. Gosse says that the Chaucer of 1651 contains a number of poems attributed to himself and Lydgate " which are merely pieces in rhyme-royal, so arranged as to imitate the French ballade : without its severity of form."

The following is a roundel attributed to Chaucer :—

I.—BURDEN.

So hath your beauty fro your hertè chased
　Pitee, that mee availeth not to pleyne ;
　For daunger* halt your mercy in his cheyne.

II.

Giltles my deth thus have ye purchased,
　I sey you soth, me nedcth not to fayne ;
So hath, etc.

III.

Alas, that Nature hath in you compassed
　So grete beaute, that no man may atteyne
　To mercy, though he stewet for the peyne.
So hath, etc.

This is given in Furnival's *Trial-Forewords to Chaucer's Minor Poems*, and is especially interesting in connection with the history of the forms in English use.

Of his immediate followers, Lydgate, a monk of Bury, author of *London Lyckpenny*, is said by Guest to have written a "roundle," and one by Thomas Occleve is printed in Morley's *Shorter English Poems*.

John Gower (1340-1408), author of *Confessio Amantis*, at the coronation of Henry IV. presented the king with a collection of fifty *Ballades*, written in the Provençal manner, "to entertain his noble court." The thin oblong MS., on vellum, which contains them is still extant in the Marquis of Stafford's library at Trentham, and in 1818 it was printed for the Roxburghe Club ; but as the poems are unfortunately written in French, they do not assist in supporting a claim for the early use of the form in England. Professor Henry Morley has translated one for his *English Writers;* it follows the rhymes accurately, but has a somewhat trite subject. A critic has well said of it, that the poets of Gowers's day "were not burdened with solving 'the riddle of

---

* Dominicn, power.　　　† Sterve.

the painful earth.'   It may be that a good deal of
their guileless delight in things fresh and young was
feigned, but then so is much of our more pretentious
philosophy." From its special interest it is quoted here—

> Winter departs, and comes the flowery May,
>   And round from cold to heat the seasons fly;
> The bird that to its nest had lost the way
>   Rebuilds it that he may rejoice thereby.
>   Like change in my love's world I now descry,
> With such a hope I comfort myself here,
>   And you, my lady, on this truth rely:
> When grief departs the coming joys are near.
>
> My lady sweet, by that which now I say
>   You may discover how my heart leaps high,
> That serves you, and has served you many a day,
>   As it will serve you daily till I die.
>   Remember, then, my lady, knowing why,
> That my desire for you will never veer
>   As God wills that it be, so be our tie:
> When grief departs the coming joys are near.
>
> The day that news of you came where I lay,
>   It seem'd there was no grief could make me sigh;
> Wherefore of you, dear lady mine, I pray
>   By your own message—when you will, not I—
>   Send me what you think best as a reply
> Wherewith my heart can keep itself from fear;
>   And, lady, search the reason of my cry—
> When grief departs the coming joys are near.
>
> *Envoy.*
>
> O noble Dame, to you this note shall hie,
>   And when God wills I follow to my dear.
> This writing speaks, and says, till I am by,
>   When grief departs the coming joys are near.

John Shirley, who lived about 1440, made a collection
of *Ballades, Roundels, Virelais,* and Tragedies, in MSS..
which are still extant in the Ashmolean Museum at
Oxford. After noticing Gower, who wrote ballades in

French, Charles d'Orléans, who wrote rondels in English, comes as another instance of the early use, but again as a mere exception, since the accident which led both writers to adopt exotic forms is outside the history of our native poetry, and cannot be brought forward to prove their early naturalisation. Of Charles d'Orléans much might be said worth saying, but there are so many sources of information open, that here we need note only the poems written during his captivity. He is said to have been our prisoner for about twenty-five years, and during that time to have acquired a taste for our language. The Abbé Sallier, who unearthed the manuscript of his poems in the Royal Library at Paris during the last century, says he wrote but two in English; but in the MS. at the British Museum, the Rev. H. F. Cary, the translator of Dante, found three, quoted in his *Early French Poets* (Bohn, 1846). The editor of that volume, the Rev. Henry Cary, son of the author, mentions in a footnote a large collection among the Harleian MSS., attributed to Charles d'Orléans, but throws doubt on their being more than translations. Into this question there is no space to enter. These are the three from Cary's book:—

> Go forth, my hert, with my lady;
> Loke that ye spar no bysines
> To serve her with such lolyness
> That ye gette her oftyme prively
> That she kepe truly her promes.
> Go forth, etc.

> I must, as a helis-body,[*]
> Abyde alone in hevynes;
> And ye that dwell with your mastris
> In plaisaunce glad and mery,
> Go forth, etc.

[*] *Helis-body*—One deprived of health or happiness.

My hertly love is in your governīs,
And ever shall whill that I live may.
I pray to God I may see that day
That ye be knyt with trouthful alyans.
Ye shall not fynd feyning or variaunce
As in my part ; that wyl I truly say.
My hertly, etc.

Bewere, my trewe innocent hert,
How ye hold with her aliauns,
That somtym with word of plesūns
Resceyved you under covert.
Thynke how the stroke of love comsmert*
Without warnyng or deffiauns.
Bewere, my, etc.

And ye shall pryvely or appert
See her by me in loves dauns,
With her faire femenyn contenauns
Ye shall never fro her astert.
Bewere, my, etc.

Spenser (1553-1599) is said (but I cannot trace the authority) to have used some of these forms. Again, Sir Philip Sidney's (1554-1586) famous ditty, "My true love hath my heart," recalls the rondel, but cannot claim to be one. Drummond of Hawthornden (1585-1649) has a fine sestina (too long for quotation), "Sith gone is my delight and ouly pleasure."

The Trivial Poems, and Triolets of Patrick Carey deserve mention. This volume was unknown until the beginning of the present century, although dated Warnefurd, 1651. The poems were brought into notice by Sir Walter Scott, who obtained the MSS. from John Murray, and after inserting a few in the *Edinburgh Annual Register*, 1810, published the whole for the first time in 1819. The following specimen is taken from Scott's reprint, p. 43 :—

Worldly designes, feares, hopes, farwell !
Farwell all earthly joyes and cares !

* *Comsmert*—Can smart, or comes smart.

> On nobler thoughts my soule shall dwell
> Worldly designes, feares, hopes, farwell !
> Att quiett, in my peacefull cell,
> I'le thincke on God, free from your snares ;
> Worldly designes, feares, hopes, farwell !
> Farwell all earthly joyes and cares.

In the *Athenæum*, May 7, 1887, is a long article on Carey, signed C. F. S. Warner, M.A. Charles Cotton, the friend of Izaak Walton, wrote a rondeau, "a very ungallant example," cited in Dr. Guests' *History of English Rhythms*. There is also one unquotable, by reason of its subject, among the correspondence of Alexander Pope (1638-1744), and in the *Rolliad*, 1784, a volume of satires in prose and verse, that enjoyed a great popularity for a time, there is a set of five rondeaus, written in pure form after the Voiture model. They satirise North, Eden, Pitt, and Dorset, and are perfect in construction, and vigorous in their ridicule. The popularity of these effusions led to many imitations in the periodical prints at the beginning of this century, few, however, of sufficient merit to be worth reviving. By the courtesy of Mr. Austin Dobson, the owner, I am able to extract a specimen from a scarce and little-known book, entitled *Rondeaulx ; translated from the Black Letter French Edition of 1527, by J. R. Best, Esq.* :—

Rondeaulx en Nombre trois cens cinquante.
Singuliers et a tous propos. Nouvellement
Imprimez a Paris. Avec Privelege
On les bend en la grant salle du palays au
Premier pillier en la boutique de Galliot du
Pre marchaut librarie jure de Luniversite.

The dedication to Robert Studley Vidal, Esq., is dated 1838. The first poem is preceded by a quaint apology, that unfortunately is too long to quote, but the rondeau itself, if its rhythm is faulty and its

language ungraceful, shows that the original had
sterling advice to offer, and that the translator was
not ignorant of the true rules of the form.

UNG BON RONDEAU

A good rondeau I was induced to show
To some fair ladies some short while ago;
   Well knowing their ability and taste,
    I asked, should ought be added or effac'd,
And prayed that every fault they'd make me know

The first did her most anxious care bestow
To impress one point from which I ne'er should go:
   " Upon a good beginning must be based
       A good rondeau."

Zeal bid the other's choicest language glow:
She softly said, " Recount your weal or woe,
   Your every subject free from pause or haste:
   Ne'er let your hero fail, nor be disgraced."
The third—" With varying emphasis should flow
       A good rondeau."

In Mr. Oxenford's *Book of French Songs,* now published
with Miss Costello's *Specimens of the Early Poetry of
France,* in a volume of the *Chandos Classics,* there
is one ballade given (with its original French, both
without envoy); but although noting the peculiarity
that each stanza has the same terminations, Mr.
Oxenford has not kept it in his translation, nor has
Miss Costello, in a numerous collection of ballades,
rondels, lais, and other forms, once paraphrased them
accurately, usually varying even the refrain; nor can I
see, in her voluminous notes, that she draws attention
to this important feature, although she gives the
particulars of the eccentricities of rhyming known as
Fraternisée, Brisée, and the like, and condemns their
triviality rather strongly. In the edition before me no
date is given; the authoress died in 1870. The oft-quoted
Rondeau by Leigh Hunt is so beautiful in itself that

all its shortcomings in the matter of form may be readily pardoned, and if—but the saving clause is great—others as beautiful could be built on the same shape, a "Leigh Hunt" variation would be a welcome addition to the forms in English ; but it is no *rondeau*, and has not the faintest claim to be so styled. Probably it is familiar to all readers, but in case even one should not know it, it is quoted here :—

> " Jenny kissed me when we met,
>   Jumping from the chair she sat in.
> Time, you thief, who love to get
>   Sweets upon your list, put that in !
> Say I'm weary, say I'm sad ;
>   Say that health and wealth have missed me ;
> Say I'm growing old, but add—
>   Jenny kissed me."

If Mr. Swinburne's examples of the forms in his earlier volumes be not counted (since he then ignored many of the rules that, as his later books show, he can use with such splendid mastery), to Mr. Andrew Lang's *Lays and Lyrics of Old France* (Longman, 1872) must be assigned the honour of leading the way in the reproduction in English of the old French metrical forms, made in conformance to their ascertained laws. How far that volume led the way to the modern employment of these forms for original poetry in our own tongue, is not so easily proved. One thing, at least, is certain, that Mr. Austin Dobson, Mr. Edmund Gosse, Mr. W. E. Henley, Mr. Payne, and one or two other writers, were each, unknown to the rest, trying the new measures. In the words of one of these, " the study of French literature was in the air ; " and naturally, as we now see, the new movement began simultaneously to adapt its rules to English conditions. To Mr. Bridges belongs the honour of printing the first Triolet in modern English ; but he expressly disclaims being looked upon as the apostle for the naturalisation of the exotic forms, for which he had no peculiar sympathy, and after his *Poems*, 1873, ceased to use. So little were his experiments appreciated, that their presence in his volume was considered prejudicial to its success, by competent authorities of the day, who little foresaw the rapid growth that would so soon spring up. To Mr. Austin Dobson is assigned the first *ballade*, "The Prodigals;" to Mr. Edmund Gosse the first *villanelle* and *chant royal;* and to Mr. W. E. Henley the first *double ballade*, and a few other variations. But it is most likely that the priority of some of these was due to the mere accident of publication, and that it is more near the truth to regard the whole as a contemporaneous movement toward French rhythms, thought out and experimented upon by many writers, ignorant of the fact that they were not alone in the study, and that others were working upon the same lines. One of the first who made trial of these French rhythms has (I believe) never published any ; yet examples of their use by the author of *A Child's Garden of Verse* would have added greatly to the interest of this collection, but the author has willed that they should remain unquoted, so I can only regret their absence.

From 1873 to 1877 a fair number had appeared, but these were produced almost entirely by the writers already named. From 1877, however, the number of those who made them increased rapidly. In that year Mr. Dobson's *Proverbs in Porcelain* was published, containing a series of these forms, which, as internal evidence of much subsequent work shows, have been accepted as typical models to be followed in their English use. The series in *The London* noticed elsewhere, during this year and 1878, also increased their popularity, while the later English use may be traced to some extent by the examples here collected. In America about the same time the new fashion in verse-making was taken up very warmly, and to the present day the Americans have shown themselves more cordial towards the Gallic measures than even our own country-men. In the popular periodicals of the United States there are more specimens than in our English magazines, and the appearance of so many examples in this book show that the American poets have caught a great deal of the peculiar quality, hard to define but easy to recognise, which the forms demand. Then came Mr. W. Davenport Adams's *Latter Day Lyrics*, with a section devoted to these forms, and "A Note on Some Foreign Forms of Verse," by Mr. Dobson. Since then the poems written in these styles have been increasing in number, until the idea of collecting them in one volume, long in my mind, was favourably entertained by Mr. William Sharp, the general editor of the series in which this book appears.

The taste for these *tours de force* in the art of verse-making is no doubt an acquired one; yet to quote the first attempt to produce a lyric with a repeated bur-den would take one back to the earliest civilisation. The use of the refrain and conventional arrangement of rhyme in these forms differs as widely from the burdens of the old examples, as the purely conven-tional design of Greek art from the savage patterns of its ancestral stock. Whether the first refrains were used for decorative effect only, or to give the singer time to recollect or to improvise the next verse, it matters little, since the once mere adjunct was made in later French use an integral and vital part of the verse. The charm of these strictly written verses is undoubtedly increased by some knowledge of their technical rules. As a subtle harmony of colours may reveal, to those who can grasp it, a miracle of skill and science, while it is no more nor less than "a pretty picture" to others—or polyphonic harmony, with all the resources of the science of music, may be employed to enrich a clear popular melody, to which the unmusical can yet nod their heads and fancy they understand it all; so a ballade or rondeau may be so deftly wrought, with an infinity of care and grace, that those who read it simply as a dainty poem never suspect the stern laws ordering the apparent spontaneity of the whole. To approach ideal perfection, nothing less than implicit obedience to all the rules is the first element of success; but the task is by no means finished there. Every quality that poetry demands, whether clearness of thought, elegance of expression, harmonious sound, or faultless rhythm, is needed as much in these shapes as in unfettered verse, and not until all those are contributed comes the final test of the poem itself; whether it utters thoughts worth uttering, or suggests ideas worth recalling. It may be said, without fear of exaggeration, that all the qualities required to form a perfect lyric in poetry are equally needful here, *plus* a great many special ones the forms themselves demand. To the students of any art there is always a peculiar charm when the highest difficulties are surmounted with such ease, that the consummate art is hidden to all who know not the magic password to unveil it. But for those who have no special knowledge of poetry, it is pertinent to inquire what good these ingenious *tours de force* achieve, and why the poem could not please as well if it was written in ordinary verse? This is hard to answer; but the fact remains that in every phase of art, whether music, picture, or poem, such technical achievements have invariably found admirers in any period of advanced civilisation. It has been said that these forms display no higher aim than the verses printed to resemble an hour-glass or altar, in some of our early poets; but such an accusation is hardly worthy of serious reply. If the sonnet in

Italian form has gained world-wide fame, the principle of fixed form is at once shown to be acceptable to the majority of scholars, and it becomes only a question of degree whether these rondeaus and ballades gain so prominent a place. It is hardly fair to expect to find among these forms a lyric that has caught the ear of the public, and won its way to the hearts of everyone; fifteen years of use is all they may claim, and compared with the lyric poetry guileless of bonds, during the same period, they at least hold their own. It must also be remembered that they were adopted by the younger men, who won no small amount of their present fame by these pretty devices.

On the Rules of the Various Forms.—There are several general laws governing these fixed metrical forms that must be insisted on at the outset. The rule of the limited number of rhymes holds good of nearly all. One feature prominent in the French rules is impossible in English, as the difference between the rhyme masculine on words that have not the *e* mute for their final letter, and the rhyme feminine on words that possess the *e* mute, is unknown to us; but side by side with the release from one binding law in French verse, a new one is imposed. In that language, words of exactly similar *sound and spelling* may be used to rhyme together, provided the meaning of the words is distinct —such license the most doggerel bard would reject in English—in spite of the precedent Milton offers, having "Ruth" and "ruth" in one of his sonnets. Purists forbid in our tongue the use of words of distinct spelling, bnt identical sound, as "sail" and "sale," "bear" and "bare;" nor would they allow words closely allied, as "claim," "disclaim," "reclaim," to be employed, the strict rule being, *that no syllable once used as a rhyme can be used again for that purpose throughout the poem, not even if it be spelt differently while keeping the same sound; nor if the whole word is altered by a prefix; the syllable that rhymes must always be a new one both in sense and sound.* It is this feature of the many rhymes to be found on a limited root-sound that proves the initial difficulty in these shapes.

If the above rule is thought too strict—and it must be owned very few writers acknowledge it to the extent of excluding such words as "claim, acclaim, prove, re-prove," etc.—at least such words should be kept as far apart as possible, not used in the same stanza, if it can be avoided, and never to rhyme with one another. Next in order, but of equal, perhaps primary importance, is the use of the refrain. This recurrent phrase is common in many languages; but the way these ballades, rondeaus, and other shapes employ it, differs from all others. In most old ballads and folk-songs the refrain comes as a mere jingle, or, at best, an interlude, not reflecting the idea of the verse it closes, nor varying its sense in spite of retaining its sound, as it does in a perfect example of these forms. An ordinary refrain in other poetry is usually kept to one note resounding through the whole poem, much as the drone-bass in "pifferari" or "musette" music is kept going throughout. In music there is another form of bass always kept continuous—the ground-bass, on which Handel and Bach built some mighty choruses; but in this the repeated sequence of notes in the phrase, although they occur again and again unaltered, have the superstructure welded into them, one splendid harmony—not, as in the other, a melody merely floating over the accompaniment of the one note or chord of the drone bass. It may be a somewhat forced parallel, but in the instance quoted, and the fugue, canon, and other contra-puntal laws of classical music, there is much in common with these laws of strict metrical verse. The enormous use of set forms in the masterpieces of tone-art may be a happy augury to the future that yet awaits them in word-art. It may be said that at present the poems dare claim no such success as the contrapuntal devices in music can show, where the greatest works employ such devices frequently ; yet the leap from the simple forms of counterpoint to the works of the mighty John Sebastian took but comparatively few years, although the distance was so great. But fanciful parallels of this sort are rarely satisfactory to any, except their maker, and need not be dwelt on here. The refrain in each case is noticed more especially among the laws of each form, but with regard to all the forms it is necessary to insist on the importance of introducing it unaltered in sound on each recurrence; it is sometimes changed by using, say, "and" for "but," or "then" for "if;" but, without condemning any who take this license, it is better to avoid it. Still, any change of meaning that be obtained by alteration of punctuation, accent, or even of spelling, provided the sound is un-changed, is not merely allowable but desirable, in lighter verse especially. Without recommending the use of the pun pure and simple, where its easy vulgarity would quickly be fatal to the dainty conceits that mark the best humorous verse in these forms, yet any pretty play upon words, or a sentence with new meaning read into it by the context, is more than permissible, being present in the best models of the Voiture rondeau and many triolets and ballades. This applies chiefly to poems of the class called *Vers de Société*, for want of an English synonym. The comic papers of our own country show no use of the form quite so fine in burlesque treatment as some of the American ones, notably the chant royal, *Mrs. Jones*, by Mr. H. C. Bunner ; in the burlesque examples printed in this book it will be seen that the forms can be made to give added zest to satire or humour, beside imparting a certain scholarly finish, that itself raises them from the terribly dead level of much of our so-called comic poetry. A few shapes yet await presentation in English dress. I have not succeeded in finding specimens of the *glose* or the *virelai* (rhythme d' Alain Chartier), while the example of the *virelai* (*nouveau*), Mr. Dobson's "July," is the only one brought to light. The *lai* and the *rondelet* are also very little used, so that anyone interested in these old measures will yet find plenty of unhackneyed forms for experimenting upon. It is curious that the sonnet, no less exacting in its technical rules, and far more imperious in the treatment it demands, finds so many eager followers, for with its wealth of literature, the chance of attaining to the second rank even, among such splendid poems, requires a high amount of talent, if not absolute genius. In the rondeau, or ballade, many writers who are ignored in the ampler crowd of sonnet-makers might find pleasing forms, not merely to display true poetic thoughts (if they have the power to do so), but verse that has in its shape some air of novelty still, and would sound less like the faint re-echoes of a stronger song, the frequent effect of many a modern sonnet.

These few prefatory lines may well close with De Banville's own words (in Mr. Lang's English)—"This cluster of forms is one of our most precious treasures, for each of them forms a rhythmic whole, complete and perfect, while at the same time they all possess the fresh and unconscious grace which marks the production of primitive times." As the translator adds, "There is some truth in this criticism, for it is a mark of man's early ingenuity in many arts to seek complexity (where you would expect simplicity), and yet to lend to that complexity an infantine naturalness. One can see this phenomenon in early decorative art, and in early law and custom, and even in the complicated structure of primitive languages.   Now, just as early and even savage races are our masters in the decorative use of colour and of carving, so the nameless master-singers of ancient France may be our teachers in decorative poetry—the poetry some call *vers de société*."

In analysing the structure of these forms, it would be, no doubt, possible for a master to present them in English, as terse and epigrammatic as the French of de Banville or de Gramont.   But there would be a danger in so doing.   A famous prelate is said to have apologised for a long letter, on the ground that he had not time to write a short one: this anecdote may be paraphrased here, for it often happens that many have time to run through a discursive, gossipy description, when they could not devote the attention needful to *read* a short one.   If every word is carefully chosen, and used in an exact way to convey as much as possible, it requires no less careful reading ;—as in some of our Science Primers, where the material for an ordinary chapter is condensed and reduced to the crystal of a single sentence, that demands almost equal exactness in obtaining its solution, if one would absorb all the learning compressed in so small a compass.   This excuse may serve in lieu of a better for the somewhat prolix method in which these rules are presented.   Let no one imagine that the most perfect knowledge of the laws of these forms is enough to start him in writing poetry ; for such rules are but what the fundamental rules of arithmetic are to astronomers—all important as the basis, but powerless, without genius and science, to discover new worlds, or formulate an hypothesis for the existence of known ones.   If such books as those the present chapter follows are looked upon as handbooks to making *poetry*, that one stupendous flight of imagination is probably the only one its author is fated to achieve.

The Ballade.—In the alphabetical sequence adopted in the arrangement of this volume, the *Ballade* happily comes first. This is as it should be, since no other of these forms has been more frequently used in English, nor, it may be, is any other so capable of variety, since among its successful examples many different treatments will be found. This form adapts itself to its subject, and may be sonorous or stately, playful or easy, at the will of its writer, as, in capable hands, it can strike any note in the gamut of passions, from religious exaltation or fierce grim satire, to actual pathos, or, if needful, pure burlesque. It is possible the *Ballade* will never be written so strictly to one model as the sonnet, but that many variations—to be noticed presently—will each find admirers; but the existing examples warrant a belief that the shape will continue in our poetry, for it is impossible, in face of many hundred examples, to style it an exotic at the present day.

The construction of the *Ballade*, although not less stern in insisting on the introduction of a refrain than many of the other shapes, uses it at wider intervals, and so escapes the besetting danger of such forms as the *villanelle* or *triolet*, where its constant recurrence may easily become as senseless as the " with a fal, la, la " of the old madrigal writers, unless it be very skilfully brought in. Again, its length, generally of twenty-eight or thirty-five lines, with the refrain in either case appearing but four times, allows room to display the subject, and yet forbids the diffuseness of many ordinary lyrics, where one fancies a happy rhyme-sound is often responsible for the intrusion of an additional couplet or quatrain, that weakens the whole poem. Its length, moreover, strictly within hard and fast limits though it be, is not so cramped as the fourteen lines of the true sonnet, nor has tradition fixed the style of treatment of the central idea. The narrative ballade is perfectly legitimate, provided the writer has sufficient power to overcome the extreme difficulty it presents. It is often urged that the unalterable sequence of rhymes, which must be found after the set of three or five are once chosen, proves a hindrance to the imagination of the poet who uses it. M. Lemâitre has answered this objection very aptly. He says—" The poet who begins a ballade does not know very exactly what he will put into it. The rhyme, and nothing but the rhyme, will whisper things unexpected and charming, things he would never have thought of but for her, things with strange and remote relations to each other, all united in the disorder of a dream. Nothing, indeed, is richer in suggestion than the strict laws of these difficult pieces; they force the fancy to wander afield, hunting high and low; and while she seeks through all the world the foot that can wear Cinderella's slipper, she makes delightful discoveries by the way."*

The BALLADE, in its normal type, consists of three stanzas of eight lines, followed by a verse of four lines, known as the envoy, or three verses of ten lines, with envoy of five, each of the stanzas and the envoy closing with the refrain. The most important rules for the ballade may be put briefly:—*First*, The same set of rhymes in the same order they occupy in the first stanza must repeat throughout the whole of its verses. *Secondly*, No word once used as a rhyme must be used again for that purpose in the whole length of the poem. *Thirdly*, Each stanza and the envoy must close with the refrain; the envoy always taking the same rhymes as the last half of the preceding verse, in the same order. For the eight-lined ballade, but three rhymes are allowable. In ordinary rhyme formula the sequence of

---

* Mr. Andrew Lang, *Longman's Magazine*, April 1887.

these is A, B, A, B, B, C, B, C, for each of the three verses, and B, C, B, C, for the envoy. The importance of the refrain must now be noticed. Old writers and purists of our own time insist that the length of the refrain should govern not only the length of each line, but the number of the lines; in other words, that a refrain of eight syllables involves the choice of an eight-lined stanza, while the refrain of ten syllables demands a ten-lined verse. This is the strict rule of the ballade as written by Clement Marot, and by some modern writers; but it must be clearly understood that it is only the rule for the ideally pure form, and that variations in this respect are perfectly allowable. Now the importance of the refrain in one aspect is given, a still more vital point must be named—namely, that the sense of the refrain must be supreme throughout the ballade, the culminating line of each stanza always brought in without effort as the natural close of the verse. In the verses a special feature must not be overlooked, namely, that the stanza (of eight or ten lines, as the case may be) should carry an unbroken sense throughout, and not split into two verses of four lines or five lines, that are by chance printed as though they were one. The needful pauses for punctuation are of course allowed, but the sense should not finish at the end of the first quatrain (or quintain), but demand the rest of the verse to complete the idea presented. All these apparently trivial details must be regarded if the ballade is attempted. The advice given in *Alice in Wonderland*, "Take care of the sense and the sounds will take care of themselves," whether in that way or its inversion, "Take care of the sounds and the sense will take care of itself," is exactly the direct opposite of the true rule. Neither sense nor sound may be scamped here. If you neglect the sounds it is no ballade; if you neglect the sense—why write it at all? No one is compelled to use these complex forms, but if chosen, their laws must be obeyed to the letter if success is to be attained. The chief pleasure they yield consists in the apparent spontaneity, which is the result of genius, if genius be indeed the art of taking infinite pains ; or, if that definition is rejected, they must yet exhibit the art which conceals art, whether by intense care in every minute detail, or a happy faculty for naturally wearing these fetters. The dance in chains must be skilful, the chains worn as decorative adjuncts, and the whole with as much apparent ease as the unfettered dancer could produce, or woe betide the unlucky wight who attempts to perform in them.

The ENVOY is so peculiarly a feature of the Ballade and Chant Royal, that it is needful to draw our attention to the invocation which with it invariably commences. Of old this envoy was really addressed to the patron of the poet, or at least to the high dignitary to whom he dedicated his ballade. So that we find Prince ! or Princess ! Sire ! or some mythical or symbolical personality invoked in the opening word. Often the person chosen was in very truth a noble of the rank assigned, but the custom of opening the envoy in this fashion grew so common that it lost its special fitness, and was often employed as a conventional ascription to those not of noble rank, while in some instances all the lovers' ballades intended for their own ladies were yet ascribed by the poets to the " Princess " of the court, who quite understood the fiction employed, and accepted praise of the golden hair and blue eyes of the rightful owner of the poem, while possibly her royal tresses were black and her eyes brown. In the number of ballades included in this collection the larger number will still be found to follow the old custom, which is so marked that the use of this dedication certainly carries out the spirit of the poem, in accordance with its original design. The envoy is not only a dedication, but should be the peroration of the subject, and richer in its wording and more stately in its imagery than the preceding verses, to convey the climax of the whole matter, and avoid the suspicion that it is a mere postscript, as it were, to the ballade.

In the ballade with stanzas of ten lines, usually of ten syllables each, four rhymes are permitted in this order—A, B, A, B, B, C, C, D, C, D, with C, C, D, C, D for the envoy.   It is not needful to quote examples, or describe varieties with eight or ten-lined stanzas, that have lines of equal or unequal length, but in other respects follow all the true rules.   De Gramont has observed that the strict laws of the *ballade* belong more to the prosodists who studied the form after it had ceased to be in current use, and that the writers of the *ballade* themselves frequently took great liberty.   In some by Marot there are verses of eleven or twelve decasyllabic lines, and in poets who preceded him, some with thirteen and fourteen lines to the stanza, while the number of verses has also been flagrantly disregarded, some even using four or five verses, and still worse, having different rhymes to them ; but in such cases the poem must not be regarded as an irregular ballade, nor a ballade at all, but simply as a set of verses with refrain.

The *Ballade with double refrain*, of which the " Frere Lubin " of Clement Marot is the only well-known example in old French, is said by Thomas Sibilet, in his *Art Poétique*, 1555, to be "*autant rare que plaisante.*" Its point of difference is that a second refrain is introduced at the fourth line of each stanza, and the second of the envoy. This necessarily alters the order of the rhymes of the envoy. In the best known English example the rhyme order is A, B, A, B, B, C, B, C, with B, B, C, C, for the envoy.

There are several in modern English, and some in
recent French.

The *Double Ballade* consists of six stanzas of eight
or ten lines, and is written usually without an envoy.
The "Ballade of Dead Lions," in *London*, January 12,
1878, was the first English specimen ; it is not quoted
here, as its subject is now out of date. De Banville has
written several. "*Pour les bonnes gens*," "*Des sottises de
l'aris*" are two in his "*Trente-six Ballades Joyeuses*"
written in this form.

M. de Banville humorously reveals a secret of the
poet's workshop, and gives a method to construct a
"correct" ballade in a mechanical fashion, dispensing
with genius, and easy to work—First, at one sitting
write the last half of all the verses, and at another
time the first half, then join them together, and the
result will be an irremediably bad ballade; but elsewhere he writes, in all seriousness this time, "All the
art is to bring in the refrain without effort, naturally,
gaily, and at each time with novel effect and with
fresh light cast on the central idea. 'Now you can'
teach 'no one to do that, and M. de Banville never
pretends to give any receipts for cooking *rondels* or
ballades worth reading.' Without poetic vision all is
mere marqueterie and cabinetmaker's work ; that is, so
far as poetry is concerned, nothing."*

The Chant Royal is now accepted by most writers as
merely a larger form of the ballade, written with five
verses of eleven lines, and envoi of five. De Gramont
treats the idea to regard it as a distinct form as a mere
fanciful attempt of prosodists, founded chiefly on the
fact that Clement Marot has left four so named which
conform to the above rule ; but he shows that on the one
hand there are ballades with stanzas of eleven lines, and
on the other chants royal with ten only. It has been

* A. Lang on De Banville, *New Quarterly Magazine*, Oct. 1878.

suggested that the *Chant Royal* derived its name from the subjects that are more usually dedicated to its use; but while these are generally sublime topics treated in dignified allegory, yet there are examples extant entirely devoid of these characteristics. Again, the idea that it owes its name to being a form selected for competition before the king for the dignity of laureate, and hence dubbed royal-song, he also rejects, and points out that its name simply denotes that it is the most excellent form of the ballade (as we might say, the "king of ballades" in English), one that, from the increased length, both in stanzas and number of lines in each, largely augments the difficulties of construction met with in the true ballade, and marks it as "the final *tour de force* of poetic composition." Henry de Croï derives the title of this form from the fact that persons excelling in the composition of chants royal were worthy to be crowned with garlands like conquerors and kings. It is a moot point with students whether the ballade or chant royal is the earlier and original poem. The chant royal in the old form is usually devoted to the unfolding of an allegory in its five stanzas, the envoy supplying the key; but this is not always observed in modern examples. Whatever be the subject, however, it must always march in stately rhythm with splendid imagery, using all the poetic adornments of sonorous, highly-wrought lines and rich embroidery of words to clothe a theme in itself a lofty one. Unless the whole poem is constructed with intense care, and has intrinsic beauty of its own of no mean order, the monotony of its sixty-one lines rhymed on five sounds is unbearable. In spite of the increased burden imposed by the necessity of so many similar rhymes, no shadow of "poetic" or other license must be taken. Nothing short of complete success can warrant the choice of this exacting form, which demands all that can be given to it; enriched with

all the elaboration of consummate art in its every detail,
and rising stanza by stanza, until the climax is reached
in the envoy.

The laws of the ballade apply to the chant royal, with
some added details of its own. The rhyme order is
usually—a, b, a, b, c, c, d, d, e, d, e, with envoy of
d, d, e, d, e. An example by Deschamps, " *Sur le mort
du Seigneur de Coucy,*" observes this order, a, b, a, b,
b, c, c, d, c, d, and envoy, c, c, d, c, c, d. In either
case the rhyme-order must be kept the same for each
stanza, and the envoy commenced with an invocation as
in the old ballades.

CHAIN VERSE.—There is one beautiful poem in so-
called chain verse, which has so much likeness to these
once-exotic forms that it deserves quotation in full, if
only as an example of a native specimen of poetic
ingenuity. It has little affinity with the chain verse of
French art, as then the one word only grew from each
line into the other (La rime Enchaînée).

> Dieu des Amans, de mort me garde
> Me gardant donne-moi bonheur,
> Et me le donnant prend ta darde
> Et la prenant navre son coeur
> Et le navrant me tiendras seur.
> . . . . . —*Clement Marot.*

The following hymn was written by John Byrom, and
published in vol. ii. of his *Posthumous Poems*, 1773 :--

THE DESPONDING SOUL'S WISH.

> My spirit longeth for Thee,
> Within my troubled breast,
> Although I be unworthy
> Of so Divine a Guest.

> Of so Divine a Guest
> Unworthy though I be,
> Yet has my heart no rest,
> Unless it comes from Thee.

Unless it comes from Thee,
In vain I look around ;
In all that I can see
No rest is to be found.

No rest is to be found
But in thy blessèd love :
Oh, let my wish be crowned,
And send it from above.

The Answer.
Cheer up, desponding soul,
Thy longing pleased I see :
'Tis part of that great whole
Wherewith I longed for Thee.

Wherewith I longed for Thee
And left my Father's throne,
From death to set thee free,
To claim thee for my own.

To claim thee for my own
I suffered on the cross :
O ! were my love but known,
No soul need fear its loss.

No soul need fear its loss,
But, filled with love divine,
Would die on its own cross
And rise for ever thine.

This has so many points resembling the forms in this book, that it seemed worth quoting, if only to compare with the Malay Pantoum, the Villanelle, and the Rondel.

KYRIELLE.—The *Kyrielle* is so simple, and so widely used by writers, all unwittingly, that but for M. de Banville including it, it would be left unnoticed here. It is merely a poem in four-lined verses of eight-syllable lines, having the last line of each the same. Our hymn books show many, witness

" Jesus ! Son of Mary, hear," or " Jesus, our Love, is crucified." It is a device so evident that it has naturally been used in almost all schools of poetry, and may be dismissed with no more words here.

PANTOUM.—The *Pantoum*, at first sight, has little reason for being included in a volume of verse in strict traditional forms, that are nearly all of French origin, since it is of Malay invention ; but being introduced by M. Ernest Fouinet, and reproduced by M. Victor Hugo in the *Orientales*, it has found a place in the group of these forms given by De Banville, De Gramont, and others. The Pantoum is written in four-line stanzas. The second and fourth line of each verse form the first and third of each succeeding one, through an indefinite number of quatrains. At the close, to complete the unity of the work, the second and fourth line of the last stanza are made from the first and third of the first verse. The rhymes are a b, a b,—b c, b c,—c d, c d,— d e, d e, and so on, until the last (which we may call z) z a, z a. In Mr. Austin Dobson's " In Town " and Mr. Brander Matthews' " En route "—as the latter him-self points out in *The Rhymester*—" there is an attempt to make the constant repetitions not merely tolerable but subservient to the general effect of monotonously recurrent sound—in the one case the buzzing of the fly, and in the other the rattle and strain of the cars."

The RONDEL, RONDEAU, and ROUNDEL, a group having a common origin, are now to some extent classified, by each accepted variety using one form of the common name to denote its shape, but this division is purely arbitrary and a modern custom, only followed here, both in these notes and in the arrangement of the volume itself, to facilitate reference.

The RONDEL is merely the old form of the word rondeau ; like *oisel* for *oiseau*, *chastel* for *chateau* so *rondel* has become *rondeau.* It is one of the earliest of these forms, and freely used in the fourteenth century by Froissart, Eustache Deschamps, and others. It probably arose in Provence, and passed afterwards into use in Northern France. The name (rondel) is still applied to forms written after its early shape, the later spelling of the name being kept for the more recent variations of its form. In its origin the rondel was a lyric of two verses, each having four or five lines, rhyming on two rhymes only. In its eight (or ten) lines, but five (or six) were distinct, the others being made by repeating the first couplet at the end of the second stanza, sometimes in an inverse order, and the first line at the end of its first stanza. The eight-lined rondel is thus, to all intents and purposes, a triolet, although labelled a rondel. Here is a fourteenth century one by Eustache Deschamps :—

> Est ce donc vostre intencion
> De voloir retrancher mes gaiges
> Vingt livres de ma pension ?
> Est-ce donc vostre intencion ?
> Laissez passer l'Ascension,
> Que honni soit vostre visaige !
> Est-ce donc vostre intencion
> De voloir retrancher mes gaiges ?

Nor are these rondel-triolets exceptions ; they are quite common till the beginning of the fifteenth century. With Charles d'Orléans the rondel took the distinct shape we now assign to it, namely, of fourteen lines on two rhymes, the first two lines repeating for the seventh and eighth, and the final couplet (see page 135). In this, the true type of the rondel, the two-lined refrain occurring three times in its fourteen makes it an unwieldy form to handle. In later French ones the last refrain uses but one of its lines. In Mr. Austin Dobson's "The Wanderer, " the rhymes are in this order :—

A. B. b. a.—a. b. A. B.—a. b. b. a. A. (the refrain being marked by capital letters). In another by the same author, "How hard it is to Sing," the rhyme order is A. B. a. b.—b. a. A. B.—a. b. a. b. A. B ; the rondel of Charles d'Orléans having A. B. b. a. a. b, A. B.— a. b. b. a. A. B. The length of the lines is not confined to any particular number of syllables in modern examples.

By the time of Octavieu de Saint Gelais (1466-1502) the rondel has nearly become the rondeau as we know it. Still rhymed on but two sounds, it repeats the first line only, nor always the whole of that, as the quoted examples show :—

> De ce qui est au pouvoir de Fortune
> Nul ne se doit vanter ny tenir fort :
> Car ung jour sert de plaisir et confort,
> Et l'autre apres, de courroux et rancune.
>
> Aux ungs est bonne, aux autres importune,
> Estrange à tous, car nuls n'entent le sort
> De ce qui est au pouvoir de Fortune.
>
> Les ungs ont d'elle honneur, sçavoir, pecune ;
> L'autres n'ônt que pitié et remort,
> Et povreté, qu'est pire que la mort.
> Est-il aucun qui soit seur soubz la lune
> De ce qui est au pouvoir de Fortune ?

Here it is formally divided into three parts with the rhymes—a, b, b, a ; a, b, a ; a, b, b, a, a. The refrain, too, is no longer a mere reiteration of the text, but linked with the preceding verse, as a refrain should be, and absorbed into the sense of the whole stanza to which it belongs. This change is still more noticeable in the rondel, using but half the first line for its refrain, as in this example :—

> Je vous arreste de main mise.
> Mes yeulx; emprisonnez serez.
> Plus mon coeur ne gouvernerez
> Desormais, je vous en advise.
>
> Trop avez fait à vostre guise;
> Par ma foy plus ne le ferez,
>   Je vous arreste.
>
> On peut bien pour vous corner prise :
> Pris estes, point n' eschapperez.
> Nul remede n'y treuverez;
> Rien n'y vault appel ne franchise :
>   Je vous arreste.

Here we pass into the later form called (for convenience only) the *Rondeau.* In these few examples the evolution of the *Voiture* type, from the Charles d'Orléans original, is clearly traceable. The rondel, however, still continues to be used, but much less frequently. De Banville often omits the thirteenth line, while otherwise following the model of Charles d'Orléans. Again, the order of the rhymes is sometimes changed, but the examples quoted in this collection will show more clearly the deviations from the true rondel than any description would do.

The RONDEAU after Voiture's model is without doubt the most popular variety of the form now in use. It is written throughout on two rhymes, being composed of thirteen lines and two unrhymed refrains. The lines are now nearly always of eight syllables only, in many of the old ones they were of ten. The refrain is usually made from the first half of the first line, but it is not uncommon to find the first word only taken for this use. Its thirteen lines are grouped in three stanzas, the first and third having five lines each, the second consisting of three only. The refrain occurs at the end of the second stanza, and at the close of the poem. The usual rhyme order is a, a, b, b, a, —— a, a, b (and refrain)—a, a, b, b, a, and refrain. The refrain is not counted among the lines of the verse, but is added to the thirteen, and in the neatness of its introduction, and in the way each of the two verses to which it belongs flow into it, so that it forms an integral and inseparable part of the stanza, the chief difficulty of the rondeau lies. If, like an " Amen " to a hymn, the refrain comes merely as an extraneous comment on the preceding lines, it is no true rondeau. At the risk of reiteration of a warning given in the description of each of these poems that use a refrain, this point must be insisted on, as the most vital one. The mechanical laws of the poem may be obeyed with scrupulous exactitude, and every technical rule complied with, while the still more important quality of sense is overlooked. The thought of the poet must so find its expression that the refrain completes it, and forms the true climax of his speech—the culminating phrase of his sentence. The refrain is the very text of the whole discourse, in itself an epitome of the subject of the whole poem, otherwise the reason for its existence in one of these fixed shapes is wanting, and the poem would be better in free verse. In the refrain the sound must reappear exactly, but the sense may be altered ; in fact, this playful variation of its meaning is one of the charms of the verse when used for lighter and more dainty subjects. The good taste of the author must decide how far an actual pun is allowable. There are precedents for the use of the pun pure and simple—" votre beau thé " " 'vôtre beauté," or, " à la fontaine," used in its literal sense, and also with reference to the famous fabulist. But in English use the pun has fallen into disrepute, perhaps from the execrable word-contortions of our so-called comic papers and its terrible vulgarity in stage burlesques, the intrusion of one is fatal to the delicacy and refinement which are the peculiar charm of the rondeau. But if a play upon words of a scholarly kind, or a new reading given either by punctuation, or the use of the words with a new light thrown on them by the lines leading up to the refrain, can be secured, every effort should be made to vary the refrain by so doing.

This quality of dainty and spontaneous wit is the secret of the rondeau, only revealed, if it is to be found at all, by close analysis of the best examples. De Banville quotes three of Voiture's—" Je ne sçaurois," " L'Amour," and " Penser "—especially for this all-important feature ; but in this volume may be found examples equally worthy of study. It would be invidious to draw attention to the best of those that have been allowed to appear here, but if the wit of the would-be rondeau-maker fails to discover the success-ful use of the refrain, and to pick out the best examples, it is in itself evidence that he had better abstain from trying to produce rondeaus that would certainly lack the airy grace and caressing tenderness which should be an element of this verse. A famous example of Voiture's is quoted on page 134.

The following is its English paraphrase by Mr. Austin Dobson, withdrawn from his later editions, but quoted now by his consent :—

> You bid me try, BLUE-EYES, to write
> A Rondeau. What ! forthwith ?—To-night ?
>   Reflect. Some skill I have, 'tis true ;
>   But thirteen lines !—and rhymed on two !—
> " Refrain," as well. Ah, hapless plight !
> Still there are five lines—ranged aright.
> These Gallic bonds, I feared, would fright
>   My easy Muse. They did, till you—
>   *You* bid me try !
>
> " That makes them eight.—The port's in sight :
> Tis all because your eyes are bright !
>   Now just a pair to end in " oo,"—
>   When maids command, what can't we do !
> Behold ! The RONDEAU—tasteful, light—
>   *You* bid me try !"

A study of rondeaus will show, both in ancient and modern examples, some little alteration of the rhyme-order, and a few trivial differences in other respects. But as the sonnet has evolved through many stages into one accepted shape that is now permanently fixed as its true type, so the rondeau of Voiture may be taken as the typical form to be imitated—the one that has, by process of selection, been proved to be the best to display the subject of the poem, and to work-in the refrains to the best advantage. Like the sonnet, the perfected form is jealously guarded. The genius which consists in breaking rules is looked upon with suspicion in all these forms, but especially in this one. There are some beautiful variations in old and new examples where the shape is widely varied, but these stand apart from the pure rondeaus of Voiture, and are generally still more difficult to construct by reason of the additional laws the writers have imposed on themselves. But the trifling evasion of the rhyme-order, a want of exactitude on the repetition of the refrain, is apt to be taken as evidence of lack of power to conform gracefully to the bonds, and not as an outburst of genius that is too strong to be confined in such puny fetters. But there are a few *poems* in these forms written fairly near the true shape, which, like some irregular, but yet in themselves beautiful sonnets, are not to be condemned solely for being impure in form. For the sake of poetry one is ready to forgive much, but it must be only real *poetry* that takes such liberty; and all the time comes a wish that having gone so near perfection of shape as well as of sense, the poet had taken the last steps needful to make his poem perfect in each respect.

There is another form than Voiture's, which is equally a true rondeau—that used by Villon. This is quoted, with Mr. Payne's translation, to show clearly the ten-lined rondeau :—

LAY OU PLUTOST RONDEAU.

Mort, j' appelle de ta rigueur,
Qui m'as ma maistresse ravie,
Et n'es pas encore assouvie,
Se tu ne me tiens en langueur.
Onc puis n'euz force ne vigueur
Mais que te nuysoit-elle en vie,
   Mort?

Deux estions, et n'avions qu' ung cueur;
S'il est mort, force est que devie,
Voire, on que je vive sans vie,
Comme les images, par cueur.
   Mort !

      —François Villon.

LAY, OR RATHER RONDEAU.

Death, of thy rigour I complain,
 That hast my lady torn from me,
 And yet wilt not contented be,
Till from me too all strength be ta'en
For languishment of heart and brain.
 What harm did she in life to thee,
   Death?

One heart we had betwixt us twain ;
 Which being dead, I too must dree
 Death, or, like carven saints we see
In choir, sans life to live be fain,
   Death !

      —John Payne.

Mr. Austin Dobson's *Rose*, which appeared in *The Spectator*, was one of the earliest, if not the very first, of the few examples of this variety in English use.

The ROUNDEL, which, it must again be said, is simply a variation of the rondeau, and not a distinct form, is grouped apart in this collection for the sake of convenience. Since Mr. Swinburne devoted a volume, entitled *A Century of Roundels*, to this particular form of the rondeau, it has been used by other writers, and the name applied by him has been kept by those who chose to follow the same form.   Probably Mr. Swinburne, during his readings in early French poetry, found poems of this shape extant, or it may be that, for reasons of his own, he formulated this variety, which slightly differs from any I have been able to find.   In Marot's *De l'Amoureux Ardant* there is a likeness to this shape, and in Villon's *Mort* there is also a resemblance, but Mr. Swinburne's roundel has eleven lines always, while Villon's has twelve, rhyming a.b.b. a.a.b. refrain, a.b.b.a. refrain. Again, Mr. Swinburne's roundel not only has a new rhyme order, A.B.A. refrain ; B.A.B. ; A.B.A. refrain ; but when the refrain consists of more than a single word it rhymes with the B lines.   The rhythm, too, of Mr. Swinburne's are in every possible and—in any hands but his—impossible variety.   The lines vary from four to sixteen syllables, but are generally identical in length in the same roundel.   As an experiment in rhythm the *Century of Roundels* will, no doubt, always command attention, and there are not wanting signs that his *Roundel*, keeping its length and other details, may become a recognised shape in English verse ; but it must be distinctly understood that Mr. Swinburne is responsible for its introduction, and to him, not to the early French poets, must be awarded the honour of its invention, unless he himself refers it to an earlier source for its authority ; but it may be that with admiration for the old shapes, he yet saw that for English use a variation was preferable, and so rearranged the lines and the refrain of the olden form in the way he considered best suited to our tongue.

The *Rondelet* is a little form not noticed in De Gramont or De Banville.   Boulmier has printed several in his " Poésies en language du XVe. Siècle " at the end of his volume, entitled *Les Villanelles*.   Here is one.

François Villon,
Sur tous rithmeurs, à qui qu'en poisa,
François Villon
Du mieulx disant eut le guerdon
Né de Paris empres Pontoise
In ne féit oncq vers à la toise
François Villon.

Here we find he adopts a seven-line stanza with four eight-syllable lines, and three of four syllables on two rhymes, a, b, a, a, b, b, a. While strongly resembling the triolet and the early rondel, it yet seems worth noting as a pretty variety for trifling subjects. There are several in English verse.

The Rondeau Redoublé would fail to suggest kinship with either form of the Rondeau, did not it include the name in its designation, as De Banville notes. It is probable that many more poems were grouped under the word Rondeau than we now are able to trace. The one we are now describing is in no way a doubled rondeau, and hardly suggests that form more than any of these that have the features of limited rhyme sounds, and more or less frequent reiteration of a refrain. The Rondeau Redoublé is written in six octosyllabic quatrains, rhyming on two alternate rhymes, with half the initial line used (unrhymed) after the last verse. Its one distinctive feature is this :—Each line of the first quatrain is used again in the same order to serve for the last line of verses two, three, four, and five ; while the last line of the sixth has a new wording for itself, but takes, in addition, a final refrain of the first half of the initial line of the poem to conclude the whole. As the rhymes of the first quatrain are a. b. a. b., it must necessarily—to use as refrain the first line rhyming on *a*—reverse the order for the second verse, which is therefore b. a. b. a., and so on alternately until the end of the rondeau redoublé. Specimens of its use are extant by Marot, La Fontaine, Benserade, and others, while in modern French it is not infrequent, but in English it is rare. The examples quoted in this book comprise all that diligent search could discover except one of too fugitive a character to reprint. As the poems written in this form in English show the rules of the verse as plainly as the original French, it has not been thought needful to quote one in its native tongue, especially as De Gramont, De Banville, and Jullien reprint specimens in their handbooks. A form so simple that, if well wrought, and the refrain brought in with skill, it can be read in a casual way, without discovering that it was written to exact rules, deserves more use. The disposition of the subject is excellently laid out; a "text," four "divisions," and "in conclusion," with the text repeated, is a method so familiar to Englishmen on Sundays that the order for variations on the initial theme is peculiarly easy : nor need the result be the least like a sermon, although this description of its shape is suggestive of one.

Another form, the GLOSE, resembles the Rondeau Redoublé in many ways ; indeed, it may be almost looked upon as a freer form of that poem. It appears, however, to be of distinct origin, and very rare in French poetry, although much used in Spanish and Portuguese verse. It begins, like the Rondeau Redoublé, with a quatrain, here called the *texte ;*—this is usually a quotation from a former poet. This text the Glose proceeds to comment on, or amplify, in four stanzas of ten lines, closing each as in the rondeau redoublé, with one of the lines of the text in the original order ; but the necessity for restricting the rhymes to two is not observed here. Each stanza has the sixth, ninth, and tenth (the refrain) line, rhyming on the same sound, but the others appear to be chosen at the fancy of the writer, while the final refrain of the rondeau redoublé

is also wanting in the glose. First employed solely
for serious themes of religion or philosophy, it is now in
France, like the once sacred triolet, devoted to parody
and the lightest forms of humour. Owing to the
impossibility of collating the mass of periodical literature of the last ten or fifteen years, it would be rash
to say that the *glose* has never appeared in English, but
not one has been discovered to include in this book. Yet,
as De Gramont places the shape among those he includes
as frequently used in France, it seemed best to give
here a brief outline of its form. De Banville quotes
one by Jean François Sarazin formed on the sonnet "de
IOB" by Benserade, where fourteen quatrains are ended
by the lines of the sonnet, employed in their original
order. This form offers a field for serious comment or
sarcastic parody that deserves working.

The SESTINA, invented by the famous troubadour,
Arnaut Daniel, at the end of the thirteenth century,
has not been used in French poetry so often as the
ballade and rondeau. There are specimens in the poetry
of Pontus de Thyard, and one in the Pleiade of the
sixteenth century, besides many others, but it has been
comparatively an exotic in French poetry, as in
English, until recent years. That it was used and
admired by Dante and Petrarch, alone gives the sestina
a royal precedence over all of the other forms. Many
judges consider it to be the supreme work of poetic art
in fixed forms, while others claim similar distinction for
the chant royal, and not a few for the sonnet. To
distinguish between the charms of these three royal forms
would need a Paris, nor is it necessary to do so, since
each will to his own taste, no matter who claims authority on the ever-disputed question of supreme beauty.
Mr. Hueffer in his "Troubadours" has a chapter so
full of interest and teeming with information of the
growth of the stanza, that in despair of condensing its

knowledge within the space possible here, the mere notice of it must suffice. De Gramont give the rules of the poem as written by the originator and followers in Italy, Spain, and Portugal :—

1st.—The Sestina has six stanzas, each of six lines, these being of the same length.

2nd.—The lines of the six verses end with the six same words, not rhyming with each other; these end words are chosen exclusively from two syllabled nouns.

3rd.—The arrangement of these six terminal words follows a regular law (a somewhat complex one, which is replaced in modern poetry by the one given below).

4th.—The piece closes with a three-line stanza, using the six words, three at the end ; the other three, placed in the middle of its lines.

But, as now written, the words of the sestina at times rhyme with each other; if so, De Banville says they should be in two rhymes alone (as Mr. Swinburne uses them), but other writers allow three rhymes. But these details all belong to the subtle laws of the verse which it is not possible to include here. De Gramont's *Sestines* is, perhaps, the best authority for study.

For our purpose, enough to say that the six end-words must repeat unchanged in sound and spelling throughout each succeeding verse. The order in which they occur is best expressed by a numerical formula. If the rules themselves were compressed, a more complex and incomprehensible jargon of firsts and seconds and thirds, etc., could hardly be found. The first verse has, of course, the initial order, 1, 2, 3, 4, 5, 6; the second, 6, 1, 5, 2, 4, 3 ; the third, 3, 6, 4, 1, 2, 5 ; the fourth, 5, 3, 2, 6, 1, 4 ; the fifth, 4, 5, 1, 3, 6, 2 ; the sixth, 2, 4, 6, 5, 3, 1 : he last half-stanza ends with 2, 4, 6, and uses 1, 3, 5 at the beginning (not the first word always) of the line,

or at the half-line in rhymes that permit their introduction there. It will be seen that no end-word occurs
more than once in the same place, and that the end-word
of every stanza is invariably chosen to take its place as
terminal of the first line of the next verse.

As though this feat in rhyming were not complex
enough, a double sestina of twelve verses of twelve lines
has been sometimes written. There are two, at least, of
these *tours de force* in English—one, "The Complaint of
Lisa," in Mr. Swinburne's *Poems and Ballads*, Second
Series ; another, by Mr. George Barlow, in *A Life's Love*,
entitled "Alone." It was hoped to include these, but
the required space in this little book would have
excluded so many specimens of smaller poems, that the
desire to make this collection as widely varied and
representative as possible forbade their quotation.

The Triolet, as we know it, may be regarded as
almost an epitome of the other forms, in its limited
space. It introduces one refrain three times, and the
second refrain twice, keeps strictly to two rhymes,
and is inflexible in its laws, brief though it be.
One poet says of it, "It is charming—nothing can
be more ingeniously mischievous, more playfully sly,
than this tiny trill of epigrammatic melody turning
so simply upon its own innocent axis." Those who
are unaware of the rules that govern this little stanza,
yet often fall in love with the verse itself, possibly
because a good example has a pretty sequence of
sound, that allures the ear by its musical jingle,
and reads like a spontaneous and easy impromptu.
Nevertheless, the subtle art needed to acquire the
ease that is the charm of a good triolet is generally
the result of infinite care. Few things are more
simple than to write a triolet—of a sort—yet the
triolet affords so little space to explain its motif, and
within its five lines must tell its story, and also carry the

three other repeated ones easily, and with a definite meaning. To introduce the refrain naturally as the only thing to say, and yet with an air of freshness and an unexpected recognition of a phrase heard before, is in itself no mean difficulty, even in the ballade and rondeau ; but when it comes three times in eight lines, and has a second line attached to it on its first and last appearance, it is a matter of small wonder that the successful triolets are not very numerous. That the ideally perfect triolet is as yet unwritten, or at least represented by very few, it may be urged ; but if that be true, it should only provoke more attempts, one would fancy. It might be pertinent to ask, if this is the chief objection, how many ideally perfect poems in any set shape, or in free form, the world acknowledges ?

The triolet consists (to quote Mr. Dobson) of *eight* lines with *two* rhymes. The first pair of lines are repeated as the seventh and eighth, while the first is repeated as the fourth. The order of the rhymes is thus as follows :—a. b. a. a. a. b. a. b. The example (on page 214) by—of all persons in the world—a grave French magistrate, Jacques Ranchin, has been christened by Ménage the "King of *Triolets.*"

The first triolet known is in the Cléomadés of Adenèz-le-Roi (1258-1297), a poem of 20,000 verses. In old examples the triolet was devoted to grave verse, but, as M. de Gramont shows, it has now not only abandoned the old ten syllable lines, and is written in those of eight and often six syllables, but from the elegiac dignity of its former subjects, it has become in French verse the form especially devoted to the most ephemeral and trivial subjects. Since M. de Banville renewed its use, triolets are common in French newspapers, and with all due deference be it said—possibly only thereby exposing my own ignorance of the subtle charm conveyed to their readers by their "argot" and "idiom"

—as inferior as they are plentiful. There is one, however, that has justly won great favour since its appearance in *Odes Funnambulesque* of M. Theodore de Banville.

These two French examples (on page 214) are hackneyed by frequent quotation, but are so generally regarded as the most successful of their class that it seemed best not to omit them, nor this one by Froissart, given in most authorities, and called a rondeau by the writer (rondel, rondeau, and triolet being evidently regarded as but one form in his day—the beginning of the fifteenth century), and the modern grouping completely unknown :—

> Mon coer s'esbat en oudourant la rose
> Et s'esjoïst en regardant ma dame.
> Trop mieulz me vault l'une que l'autre chose,
> Mon coer s'esbat en oudourant la rose.
> L'oudour m'est bon, mès don regart je n'ose
> Juer trop fort, je le vous jur par m'ame
> Mon coer s'esbat en oudourant la rose
> Et s'esjoïst en regardant ma dame.
>
> *—Froissart.*

The weak point of the Triolet being the monotony of its refrain, every attempt, at giving a new accent to the words, short of actual punning, is welcomed as a relief. There is an air composed by Charles Delioux, to which all triolets in the pure form may be sung. De Banville quotes the melody in his "Odes Funnambulesque." Most people who have attempted to make rhymes know that when once a haunting melody gains control the words and sentences will try and fit themselves to it ; so perhaps a would-be writer of triolets could secure correct form by learning this tune and writing his triolets to it. It is quite certain that this alone would not ensure a good poem, but it might keep one to the usual rhythm and exact number of syllables, with the correct musical accent, singularly near, if not identical, with the poetical one, when properly used. A quaint example found by Mr. Dobson in an old French play is given on page 214, as it has not hitherto been printed in England.

The VILLANELLE has been called " the most ravishing jewel worn by the Muse Erato." The large number of Villanelles in modern English was the most unexpected find that came to light in the course of collecting material for the present volume. Many of these fulfil a condition now held strictly binding, since promulgated by Joseph Boulmier in his own Villanelles—that is, that their length should imitate the example of Jean Passerat's famous model, and be complete in nineteen lines. The rules sound simple, and the result must read easily ; but the ease is only to be attained by an elaborate amount of care in production, which those who read only would hardly suspect existed. The accepted model for all to follow will be found on page 242. The example that follows is an interesting translation by Boulmier of Mr. Dobson's Villanelle, " When I saw you last, Rose," first printed by his permission in *Longman's Magazine* (under the heading "At the Sign of the Ship") for July 1887 :—

ROSE.

Vous étiez encore petite
Rose, la dernière fois . . .
Dieu ! que le temps passe vite.

Fleur innocente qu'abrite
Tendrement l'ombre des bois
Vous étiez encore petite.

Et déjà la marguerite
Va s' effeuillant sous vos doigts . . .
Dieu ! que le temps passe vite !

Oh, comme se précipite
La vie. A peine j'y crois . . .
Vous étiez encor petite.

> Dans votre sein qui palpite
> Se glisse un hôte sournois . . .
> Dieu ! que le temps passe vite.
>
> Chez vous Cupidon s' invite :
> Adieu la paix d' autrefois !
> Vous étiez encore petite :
> Dieu ! que le temps passe vite !

The Villanelle is written in five three-lined stanzas, concluding with one of four lines. It will be seen that the refrain occupies eight of the nineteen lines, and is of paramount importance ; taken from the first and third line of the first stanza, the two supply alternately the last lines from the second to the fifth verse, and both conclude the quatrain which ends the villanelle. Two rhymes only are allowed. The refrains must repeat in the order quoted in the example, the first refrain to conclude the second and fifth stanzas, the second refrain for the first, third, and fifth, and both for the sixth.

"The primitive *Villanelle* was, in truth, a 'shepherd's song,' and, according to custom, its 'thoughts should be full of sweetness and simplicity,'" a hint given in a "Note on some Foreign Forms of Verse" that has been taken to heart by later writers, who almost invariably select pastoral or idyllic subjects for this most artificial but dainty lyric. Mr. Joseph Boulmier's "*Les Villanelles*," Paris, 1878, contains a valuable essay on the history and construction of the poem, and a series of forty original Villanelles, with twenty-two other poems, all of singular beauty.

The LAI and the VIRELAI are so nearly related that they must be considered together. De Gramont says, that the *lai* has been unused since the earliest days in French poetry, but as it is invariably quoted in all treatises on the art, he prints a seventeenth century one, evidently written as a specimen to illustrate its

laws.   De Banville cites the following by Pere Mourgues,
from his *Traité de la Poesie* :—

LAI.

> Sur l'appui du Monde
> Que faut-il qu'on fonde
> D'espoir?
> Cette mer profonde
> Et débris féconde
> Fait voir
> Calme au matin l'onde ;
> Et l'orage y gronde
> Le Soir.

As no examples of the Lai are included in this volume,
by the courtesy of the author I am allowed to quote the
following :—

FROM OVERSEA.

> From oversea—
> Violets, for memories,
> I send to thee.
>
> Let them bear thought of me,
> With pleasant memories
> To touch the heart of thee,
> Far oversea.
>
> A little way it is for love to flee,
> Love wing'd with memories,
> Hither to thither oversea.

—William Sharp.

In the French example the form is seen to be composed
of couplets of five syllable lines, all on the same rhyme,
separated by single lines of two syllables, also on one
rhyme throughout the stanza, which therefore employs
but two rhymes.   The number of lines in each verse
was not fixed, nor the number of verses in the complete
poem.   The LAI has preserved a curious old tradition

in the form it appears either in writing or print. As in the verse quoted, the first letter of each line begins exactly under the preceding one; not with the short line indented—that is coming under the middle of the larger ones—usual in other poems composed of lines of irregular length. This detail was called *Arbre fourchu* (a forked tree), from the fanciful resemblance of a trunk with bare branches projecting, found by imaginative persons in its appearance on paper.

In the Lai each fresh stanza of the poem has its own two rhyme sounds, without reference to the preceding ones. By curtailing this liberty, and compelling each succeeding stanza to take the rhyme for its longer lines, from the short line of the preceding verse the Virelai is produced.

THE VIRELAI (ancien) is a lai that preserves a sequence of rhymes throughout. For example, in a twelve-line stanza the rhymes are A. A. b. A. A b. A. A. b. A. A. b. (the long lines being marked by capital letters, and the shorter by small ones). Therefore, to follow the rules of the virelai, the next verse must have its rhymes B. B. c. B. B. c. B. B. c. B. B. c., and the next C. C. d. C. C. d., and so on until the last verse (taking seven verses for an example) would have G. G. a. G. G. a. G. G. a. G. G. a., its short lines rhyming with the two first lines of the poem. Thus each rhyme appears twice, once in its longer couplets, once in the short single lines. In the English examples this rule is preserved, but the length of the lines are frequently varied.

The VIRELAI (Rhythme d'Alain Chartier) by Boulmier may be quoted as a form yet unused (I believe) in England.

> TRISTE remembrance !
> Hé ! Dieu ! quand i'y pense
> Ce m'est grand penance :
> Las ! de ma iouuence
> A passé la flour.

Sanz doubter meschance,
Bercé d'esperance
Plain de desirance
Auecq Oubliance
Ay faict long seiour.

Nice troubadour
Assoty pastour
Serf ie feus d' Amour
Mais de ma folour
Ie n' ay repentance.

Ouyl, mangré Donlour
Bel Aage engignour
En mog fay retour,
Ne fust-ce qu' vng iour. . .
Et ie recommence.

The rhymes are a, a, a, a, b; a, a, a, b; b, b, b, b, a; b, b, b, b, a. As but one example has come to notice, so it must speak for itself, for it would be unfair to deduce rules from a single specimen. Before leaving this heading there is another form, the *Virelai nouveau*, singularly unlike its name. It is curious that both the Rondeau Redoublé and this one, masquerading under the names of well-known forms, should be each unlike their unqualified title, and yet so nearly akin to the other.

The *Virelai nouveau* is written throughout in two rhymes. Like the *rondeau redoublé*, its first stanza serves as refrain for the later ones, but its initial verse is but a couplet, and the two lines close each stanza alternately until the last, where they appear both together, but in inverse order. Unfortunately, space forbids an example being quoted in its complete length. The one usually chosen is "Le Rimeur Rebuté;" this commences with the couplet—

Adieu vous dy, triste Lyre,
C'est trop apprêter à rire.

  INTRODUCTION.

Then follows a five-line stanza, rhyming a, a, b, a, a, with " Adieu vous dy," etc., for its last line ; then an eight-lined one rhymed a, b, a, a, b, a, b, a, the last line being " *C'est trop*," etc. ; that is followed by a four-line one closing with first line ; then a sixteen-line one, using the second line for its refrain ; then a seventeen-line one, with first line ending it ; and finally a five-line stanza, its last lines being—

> C'est trop apprêter à rire,
> Adieu vous dy, triste lyre.

If this description conveys its intended meaning, it will be seen that the verses are singularly irregular in form, and choose both the order of the rhymes and the length of the verses exactly at the will of the poet ; but each paragraph must not only use its proper refrain to close with, but must bring it in naturally and easily as an inherent part of the verse. The last two lines in the inverted order must also be worked in with equal skill. Excepting one by Mr. Austin Dobson, that appeared in *Evening Hours* about 1878, this form has been unused, or at least unpublished, in English verse.

The poems in the following collections have been chosen for several reasons—some for their intrinsic excellence, some as examples of pure form, some for their bold attempts to produce variations from the typical models. There has been no limit to the subjects, since the purpose was to give a representative group of the rhythms, treated in the most diverse ways. Even burlesque and diatribe of the use of the forms, masquerading in guise of the enemy they professed to attack, have been welcomed, as the points of the construction of the verse are often seen more clearly in such examples. For similar reasons the parody of the pioneer Ballade, Mr. Austin Dobson's *Prodigals*, is quoted, since the doubtful honour of parody is at least a proof of wide popularity, the only others marked in this way being Mr. Swinburne's ' *Dreamland* ' and Mr. Lang's ' *Primitive Man.* ' Here, too, in default of a better place, it may be noted that Mr. Henley's ' Villonism ' is not an imitation of the incomprehensible ballades in ' Jargon ' or ' Jobelin,' but a paraphrase in thieves' patter of to-day of Villon's *Ballade of Good Counsel.*

It may be that such a medley of themes handled in so many different ways, was never of set purpose grouped side by side before, but is to be hoped that a method in the madness will be found. While conscious of a few noteworthy examples, Rossetti's *Translations from Villon* to wit, being not included for reasons beyond my control, so it may be that one or two here inserted would have been replaced by later comers, had they not gone to the printer's eternity of stereotype. Started as a collection, but turned perforce to a selection, from the increasing number available, they yet do not aim so much at being a selection of the best work solely, as of the best and least-accessible examples. This explanation of the progress and purpose of the volume is offered in common fairness both to its readers and to those authors who have permitted their works to be included, also to those who by oversight or too late discovery on my part have no examples of their poetry included herein.

[Note to page xxxvi.—For Wyatt's Rondeaus, and alteration of the same into Sonnets by Tottel, in his *Miscellany*, 1557, see Mr. Austin Dobson's Note in the *Athenæum.*]

The Ballade, The Double Ballade, and The Chant Royal.

Ballade en huitains d' octosyllabes.

Chant de May.

En ce beau mois delicieux,
Arbres, fleurs et agriculture,
Qui, durant l' yver soncieux,
Avez esté en sepulture,
Sortez pour servir de pasture
Aux troupeaux du plus grand Pasteur:
Chacun de vous en sa nature,
Louez le nom de Createur.

Les servans d' amour furieux
Parlent de l' amour vaine et dure,
Où vous, vrays amans curieux
Parlez de l' amour sans laidure.
Allez aux champs sur la verdure
Ouir l' oyseau, parfait chanteur;
Mais du plaisir, si peu qu 'il dure
Louez le nom de Createur.

Quand vous verrez rire les Cieux
Et la terre en sa floriture,
Quand vous verrez devant vos yeux
Les eaux lui bailler nourriture,
Sur peine de grand forfaiture
Et d' estre larron et menteur,
N' en louez nulle creature,
Louez le nom de Createur.

Envoy.

Prince, pensez, veu la facture,
Combien est puissant le facteur;
Et vous aussi, mon escriture,
Louez le nom de Createur.

—CLÉMENT MAROT.

WHERE ARE THE PIPES OF PAN?

In these prosaic days
    Of politics and trade,
Where seldom fancy lays
    Her touch on man or maid,
    The sounds are fled that strayed
Along sweet streams that ran ;
    Of song the world's afraid :
Where are the Pipes of Pan ?

Within the busy maze
    Wherein our feet are stayed,
There roam no gleesome fays
    Like those which once repaid
    His sight who first essayed
The stream of song to span,
    Those spirits are all laid.
Where are the Pipes of Pan ?

Dry now the poet's bays ;
    Of song-robes disarrayed
He hears not now the praise
    Which erst those won who played
    On pipes of rushes made,
Before dull days began
    And love of song decayed.
Where are the Pipes of Pan ?

Envoy.

Prince, all our pleasures fade ;
    Vain all the toils of man :
And fancy cries dismayed,
    Where are the Pipes of Pan ?

OSCAR FAY ADAMS.

A BALLADE OF EVOLUTION.

In the mud of the Cambrian main
    Did our earliest ancestor dive :
From a shapeless albuminous grain
    We mortals our being derive.
    He could split himself up into five,
Or roll himself round like a ball ;
    For the fittest will always survive,
While the weakliest go to the wall.

As an active ascidian again
    Fresh forms he began to contrive,
Till he grew to a fish with a brain,
    And brought forth a mammal alive.
    With his rivals he next had to strive,
To woo him a mate and a thrall ;
    So the handsomest managed to wive
While the ugliest went to the wall.

At length as an ape he was fain
    The nuts of the forest to rive ;
Till he took to the low-lying plain,
    And proceeded his fellow to knive.
    Thus did cannibal men first arrive,
One another to swallow and maul ;
    And the strongest continued to thrive.
While the weakliest went to the wall.

Envoy.

Prince, in our civilised hive
    Now money's the measure of all ;
And the wealthy in coaches can drive
    While the needier go to the wall.

GRANT ALLEN.

BALLADE OF SOLITUDE.

Thank Heaven, in these despondent days,
    I have at least one faithful friend,
Who meekly listens to my lays,
    As o'er the darkened downs we wend.
    Nay, naught of mine may him offend ;
In sooth he is a courteous wight,
    His constancy needs no amend—
My shadow on a moonlight night.

Too proud to give me perjured praise,
    He hearkens as we onward tend,
And ne'er disputes a doubtful phrase,
    Nor says he cannot comprehend.
    Might God such critics always send !
He turns not to the left or right,
    But patient follows to the end—
My shadow on a moonlight night.

And if the public grant me bays,
    On him no jealousies descend ;
But through the midnight woodland ways,
    He velvet-footed will attend ;
    Or where the chalk cliffs downward bend
To meet the sea all silver-bright,
    There will he come, most reverend—
My shadow on a moonlight night.

Envoy.

O wise companion, I commend
    Your grace in being silent quite ;
And envy with approval blend—
    My shadow on a moonlight night.

WILLIAM BLACK.

A BALLADE OF BOTHERS.

From country, from coast and from city,
    From nowhere and goodness knows where,
The visitors come without pity,
    There is not a corner to spare ;
    And students with work to prepare
Must charter a captive balloon
    And study aloft in the air,
For the May Week has fallen in June.

The grinding of feet that are gritty
    So ceaseless on landing and stair ;
The notes of some drawing-room ditty
    Disturb the recluse in his lair
    And cause him to clutch at his hair
As he toils in the hot afternoon ;
    But nobody hears if he swear,
For the May Week has fallen in June.

Then the damsels supposing its pretty
    Their art-curtain patterns to wear,
And the youths who conceive they are witty,
    Came round to be stared at, and stare.
    And amateur buglers that blare,
And singers that howl to the moon,
    Are more than the system can bear ;
For the May Week has fallen in June.

Envoi.

Friend, do not be caught in the snare,
    And strive not to sing or to spoon,
Your tripos is all your affair,
    For the May Week has fallen in June.

From the ' Cambridge Meteor.'

BALLADE OF BELIEF.

Says Herbert : Pray, list to my notion,
    All ye who the truth would invite ;
Be Agnostics, and spurn the emotion
    That ghosts and the gospels excite.
    In th' Unknown do I find all delight,
And in Infinite Energy see
    All casual cravings unite—
And that's the religion for me.

Says Frederic : Pray list to *my* notion,
    Away with Impersonal Might,
To Humanity tender promotion,
    And worship the idëal wight.
    Though from stock that is Simian hight
He may trace out a pure pedigree,
    Yet to Man will I anthems recite—
And that's the religion for me.

Says Wilfrid : Pray, list to *my* notion,
    On the hip I will infidels smite ;
'Tis only through Christian devotion
    That virtues with vices can fight.
    Whate'er may Theology write,
Whatever the Church may decree,
    My soul shall acknowledge as right—
And that's the religion for me.

Envoi.
(*Voice of the bewildered one.*)

O faith full of riddle and rite,
    O philosophies deep as the sea,
In this posse of problems polite,
    Prithee, where's the religion for me ?

COTSFORD DICK.

BALLADE OF BURIAL.

The sunlight sways the summer sky,
 Quivers with breath each quicken'd blade,
The birds with one another vie
 To move to mirth the grove and glade,
 While yonder solemn cavalcade
Winds o'er the glebe in gloom august,
 Chanting a dead man's serenade,
Ashes to ashes, dust to dust.

A smile is mated to a sigh,
 One flashes ere the other fade,
Farce arm-in-arm with tragedy,
 So struts the motley masquerade.
 Youth deems for joy the world is made,
Till disappointment deals disgust,
 Disease defiles the last decade,
Ashes to ashes, dust to dast.

Within the grave our earnest eye
 Beholds a brother's body laid,
Around us sombre hirelings ply
 The unctuous usage of their trade.
 Beneath the hedgerow laughs a maid,
Held in a lover's arm robust ;
 One day for her it shall be said,
Ashes to ashes, dust to dust.

Envoi.

Life, dost thou still possess the shade
 Of him in earth so rudely thrust ?
Canst thou the sentence yet evade,
 Ashes to ashes, dust to dust ?

COTSFORD DICK.

A BALLAD TO QUEEN ELIZABETH.

Of the Spanish Armada.

King Philip had vaunted his claims ;
    He had sworn for a year he would sack us ;
With an army of heathenish names
    He was coming to fagot and stack us ;
    Like the thieves of the sea he would track us,
And shatter our ships on the main ;
    But we had bold Neptune to back us,—
And where are the galleons of Spain ?

His carackes were christened of dames
    To the kirtles whereof he would tack us ;
With his saints and his gilded stern-frames,
    He had thought like an egg-shell to crack us :
    Now Howard may get to his Flaccus,
And Drake to his Devon again,
    And Hawkins bowl rubbers to Bacchus,—
For where are the galleons of Spain ?

Let his Majesty hang to St. James
    The axe that he whetted to hack us ;
He must play at some lustier games
    Or at sea he can hope to out-thwack us ;
    To his mines of Peru he would pack us
To tug at his bullet and chain ;
    Alas that his Greatness should lack us !—
But where are the galleons of Spain ?

Envoy.

Gloriana !—the Don may attack us
    Whenever his stomach be fain ;
    He must reach us before he can rack us, . .
And where are the galleons of Spain ?

Austin Dobson.

ON A FAN THAT BELONGED TO THE MARQUISE DE POMPADOUR.

Chicken-skin, delicate, white,
    Painted by Carlo Vanloo,
Loves in a riot of light,
    Roses and vaporous blue ;
    Hark to the dainty *frou-frou!*
Picture above if you can,
    Eyes that could melt as the dew,—
This was the Pompadour's fan !

See how they rise at the sight,
    Thronging the *Œil de Bœuf* through,
Courtiers as butterflies bright,
    Beauties that Fragonard drew,
Talon-rouge, falbala, queue,
    Cardinal, Duke,—to a man,
    Eager to sigh or to sue,—
This was the Pompadour's fan !

Ah ! but things more than polite
    Hung on this toy, *voyez vous !*
Matters of state and of might,
    Things that great ministers do ;
    Things that, maybe, overthrew
Those in whose brains they began ;
    Here was the sign and the cue,—
This was the Pompadour's fan !

Envoy.

Where are the secrets it knew ?
    Weavings of plot and of plan ?
—But where is the Pompadour, too ?
    This was the Pompadour's *Fan !*

AUSTIN DOBSON.

THE BALLAD OF IMITATION.

" C'est imiter quelqu' un que de planter des choux."
—ALFRED DE MUSSET.

If they hint, O Musician, the piece that you played
  Is nought but a copy of Chopin or Spohr ;
That the ballad you sing is but merely "conveyed"
  From the stock of the Arnes and the Purcells of yore ;
  That there's nothing, in short, in the words or the score,
That is not as out-worn as the " Wandering Jew ; "
  Make answer—Beethoven could scarcely do more—
That the man who plants cabbages imitates, too !

If they tell you, Sir Artist, your light and your shade
  Are simply "adapted" from other men's lore ;
That—plainly to speak of a "spade " as a " spade "—
  You've "stolen" your grouping from three or from four;
  That (however the writer the truth may deplore),
'Twas Gainsborough painted *your* " Little Boy Blue ; "
  Smile only serenely—though cut to the core—
For the man who plants cabbages imitates, too !

And you too, my Poet, be never dismayed
  If they whisper your Epic—"Sir Éperon d' Or "—
Is nothing but Tennyson thinly arrayed
  In a tissue that's taken from Morris's store ;
  That no one, in fact, but a child could ignore
That you " lift " or " accommodate " all that you do ;
  Take heart—though your Pegasus' withers be sore—
For the man who plants cabbages imitates, too !

POSTSCRIPTUM.—And you, whom we all so adore,
  Dear Critics, whose verdicts are always so new !—
One word in your ear.   There were Critics before . .
  And the man who plants cabbages imitates, too !

AUSTIN DOBSON.

THE BALLADE OF PROSE AND RHYME.

(Ballade à double refrain.)

When the roads are heavy with mire and rut,
   In November fogs, in December snows,
When the North Wind howls, and the doors are shut,
    There is place and enough for the pains of prose ;—
    But whenever a scent from the whitethorn blows,
And the jasmine-stars to the casement climb,
    And a Rosalind-face at the lattice shows,
Then hey !—for the ripple of laughing rhyme !

When the brain gets dry as an empty nut,
   When the reason stands on its squarest toes,
When the mind (like a beard) has a "formal cut,"
    There is place and enough for the pains of prose ;—
    But whenever the May-blood stirs and glows,
And the young year draws to the " golden prime,"—
    And Sir Romeo sticks in his ear a rose,
Then hey !—for the ripple of laughing rhyme !

In a theme where the thoughts have a pedant-strut
   In a changing quarrel of " Ayes " and " Noes,"
In a starched procession of " If " and " But,"
    There is place and enough for the pains of prose ;—
    But whenever a soft glance softer grows,
And the light hours dance to the trysting-time,
    And the secret is told " that no one knows,"
Then hey !—for the ripple of laughing rhyme !

Envoy.

In the work-a-day world,—for its needs and woes,
There is place and enough for the pains of prose ;
But whenever the May-bells clash and chime,
Then hey !—for the ripple of laughing rhyme !

AUSTIN DOBSON.

THE BALLAD OF DEAD CITIES.

To A. L.

Where are the cities of the plain?
    And where the shrines of rapt Bethel?
And Calah built of Tubal-Cain?
    And Shinar whence King Amraphel
    Came out in arms, and fought, and fell,
Decoyed into the pits of slime
    By Siddim, and sent sheer to hell;
Where are the cities of old time?

Where now is Karnak, that great fane
    With granite built, a miracle?
And Luxor smooth without a stain,
    Whose graven scriptures still we spell?
    The jackal and the owl may tell,
Dark snakes around their ruins climb,
    They fade like echo in a shell;
Where are the cities of old time?

And where is white Shusan, again,
    Where Vashti's beauty bore the bell,
And all the Jewish oil and grain
    Were brought to Mithridath to sell,
    Where Nehemiah would not dwell,
Because another town sublime
    Decoyed him with her oracle?
Where are the cities of old time?

Envoi.

Prince, with a dolorous, ceaseless knell,
    Above their wasted toil and crime
The waters of oblivion swell:
    Where are the cities of old time?

EDMUND GOSSE.

BALLADE.

Love thou art sweet in the spring-time of sowing
    Bitter in reaping and salt as the seas,
Lovely and soft when the young buds are growing
    Harsh when the fruitage is ripe on the trees :
      Yet who that hath plucked him thy blossom e'er flees
      Who that hath drunk of thy sweetness can part,
    Tho' he find when thy chalice is drained to the lees
    Ashes and dust in the place of a heart ?

'Tis myself that I curse at, the wild thoughts flowing
    Against myself built up of the breeze
Like mountainous waves to my own o'erthrowing
    Strike and I tremble, my shivering knees
    Sink thro' the quicksands that round them freeze,
      From their treacherous hold I am loth to start :—
    In my breast laid bare, had you only the keys,
    Ashes and dust in the place of a heart.

The world wide over young hearts are glowing
    With high held hopes we believed with ease,
And have them still, but the saddest knowing
    Is the knowledge of how by slow degrees
    They slip from our side like a swarm of bees
      Bearing their sweetness away, and depart
    Leaving their stings in our bosom, with these
    Ashes and dust in the place of a heart.

Envoi.

Love, free on the uplands, the lawns, and leas ;
    Priced and sold in the World's base mart :
But the same in the end ; tho' at first it please,
    Ashes and dust in the place of a heart.

JOHN CAMERON GRANT.

BALLADE.—LILITH.

Lady, around thy throat
  Gleameth the one gold hair;
And none that hath taken note
  Of the first that he looked on fair,
  The moment his boyish air
    Was moved by that mystic breeze,
  But hath felt the spell of thy presence there,
    Lilith, the first Love sees!

We sail in an open boat,
  'Mid breakers that rage and tear,
And ply the oars by rote
  As over the waves we fare,
  But never a moment dare
    Gaze down at the Form by our knees,
  For her eyes that thro' Self and thro' Soul do stare,
    Lilith, the first Love sees!

Circle of wall and moat,
  Vain as the thought to wear
Cunning of knightly coat
  Steely and tempered rare,
  Against her mute despair;
    For none there is who frees
  His soul from her spell, who hath all in care,
    Lilith, the first Love sees!

L' Envoi.

Maid without mate or pair,
  From the Past's pale Presences,
Who is there but next his heart doth bear
    Lilith, the first Love sees!

JOHN CAMERON GRANT.

BALLADE OF ANTIQUE DANCES.

Before the town had lost its wits,
   And scared the bravery from its beaux,
When money-grubs were merely cits,
   And verse was crisp and clear as prose,
   Ere Chloë and Strephon came to blows
For votes, degrees, and cigarettes,
   The world rejoiced to point its toes
In Gigues, Gavottes, and Minuets.

The solemn fiddlers touch their kits ;
   The twinkling clavichord o'erflows
With contrapuntal quirks and hits ;
   And, with all measure and repose,
   Through figures grave as royal shows,
With noble airs and pirouettes,
   They move, to rhythms HANDEL knows,
In Gigues, Gavottes, and Minuets.

O Fans and Swords, O Sacques and Mits,
   That was the better part you chose !
You know not how those gamesome chits
   Waltz, Polka, and Schottische arose,
   Or how Quadrille—a kind of doze
In time and tune—the dance besets ;
   You aired your fashion till the close
In Gigues, Gavottes, and Minuets.

Envoy.

   Muse of the many-twinkling hose,
TERPSICHORE, O teach your pets
   The charm that shines, the grace that glows
In Gigues, Gavottes, and Minuets.

W. E. HENLEY.

BALLADE OF DEAD ACTORS.

Where are the passions they essayed,
  And where the tears they made to flow?
Where the wild humours they portrayed
  For laughing worlds to see and know?
  Othello's wrath and Juliet's woe?
Sir Peter's whims and Timon's gall?
  And Millamant and Romeo?—
Into the night go one and all.

Where are the braveries, fresh or frayed?
  The plumes, the armours—friend and foe?
The cloth of gold, the rare brocade,
  The mantles glittering to and fro?
  The pomp, the pride, the royal show?
The cries of war and festival?
  The youth, the grace, the charm, the glow?—
Into the night go one and all.

The curtain falls, the play is played:
  The Beggar packs beside the Beau;
The Monarch troops, and troops the Maid;
  The Thunder huddles with the Snow.
  Where are the revellers high and low?
The clashing swords? The lover's call?
  The dancers gleaming row on row?—
Into the night go one and all.

Envoy.

Prince, in one common overthrow
The hero tumbles with the thrall:
  As dust that drives, as straws that blow,
Into the night go one and all.

                          W. E. HENLEY.

BALLADE OF JUNE.

Lilacs glow, and jasmines climb,
    Larks are loud the livelong day.
O the golden summer-prime !
    June takes up the sceptre of May,
    And the land beneath her sway
Glows, a dream of flowerful closes,
    And the very wind's at play
With Sir Love among the roses.

Lights and shadows in the lime
    Meet in exquisite disarray.
Hark ! the rich recurrent rhyme
    Of the blackbird's roundelay !
    Where he carols, frank and gay,
Fancy no more glooms or proses ;
    Joyously she flits away
With Sir Love among the roses.

O the cool sea's slumbrous chime !
    O the links that beach the bay,
Tricked with meadow-sweet and thyme,
    Where the brown bees murmur and stray !
    Lush the hedgerows, ripe the hay !
Many a maiden, binding posies,
    Finds herself at Yea-and-Nay
With Sir Love among the roses.

Envoi.

    Boys and girls, be wise, I pray !
Do as dear Queen June proposes,
    For she bids you troop and stay
With Sir Love among the roses.

W. E. Henley.

BALLADE OF LADIES' NAMES.

Brown's for Lalage, Jones for Lelia,
　　Robinson's bosom for Beatrice glows,
Smith is a Hamlet before Ophelia.
　　The glamour stays if the reason goes !
　　Every lover the years disclose
Is of a beautiful name made free.
　　One befriends, and all others are foes.
Anna's the name of names for me.

Sentiment hallows the vowels of Delia ;
　　Sweet simplicity breathes from Rose ;
Courtly memories glitter in Celia ;
　　Rosalind savours of quips and hose,
　　Araminta of wits and beaux,
Prue of puddings, and Coralie
　　All of sawdust and spangled shows :
Anna's the name of names for me.

Fie upon Caroline, Madge, Amelia—
　　These I reckon the essence of prose !—
Cavalier Katharine, cold Cornelia,
　　Portia's masterful Roman nose,
　　Maud's magnificence, Totty's toes,
Poll and Bet with their twang of the sea,
　　Nell's impertinence, Pamela's woes !
Anna's the name of names for me.

Envoy.

Ruth like a gillyflower smells and blows,
　　Sylvia prattles of Arcadee,
Sybil mystifies, Connie crows,
　　Anna's the name of names for me !

W. E. HENLEY.

BALLADE OF SPRING.

There's a noise of coming, going,
  Budding, waking, vast and still.
Hark, the echoes are yeo-hoing
  Loud and sweet from vale and hill !
  Do you hear it ?   With a will,
In a grandiose lilt and swing,
  Nature's voices shout and trill. . .
'Tis the symphony of Spring !

Rains are singing, clouds are flowing,
  Ocean thunders, croons the rill,
And the West his clarion's blowing,
  And the sparrow tunes his quill,
  And the thrush is fluting shrill,
And the skylark's on the wing,
  And the merles their hautboys fill—
'Tis the symphony of Spring !

Lambs are bleating, steers are lowing,
  Brisk and rhythmic clacks the mill.
Kapellmeister April, glowing
  And superb with glee and skill,
  Comes, his orchestra to drill
In a music that will ring
  Till the grey world yearn and thrill.
'Tis the symphony of Spring !

Envoy.

Princes, though your blood he chill,
  Here's shall make you leap and fling,
Fling and leap like Jack and Jill !
  'Tis the symphony of Spring.

W. E. HENLEY.

BALLADE OF MIDSUMMER DAYS AND NIGHTS.

(Double refrain.)

With a ripple of leaves and a tinkle of streams
    The full world rolls in a rhythm of praise,
And the winds are one with the clouds and beams—
    Midsummer days ! midsummer days !
    The dusk grows vast ; in a purple haze,
While the West from a rapture of sunset rights,
    Faint stars their exquisite lamps upraise—
Midsummer nights ! O midsummer nights !

The wood's green heart is a nest of dreams,
    The lush grass thickens and springs and sways,
The rathe wheat rustles, the landscape gleams—
    Midsummer days ! midsummer days !
    In the stilly fields, in the stilly ways,
All secret shadows and mystic lights,
    Late lovers murmurous linger and gaze—
Midsummer nights ! O midsummer nights !

There's a music of bells from the trampling teams,
    Wild skylarks hover, the gorses blaze,
The rich, ripe rose as with incense steams—
    Midsummer days ! midsummer days !
    A soul from the honeysuckle strays,
And the nightingale as from prophet heights,
    Sings to the Earth of her million Mays—
Midsummer nights ! O midsummer nights !

Envoy.

And its O ! for my dear and the charm that stays—
Midsummer days ! midsummer days !
    Its O ! for my Love and the dark that plights—
    Midsummer nights ! O midsummer nights !

W. E. HENLEY.

BALLADE OF YOUTH AND AGE.

(Double refrain.)

Spring at her height on a morn at prime,
  Sails that laugh from a flying squall,
Pomp of harmony, rapture of rhyme—
  Youth is the sign of them, one and all.
  Winter sunsets and leaves that fall,
An empty flagon, a folded page,
  A tumble-down wheel, a tattered ball—
These are a type of the world of Age.

Bells that clash in a gorgeous chime,
  Swords that clatter in outsets tall,
The words that ring and the fames that climb—
  Youth is the sign of them, one and all.
  Old hymnals prone in a dusty stall,
A bald blind bird in a crazy cage,
  The scene of a faded festival—
These are a type of the world of Age.

Hours that strut as the heirs of time,
  Deeds whose rumour's a clarion-call,
Songs where the singers their souls sublime—
  Youth is the sign of them, one and all.
  A staff that rests in a nook of wall,
A reeling battle, a rusted gage,
  The chant of a nearing funeral—
These are a type of the world of Age.

Envoy.

Struggle and sacrifice, revel and brawl—
Youth is the sign of them, one and all.
  A smouldering hearth and a silent stage—
  These are a type of the world of Age.

W. E. HENLEY.

BALLADE.

The sun across the meads glows bright ;
   The river shines a silver sheet,
And mirrors back the pearly light.
   In its warm gleam the shadows fleet,
   Earth seems in joy the heaven to greet ;
Heaven's love illumes the deep blue skies,
   And birds and flowers and streams repeat,
' Where true love dwells is Paradise.'

Beneath the hedge with May-bloom white
   An old man and a child, whose feet
In cadence move to love's fond might ;
   In its warm gleam the shadows fleet ;
   Like op'ning flowers in morn's soft heat.
A youth and maid whose beaming eyes
   Flash forth the thought their hearts secrete,
' Where true love dwells is Paradise.'

Within the minster's fane the rite
   Is breathed ; down-pours His own to meet
The glory of the Infinite :
   In its warm gleam the shadows fleet ;
   Faith falls before the mercy-seat,
And knows, though veiled to mortal eyes,
   There, there in loveliness complete,
Where True Love dwells is Paradise.

Past sounding brass are love's tones sweet,
   Than gold or gems more rare its price ;
In its warm gleam the shadows fleet ;
   Where true love dwells is Paradise.

W. H. JEWITT.

BALLADE DES PENDUS.   (GRINGOIRE.)

Where wide the forest boughs are spread,
    When Flora wakes with sylph and fay,
Are crowns and garlands of men dead,
    All golden in the morning gay ;
Within this ancient garden grey
    Are clusters such as no man knows,
Where Moor and Soldan bear the sway :
    This is King Louis' orchard close.

These wretched folk wave overhead,
    With such strange thoughts as none may say ;
A moment still, then sudden sped,
    They swing in a ring and waste away.
The morning smites them with her ray ;
    They toss with every breeze that blows,
They dance where fires of dawning play :
    This is King Louis' orchard close.

All hanged and dead, they've summoned
    (With Hell to aid that hears them pray)
New legions of an army dread,
    Now down the blue sky flames the day ;
The dew dries off ; the foul array
    Of obscene ravens gathers and goes,
With wings that flaps and beaks that flay :
    This is King Louis' orchard close.

Envoi.

Prince, where leaves murmur of the May,
    A tree of bitter clusters grows ;
The bodies of men dead are they,
    This is King Louis' orchard close.

ANDREW LANG.

VALENTINE IN FORM OF BALLADE.

The soft wind from the south land sped,
    He set his strength to blow,
O'er forests where Adonis bled
    And lily flowers a-row.
He crossed the straits like streams that flow
    The ocean dark as wine
To my true love to whisper low
    To be your Valentine.

The spring-time raised her drowsy head,
    Besprent with drifted snow,
" I'll send an April Day," she said,
    " To lands of wintry woe."
He came ; wan winter's overthrow
    With showers that sing and shine
Pied daisies round your path to strow,
    To be your Valentine.

Where sands of Egypt swart and red
    'Neath suns Egyptian glow,
In places of the princely dead
    By the Nile's overflow,
The swallow preened her wings to go,
    And for the North did pine,
And fain would brave the frost, her foe,
    To be your Valentine.

Envoy.

Spring, Swallow, South Wind, even so
    Their various voice combine,
But that they crave on me bestow
    To be your Valentine.

ANDREW LANG.

BALLADE OF PRIMITIVE MAN.

(To J. A. Farrer.)

He lived in a cave by the seas,
    He lived upon oysters and foes,
But his list of forbidden degrees
    An extensive morality shows:
    Geological evidence goes
To prove he had never a pan,
    But he shaved with a shell when he chose.
'Twas the manner of Primitive Man!

He worshipp'd the rain and the breeze,
    He worshipped the river that flows,
And the Dawn, and the Moon, and the trees,
    And bogies, and serpents, and crows;
    He buried his dead with their toes
Tucked up, an original plan,
    Till their knees came right under their nose,
'Twas the manner of Primitive Man!

His communal wives, at his ease,
    He would curb with occasional blows;
Or his State had a queen, like the bees
    (As another philosopher trows):
    When he spoke it was never in prose,
But he sang in a strain that would scan,
    For (to doubt it, perchance, were morose)
'Twas the manner of Primitive Man!

Envoy.

Max, proudly your Aryans pose,
But their rigs they undoubtedly ran,
    For, as every Darwinian knows,
'Twas the manner of Primitive Man!

Andrew Lang.

BALLADE OF SUMMER.

(To Constance Arkcoll.)

When strawberry pottles are common and cheap,
   Ere elms be black, or limes be sere,
When midnight dances are murdering sleep,
   Then comes in the sweet o' the year !
   And far from Fleet Street, far from here
The Summer is Queen in the length of the land,
   And moonlight nights they are soft and clear,
When fans for a penny are sold in the Strand.

When clamour that doves in the lindens keep,
   Mingles with musical plash of the weir,
Where drowned green tresses of crowsfoot creep,
   Then comes in the sweet o' the year !
   And better a crust and a beaker of beer,
With rose-hung hedges on either hand,
   Than a palace in town and a prince's cheer,
When fans for a penny are sold in the Strand !

When big trout late in the twilight leap,
   When cuckoo clamoureth far and near,
When glittering scythes in the hayfield reap,
   Then comes in the sweet o' the year !
   And it's oh to sail, with the wind to steer,
Where kine knee-deep in the water stand,
   On a Highland loch, or a Lowland mere,
When fans for a penny are sold in the Strand.

Envoi.

   Friend, with the fops while we dawdle here,
   Then comes in the sweet o' the year !
And Summer runs out like grains of sand,
When fans for a penny are sold in the Strand.

ANDREW LANG.

BALLADE OF YULE.

" Heigo-ho, the holly !
This life is most jolly."

This life's most jolly, Amiens said
    Heigh-ho, the Holly !   So sang he
As the good duke was comforted
    By these reflections, so may we !
The years may darken as they flee,
    And Christmas bring his melancholy ;
But round the old mahogany tree
    We drink, we sing *Heigh-ho, the Holly !*

Though some are dead and some are fled
    To lands of summer over sea,
The holly berry keeps his red,
    The merry children keep their glee ;
They hoard with artless secresy,
    This gift for Maude, and that for Molly,
And Santa Claus he turns the key
    On Christmas Eve, *Heigh-ho, the Holly !*

Amid the snow the birds are fed,
    The snow lies deep on lawn and lea,
The skies are shining overhead,
    The robin's tame that was so free.
Far North, at home, the " barley bree "
    They brew ; they give the hour to folly.
How " Rab and Allen cam' to prie "
    They sing ; we sing *Heigh-ho, the Holly !*

Envoi.

Friend, let us pay the wonted fee,
    The yearly tithe of mirth : be jolly !
It is a duty so to be,
    Though half we sigh, *Heigh-ho, the Holly !*

                    ANDREW LANG.

BALLADE OF MIDDLE AGE.

Our youth began with tears and sighs
    With seeking what we could not find ;
Our verses all were threnodies,
    In elegiacs still we whined ;
    Our ears were deaf, our eyes were blind,
We sought and knew not what we sought.
    We marvel, now we look behind :
Life's more amusing than we thought !

Oh ! foolish youth, untimely wise !
    Oh ! phantoms of the sickly mind !
What ? not content with seas and skies,
    With rainy clouds and southern wind,
    With common cares and faces kind,
With pains and joys each morning brought ?
    Ah, old and worn, and tired we find
Life's more amusing than we thought !

Though youth "turns spectre-thin and dies,"
    To mourn for youth we're not inclined ;
We set our souls on salmon-flies,
    We whistle where we once repined.
    Confound the woes of human-kind !
By Heaven we're "well deceived," I wot ;
    Who hum, contented or resigned,
" Life's more amusing than we thought ! "

Envoy.

O nate mecum, worn and lined
Our faces show, but that is naught ;
    Our hearts are young 'neath wrinkled rind—
Life's more amusing than we thought !
ANDREW LANG.

BALLADE FOR THE LAUREATE.

(After Theodore de Banville.)

Rhyme, in a late disdainful age,
    Hath many and many an eager knight,
Each man of them, to print his page,
    From every quarter wings his flight !
What tons of manuscript alight
    Here in the Row, how many a while
For all can rhyme, when all can write—
    The master's yonder in the Isle !

Like Otus some, with giant rage,
    But scarcely with a giant's might,
Ossa on Pelion engage
    To pile, and scale Parnassus' height !
    And some, with subtle nets and slight,
Entangle rhymes exceeding vile,[1]
    And wond'rous adjectives unite—
The master's yonder in the Isle !

Alas, the Muse they cannot cage
    These poets in a sorry plight !
Vain is the weary war they wage,
    In vain they curse the Critic's spite !
While grammar some neglect outright,
    While others polish with the file,
The Fates contrive their toil to blight—
    The master's yonder in the Isle !

Envoy.

Prince, Arnold's jewel-work is bright,
    And Browning, in his iron style,
Doth gold on his rude anvil smite—
    The master's yonder in the Isle !

ANDREW LANG.

[1] For example 'dawning' and 'warning,'

BALLADE OF THE SOUTHERN CROSS.

Fair islands of the silver fleece,
  Hoards of unsunned, uncounted gold.
Whose havens are the haunts of Peace,
  Whose boys are in our quarrel bold ;
Our bolt is shot, our tale is told,
  Our ship of state in storms may toss,
But ye are young if we are old,
  Ye Islands of the Southern Cross !

Aye, *we* must dwindle and decrease,
  Such fates the ruthless years unfold ;
And yet we shall not wholly cease,
  We shall not perish unconsoled ;
Nay, still shall Freedom keep her hold
  Within the sea's inviolate fosse,
And boast her sons of English mould,
  Ye Islands of the Southern Cross !

All empires tumble—Rome and Greece—
  Their swords are rust, their altars cold !
For us, the Children of the Seas,
  Who ruled where'er the waves have rolled,
For us, in Fortune's books enscrolled,
  I read no runes of hopeless loss ;
Nor—while *ye* last—our knell is tolled,
  Ye Islands of the Southern Cross !

Envoy.

Britannia, when thy hearth's a-cold,
  When o'er thy grave has grown the moss,
Still *Rule Australia* shall be trolled
  In Islands of the Southern Cross !

ANDREW LANG.

A BALLADE OF OLD SWEETHEARTS.

(To M. C.)

Who is it that weeps for the last year's flowers
  When the wood is aflame with the fires of spring,
And we hear her voice in the lilac bowers
  As she croons the runes of the blossoming?
  For the same old blooms do the new years bring.
But not to our lives do the years come so,
  New lips must kiss and new bosoms cling.—
Ah! lost are the loves of the long ago.

Ah! me for a breath of those morning hours
  When Alice and I went awandering
Through the shining fields, and it still was ours
  To kiss and to feel we were shuddering—
  Ah! me, when a kiss was a holy thing.—
How sweet were a smile from Maud, and oh!
  With Phyllis once more to be whispering. —
Ah! lost are the loves of the long ago.

But it cannot be that old Time devours
  Such loves as was Annie's and mine we sing,
And surely beneficent heavenly powers
  Save Muriel's beauty from perishing;
  And if in some golden evening
To a quaint old garden I chance to go,
  Shall Marion no more by the wicket sing?—
Ah! lost are the loves of the long ago.

In these lives of ours do the new years bring
  Old loves as old flowers again to blow?
Or do new lips kiss and new bosoms cling?—
  Ah! lost are the loves of the long ago.

R. LE GALLIENNE.

BALLADE.

O Love, whom I have never seen,
　　Yet ever hope to see ;
The memory that might have been
　　The hope that yet may be ;
The passion that persistently
　　Makes all my pulses beat
With unassuaged desire that we
　　Some day may come to meet :

This August night outspread serene,
　　The scent of flower and tree,
The fall of water that unseen
　　Moans on incessantly,
That line of fire, where breaks the sea
　　In ripples at my feet ;
What mean they all, if not that we
　　Some day may come to meet ?

About your window bowered in green
　　The night wind wanders free,
While out into the night you lean,
　　And dream, but not of me,
As now I dream of you who flee
　　Before my dream complete
The shadow of the day when we
　　Some day may come to meet.

Envoy.

Princess, while yet on lawn and lea
　　The harvest moon is sweet,
Ere August die, who knows but we
　　Some day may come to meet ?

" Love in Idleness."

BALLADE OF DEAD THINKERS.

Where's *Heraclitus* and his Flux
    Of Sense that never maketh stay?
Or *Thales*, with whom water sucks
    Into itself both Clod and Clay?
Or He, who in an evil Day
    Νόμος and φύσις first employ'd;
And of the Sum of Things doth say,
    They all are Atoms in the Void?

Where's grave *Parmenides?* Death plucks
    His Beard: and by the *Velian* Bay
Sleeps *Zeno; Plato's* Pen their Crux
    Of *One and Many* doth portray.
Empedocles too, well-away,
    His taste for climbing, unalloy'd
By Prudence, led him far astray:
    They all are Atoms in the Void.

Where's *Socrates* himself, who chucks
    Up *Physics*, makes of *Sophists* hay,
Into *Induction* briskly tucks,
    And *Definitions* frames alway?
The good *Athenians* him did slay,
    His *Dialectic* them annoy'd;
And his Disciples, where are they?
    They all are Atoms in the Void.

Envoy.

Prince, tho' with these old names and grey
    Our peace of mind be half destroyed,
Take comfort; say they what they may,
    They all are Atoms in the Void.

                    " Love in Idleness."

A BALLADE OF ROSES.

Τὸ 'ροδον τὸ τῶν ἐρωτων.

When Venus saw Ascanius sleep
    On sweet Cythera's snow-white roses
His face like Adon's made her weep,
    And long to kiss him where he dozes ;
But fearing to disturb the boy,
    She kissed the pallid blooms instead,
Which blushed and kept their blush for joy,
    When Venus kissed white roses red.

Straight of these roses she did reap
    Sufficient store of pleasant posies,
And coming from Cythera's steep
    Where every fragrant flower that grows is,
She tossed them for the winds to toy
    And frolic with till they were dead.
Heaven taught the earth a fair employ
    When Venus kissed white roses red.

For each red rose the symbol deep
    In its sad, happy heart encloses
Of kisses making love's heart leap,
    And every summer wind that blows is
A prayer that ladies be not coy
    Of kisses ere brief life be sped.
There gleamed more gold in earth's alloy
    When Venus kissed white roses red.

Envoy.

All lovers true since windy Troy
    Flamed for a woman's golden head,
You gained surcease from life's annoy
    When Venus kissed white roses red.

JUSTIN HUNTLY MCCARTHY.

A BALLADE OF DEATH.

The furious storm takes wing ;
 Quenched is the fiery ray ;
And broken the frosty air's sting,
 For these hold mutable sway :
Pain puts an end to its stay ;
 Ills have a time to endure ;
One thing will not heal nor allay :
 For death there is no cure !

For the good that the future may bring,
 We strive to exist to-day.
With the veering vane we swing,
 When fate sweeps fortune away :
Seldom will misery slay ;
 And ever will hope allure ;
Yet one thing endureth for aye,
 For death there is no cure !

Though life be an exquisite thing,
 Death shatters the curious clay ;
Though in frenzy we cry and we cling,
 There is none who can save us that day :
So life is devoured as a prey,
 And in darkness for aye will immure ;
And silence for ever hath sway :
 For death there is no cure !

Envoi.

O man, be ye sad, be ye gay,
 In the end there is one thing sure :
Make out of life what ye may,
 For death there is no cure !

HUNTER MacCulloch.

THE BALLADE OF TOBACCO.

When verdant youth sees life afar,
    And first sets out wild oats to sow,
He puffs a stiff and stark cigar,
    And quaffs champagne of Mumm & Co.
    He likes not smoking yet ; but though
Tobacco makes him sick indeed,
    Cigars and wine he can't forego :—
A slave is each man to the weed.

In time his tastes more dainty are,
    And delicate.   Become a beau,
From out the country of the Czar
    He brings his cigarettes, and lo !
    He sips the vintage of Bordeaux.
Thus keener relish shall succeed
    The baser liking we outgrow :—
A slave is each man to the weed.

When age and his own lucky star
    To him perfected wisdom show,
The schooner glides across the bar,
    And beer for him shall freely flow,
    A pipe with genial warmth shall glow ;
To which he turns in direst need,
    To seek in smoke surcease of woe :—
A slave is each man to the weed.

Envoi.

Smokers ! who doubt or con or pro,
    And ye who dare to drink, take heed !
And see in smoke a friendly foe :—
    A slave is each man to the weed.

BRANDER MATTHEWS.

THE BALLADE OF ADAPTATION.

The native drama's sick and dying,
    So say the cynic critic crew :
The native dramatist is crying—
    " Bring me the paste !   Bring me the glue !
    Bring me the pen, and scissors, too !
Bring me the works of E. Augier !
    Bring me the works of V. Sardou !
I am the man to write a play ! "

For want of plays the stage is sighing,
    Such is the song the wide world through :
The native dramatist is crying—
    " Behold the comedies I brew !
    Behold my dramas not a few !
On German farces I can prey,
    And English novels I can hew :
I am the man to write a play ! "

There is, indeed, no use denying
    That fashion's turned from old to new :
The native dramatist is crying—
    " Molière, good-bye ! Shakespeare adieu !
    I do not think so much of you.
Although not bad, you've had your day,
    And for the present you won't do.
I am the man to write a play ! "

Envoi.

Prince of the stage, don't miss the cue,
    A native dramatist, I say
To every cynic critic, " Pooh !
    I am the man to write a play ! "

BRANDER MATTHEWS.

A BALLADE OF MIDSUMMER.

The heat wave sweeps along the street,
    And torrid ripples mark its flow ;
Successive billows follow fleet,
    And blister all things with their glow.
    No puff of air swings to and fro ;
No gentle zephyr stirs the trees.
    O for the winds that o'er ocean blow !
O for a breath of the salt sea-breeze !

Along the shadeless ways you greet
    No damsel fair, no buckramed beau—
The solitude is ruled by heat—
    A sultry, sullen, scorching woe.
    The blazing sun rides high and slow,
As if with laziness to tease
    The melting, sweltering world below—
O for a breath of the salt sea-breeze !

The laggard steed with aching feet
    Must stagger on ; for him is no
Surcease of labour, no retreat
    ' Before his stint is done.   And so
    Must man still labour on, although
He hopeless longs to take his ease,
    Or to the ocean fain would go—
O for a breath of the salt sea-breeze !

Envoi.

Princes or peasants, friend and foe,
    No man may have all that he please ;
Midsummer heat shall lay him low—
    O for a breath of the salt sea-breeze !

BRANDER MATTHEWS.

RAIN AND SHINE.

(Ballade à double refrain.)

The clouds are thick and darkly lower ;
　　The sullen sodden sky would fain
Pour down a never-ending shower :
　　I hear the pattering of the rain,
　　I hear it rattle on the pane.—
And then I see the mist entwining,
　　Nor one position long retain.
Behold ! the gentle sun is shining !

As though exulting in its power,
　　The storm beats down with steady strain ;
Upon the ivy of the tower
　　I hear the pattering of the rain ;
　　It swiftly sweeps across the plain.—
And then I see the sky refining,
　　And molten with a golden stain.
Behold ! the gentle sun is shining !

Beneath the storm the cattle cower ;
　　It beats upon the growing grain,
And as it breaks both bud and flower,
　　I hear the pattering of the rain,—
　　From where the clouds too long have lain
They turn, and show a silver lining,
　　A splendid glory comes again.
Behold ! the gentle sun is shining !

Envoy.

Although like some far, faint refrain,
I hear the pattering of the rain,
The storm is past.　No more repining—
Behold ! the gentle sun is shining !

BRANDER MATTHEWS.

AN AMERICAN GIRL.

She's had a Vassar education,
    And points with pride to her degrees ;
She's studied houschold decoration ;
    She knows a dado from a frieze,
    And tells Corots from Boldonis ;
A Jacquemart etching, or a Haden,
    A Whistler, too, perchance might please
A free and frank young Yankee maiden.

She does not care for meditation ;
    Within her bonnet are no bees ;
She has a gentle animation,
    She joins in singing simple glees.
    She tries no trills, no rivalries
With Lucca (now Baronin Räden),
    With Nilsson or with Gerster ; she's
A frank and free young Yankee maiden.

I'm blessed above the whole creation,
    Far, far, above all other he's ;
I ask you for congratulation
    On this the best of jubilees :
    I go with her across the seas
Unto what Poe would call an Aiden, —
    I hope no serpent's there to tease
A frank and free young Yankee maiden.

Envoy.

Princes, to you the western breeze
    Bears many a ship and heavy laden,
What is the best we send in these ?
    A free and frank young Yankee maiden.

BRANDER MATTHEWS.

"FROM BATTLE, MURDER AND SUDDEN DEATH, GOOD LORD, DELIVER US.

What of this prayer which myriad skies
    Hear from the shrines where tired men kneel,
Godward upturning anguished eyes,
    Clasping gaunt hands in strong appeal?
    What of this fear that worn lives feel?
Why should some strain their labouring breath,
    Since they must gain not woe but weal,
From battle, murder and sudden death !

Is it not well with him who dies
    Flushed amid smoke and flash of steel ;
Stabbed by some traitor's swift surprise ;
    Stricken by doom no signs reveal?
    Ruin and wrong can no more deal
Blows beneath which (man's record saith)
    Men ask deliverance, while they reel.
From battle, murder and sudden death !

Can one so dead be harmed by lies,
    Tortured by wounds smiles ill conceal?
Can love bring loss, or desire devise
    Vain visions, or grim fate's iron heel
    Brand both on brow and soul its seal,
Till, wretched as He of Nazareth,
    Man loathes the life he yet prays to steal
From battle, murder and sudden death ?

Envoi.

Waifs that on life's tide sink and rise,
    Chaff that each chance wind winnoweth,
Why dread God's rest that comes, a prize
    From battle, murder and sudden death ?

JOHN MORAN.

IN WINTER.

Oh, to go back to the days of June,
    Just to be young and alive again,
Hearken again to the mad, sweet tune
    Birds were singing with might and main:
South they flew at the summer's wane,
    Leaving their nests for storms to harry,
Since time was coming for wind and rain
    Under the wintry skies to marry.

Wearily wander by dale and dune
    Footsteps fettered with clanking chain—
Free they were in the days of June,
    Free they never can be again:
Fetters of age, and fetters of pain,
    Joys that fly, and sorrows that tarry—
Youth is over, and hopes were vain
    Under the wintry skies to marry.

Now we chant but a desolate rune—
    Oh to be young and alive again !
But never December turns to June,
    And length of living is length of pain:
Winds in the nestless trees complain,
    Snows of winter about us tarry,
And never the birds come back again
    Under the wintry skies to marry.

Envoi.

Youths and maidens, blithesome and vain,
    Time makes thrusts that you cannot parry ;
Mate in season, for who is fain
    Under the wintry skies to marry ?

LOUISE CHANDLER MOULTON.

BALLADE OF HIS LADY.

My lady's heart 'twere hard to touch,
    And sighs and vows she'd soon repel ;
But if she liked one twice as much,
    One would not like her half as well ;
    She careth not for sage or swell,
For guardsman stout or poet lean,
    Who haunt Parnassus or Pall Mall ;
My lady-love is just thirteen.

She loves a rabbit in a hutch
    (A fat Aquinas in his cell),
She loves an aged cat, whose clutch
    At breakfast-time exerts a spell,
    A most ungracious Florizel.
In fact it's easy to be seen,
    Were she at all averse to tell,
My lady-love is just thirteen.

Although she reads the Higher Dutch,
    On culture's peaks apart to dwell,
She feigns not ; nor of things 'as such'
    Does she discourse, nor parallel
    Dante and Dante Gabriel ;
Yet she has 'views' advanced and keen,
    On chocolate and caramel,—
My lady-love is just thirteen.

Envoy.

Madam, just homage you compel,
    Mature, self-conscious, and serene,
One heart alone you cannot quell ;
    My lady-love is just thirteen.

J. B. B. NICHOLS.

BALLADE OF EXMOOR.

Fly westward, westward, gentle wind,
    Where erst we trod the windy ways;
And wake within her wayward mind
    The memory of forgotten days.
    The stars step forth aslant the bays,
The still moon silvers tower and tree,
    And never sound the silence frays
Athwart the slumberous Severn Sea.

So soft, so strange the light that lined
    The ferny moors, the forest maze,
Till all the west was smitten blind
    With glamour of the golden haze;
    What time we watch'd the stag upraise
His lordly brow by linn and lea,
    To fright the morris of the fays
Athwart the slumberous Severn Sea.

O'er the dim passes flung behind
    The dying daylight all ablaze,
About those dainty tresses twined
    One aureole of dreamy rays,
    And many a winged lamp that strays
Darkling his weird in heaven to dree,
    Lit the rare eyne downdrops to gaze
Athwart the slumberous Severn Sea.

Envoy.

    O westward wind, whose low breath sways
Her locks, whereto night's shadows flee,
    Bear hence a lilt of summer lays
Athwart the slumberous Severn Sea.

F. S. P.

BALLAD OF PAST DELIGHT.

Where are the dreams of the days gone by,
    The hopes of honour, the glancing play
Of fire-new fancies that filled our sky—
    The songs we sang in the middle May,
    Carol and ballad and roundelay ?
Where are the garlands our young hands twined ?
    Life's but a memory, well-away !
All else flits past on the wings of the wind.

Where are the ladies fair and high—
    Marie and Alice and Maud and May
And merry Madge with the laughing eye—
    And all the gallants of yesterday
    That held us merry—ah, where are they ?
Under the mould we must look to find
    Some ; and the others are worn and grey.
All else flits past on the wings of the wind.

I know of nothing that lasts, not I,
    Save a heart that is true to its love alway—
A love that is won with tear and sigh
    And never changes or fades away,
    In a breast that is oftener sad than gay ;
A tender look and a constant mind—
    These are the only things that stay :
All else flits past on the wings of the wind.

Envoy.

Prince, I counsel you, never say,
    Alack for the years that are left behind !
Look you keep love when your dreams decay ;
    All else flits past on the wings of the wind.

JOHN PAYNE.

THE PIXIES.

The frost hath spread a shining net
    Where late the autumn roses blew,
On lake and stream a seal is set
    Where floating lilies charmed the view ;
    So silently the wonder grew
Beneath pale Dian's mystic light,
    I know my fancies whisper true,
The Pixies are abroad to-night.

When at the midnight chime are met
    Together elves of every hue,
I trow the gazer will regret
    That peers upon their retinue ;
    For limb awry and eye askew
Have oft proclaimed a fairy's spite—
    Peep slyly, gallants, lest ye rue,
The Pixies are abroad to-night.

'Tis said their forms are tiny, yet
    All human ills they can subdue,
Or with a wand or amulet
    Can win a maiden's heart for you ;
    And many a blessing know to strew
To make the way to wedlock bright ;
    Give honour to the dainty crew,
The Pixies are abroad to-night.

Envoy.

Prince, e'en a prince might vainly sue,
    Unaided by a fairy's might ;
Remember Cinderella's shoe,
    The Pixies are abroad to-night.

SAMUEL MINTURN PECK.

A BALLADE OF THE THUNER-SEE.

Soft on the lake's soft bosom we twain
    Float in the haze of a dim delight,
While the wavelets cradle the sleepless brain,
    And the eyes are glad of the lessening light,
    And the east with a fading glory is bright—
The lingering smile of a sun that is set,—
    And the earth in its tender sorrow is dight,
And the shadow that falleth hath spared us yet.

Oh, the mellow beam of the suns that wane,
    Oh the joys, ah me ! that are taking flight,
Oh, the sting of a rapture too near to pain,
    And of love that loveth in death's despite.
    But the hour is ours, and its beauty's might
Subdues our souls to a still regret,
    While the Blumlis-alp unveils to the night,
And the shadow that falleth hath spared us yet.

Now we set our prow to the land again,
    And our backs to those splendours ghostly white,
But a mirrored star with a watery train
    We hold in our wake as a golden kite ;
    When we near the shore with its darkening height,
And its darker shade on the waters set,
    Lo ! the dim shade fleeth before our sight,
And the shadow that falleth hath spared us yet.

Envoy.

From the jewelled circles where I indite
    This song which my faithless tears make wet,
We trail the light till its gemmed rings smite
    The shadow—that falleth ! and spares us yet.

EMILY PFEIFFER.

GRANDMOTHER.

Another new gown, as I declare !
   How many more is it going to be?
And your forehead all hid in a cloud of hair—
   'Tis nothing but folly, that I can see !
   The maidens of nowaday make too free ;
To right and to left is the money flung ;
   We used to dress as became our degree—
But things have altered since I was young.

Stuff, in my time, was made to wear ;
   Gowns we had never but two or three ;
Did we fancy them spoilt, if they chanced to tear?
   And shrink from a patch, or a darn ? not we !
   For pleasure, a gossiping dish of tea,
Or a mushroom hunt, while the dew yet hung,
   And no need, next day, for the doctor's fee—
But things have altered since I was young.

The yellow gig, and a drive to the fair ;
   A keepsake bought in a booth on the lea ;
A sixpence, perhaps, to break and share—
   That's how your grandfather courted me.
   Did your grandmother blush, do you think—
      not she !
When he found her, the churn and the pails among?
   Or your grandfather like her the less ? not he !
But things have altered since I was young.

Envoi.

Child ! you pout, and you urge your plea—
Better it were that you held your tongue !
   Maids should learn at their elders' knee—
But things have altered since I was young.

MAY PROBYN.

A BALLADE OF PHILOMELA.

From gab of jay and chatter of crake
    The dusk wood covered me utterly.
And here the tongue of the thrush was awake.
    Flame-floods out of the low bright sky
    Lighted the gloom with gold-brown dye,
Before dark ; and a manifold chorussing
    Arose of thrushes remote and nigh,—
For the tongue of the singer needs must sing.

Midmost a close green covert of brake
    A brown bird listening silently
Sat ; and I thought—"She grieves for the sake
    Of Itylus,—for the stains that lie
    In her heritage of sad memory."
But the thrushes were hushed at evening.
    Then I waited to hear the brown bird try,—
For the tongue of the singer needs must sing.

And I said—"The thought of the thrushes will shake
    With rapture remembered her heart ; and her shy
Tongue of the dear times dead will take
    To make her a living song, when sigh
    The soft night winds disburthened by.
Hark now !" for the upraised quivering wing,
    The throat exultant, I could descry,—
For the tongue of the singer needs must sing.

L' Envoi.

But the bird dropped dead with only a cry :
    I found its tongue was withered, poor thing !
Then I no whit wondered, for well knew I
    That the heart of the singer will break or sing.

CHARLES G. D. ROBERTS.

A BALLADE OF CALYPSO.

The loud black flight of the storm diverges
    Over a spot in the loud mouthed main,
Where, crowned with summer and sun, emerges
    An isle unbeaten of wind or rain.
    And here, of its sweet queen grown full fain,
By whose kisses the whole broad earth seems poor,
    Tarries the wave-worn prince, Troy's bane,
In the green Ogygian Isle secure.

To her voice our sweetest songs are dirges.
    She gives him all things, counting it gain.
Ringed with the rocks and ancient surges,
    How could Fate dissever these twain?
    But him no loves nor delights retain ;
New knowledge, new lands, new loves allure ;
    Forgotten the perils, and toils, and pain,
In the green Ogygian Isle secure.

So he spurns her kisses and gifts, and urges
    His weak skiff over the wind-vext plain,
Till the grey of the sky in the grey sea merges,
    And nights reel round, and waver and wane.
    He sits once more in his own domain.
No more the remote sea-walls immure.—
    But ah, for the love he shall clasp not again
In the green Ogygian Isle secure.

L'Envoi.

Princes, and ye whose delights remain,
    To the one good gift of the gods hold sure,
Lest ye, too, mourn, in vain, in vain,
    Your green Ogygian Isle secure.

CHARLES G. D. ROBERTS.

A BALLAD OF FORGOTTEN TUNES.

To V. L.

Forgotten seers of lost repute
    That haunt the banks of Acheron,
Where have you dropped the broken lute
    You played in Troy or Calydon?
    O ye that sang in Babylon
By foreign willows cold and grey,
    Fall'n are the harps ye hanged thereon,
Dead are the tunes of yesterday!

De Coucy, is your music mute,
    The quaint old plain-chant woe-begone
That served so many a lover's suit?
    Oh, dead as Adam or Guédron!
    Then, sweet De Caurroy, try upon
Your virginals a virelay;
    Or play Orlando, one pavonne—
Dead are the tunes of yesterday!

But ye whose praises none refute,
    Who have the immortal laurel won;
Trill me your quavering close acute,
    Astorga, dear unhappy Don!
    One air, Galuppi!   Sarti one
So many fingers used to play!—
    Dead as the ladies of Villon,
Dead are the tunes of yesterday!

Envoy.

Vernon, in vain you stoop to con
The slender, faded notes to-day—
    The Soul that dwelt in them is gone:
Dead are the tunes of yesterday!

A. MARY F. ROBINSON.

BALLADE OF A GARDEN.

With plash of the light oars swiftly plying,
    The sharp prow furrows the watery way;
The ripples' reach as the bank is dying,
    And soft shades slender, and long lights play
    In the still dead heat of the drowsy day,
As on I sweep with the stream that flows
    By sleeping lilies that lie astray
In the Garden of Grace whose name none knows.

There ever a whispering wind goes sighing,
    Filled with the scent of the new-mown hay,
Over the flower hedge peering and prying,
    Wooing the rose as with words that pray;
    And the waves from the broad bright river bay
Slide through clear channels to dream and doze,
    Or rise in a fountain's silver spray
In the Garden of Grace whose name none knows.

The sweet white rose with the red rose dying,
    Blooms where the summer follows the May,
Till the streams be hid by the lost leaves lying,
    That autumn shakes where the lilies lay.
    But now all bowers and beds are gay
And no rain ruffles the flower that blows,
    And still on the water soft dreams stay
In the Garden of Grace whose name none knows.

Envoi.

Before the blue of the sky grows grey
    And the frayed leaves fall from the faded rose,
Love's lips shall sing what the day-dreams say
    In the Garden of Grace whose name none knows.

ARTHUR REED ROPES.

BALLADE OF THE BARD.

Though through the cloudy ranks of morn
    The Sun-god sends no golden ray,
Though swift along the air are borne
    The feathery shafts that none may stay ;
    Though wrathful storm-blasts pangless slay,
And wan the patient plodder rues
    His lonely lot each dagging day—
He's gay who courts the merry muse !

When down the fields the tender corn
    Upsprings, and sees blue skies in May,
When budding blooms the boughs adorn,
    And flowers bespangle sprig and spray,
    When torrid summer's regnant sway
Has dimmed the foliage's fairest hues,
    And bronzèd reapers house the hay—
He's gay who courts the merry muse !

And when the hollow harvest horn
    O'erflows with autumn's rich display,
When high, with goodly grain, new-shorn,
    Is piled each lofty granary,
    When, like dark moons amid the gray
Of cornfields, where the red ear woos,
    The pumpkins lie in long array—
He's gay who courts the merry muse !

Envoy.

Prince, e'en though Fortune go astray
    And lost is wealth's bright-shining cruse,
Though dark and drear the weary way—
    He's gay who courts the merry muse.

CLINTON SCOLLARD.

BALLADE OF DEAD POETS.

Theocritus, who bore
    The lyre where sleek herds graze
On the Sicilian shore,
    (There yet the shepherd strays)—·
    And Horace, crowned with bays,
Who dwelt by Tiber's flow,
    Sleep through the silent days—
For God will have it so !

The bard, whose requiem o'er
    And o'er the sad sea plays,
Who sang of classic lore,
    Of Mab, the queen of fays—
    And Keats, fair Adonais,
The child of song and woe,
    No longer thread life's maze—
For God will have it so !

Your voices, sweet of yore,
    With honied word and phrase,
Are heard by men no more,
    They list to other lays—
    New poets now have praise,
But all in turn must go
    To follow in your ways—
For God will have it so !

Envoy.

Poets, the thrones ye raise
    Are not a " fleeting show ; "
Fame lives, though dust decays—
    For God will have it so !

CLINTON SCOLLARD.

BALLADE TO VILLON.

Where, prithee, are thy comrades bold,
    With ruffle, flounce, and furbelow,
Who, in the merry days of old,
    Made light of all but red wine's flow?
    Where now are cavalier and beau
Who joyed with thee in that bright clime?
    Ah! dust to dust!—and none may know—
Alas, for the fleet wings of Time!

Where now are they whom gleaming gold
    Led on to many a bandit blow,
Who roamed with thee the widening wold
    And vine-clad hills, and shared thy woe?
    Where they, who, in the sunset glow,
With thee heard Paris' sweet bells chime?
    Ah! they are gone!—and still men go—
Alas, for the fleet wings of Time!

And where are they, those maids untold,
    Thy lighter loves, each one thy foe?
They too are now but loathsome mould,
    With earth above and earth below.
    And she who won, aside to throw
Thy love, the promise of thy prime,
    Doth any seek her name? Ah! no—
Alas, for the fleet wings of Time!

Envoy.

Poet of ballade and rondeau,
    Prince of the tripping, laughing rhyme,
Thy name alone hath 'scaped the snow;
    Alas, for the fleet wings of Time.

CLINTON SCOLLARD.

FOR ME THE BLITHE BALLADE.

Of all the songs that dwell
        Where softest speech doth flow,
Some love the sweet rondel,
        And some the bright rondeau,
        With rhymes that tripping go
In mirthful measures clad ;
        But would I choose them ?—no,
For me the blithe ballade !

O'er some, the villanelle,
        That sets the heart aglow,
Doth its enchanting spell
        With lines' recurring throw ;
        Some weighed with wasting woe,
Gay triolets make them glad ;
        But would I choose them ?—no,
For me the blithe ballade !

On chant of stately swell
        With measured feet and slow,
At grave as minster bell
        As vesper tolling low,
        Do some their praise bestow ;
Some on sestinas sad ;
        But would I choose them ?—no,
For me the blithe ballade !

Envoy.

Prince, to these songs a-row
        The Muse might endless add ;
But would I choose them ?—no,
        For me the blithe ballade !

CLINTON SCOLLARD.

O LADY MINE.

O lady mine with the sunlit hair,
    The birds are caroling blithe and gay
In the bourgeoning boughs that sway in air
    O'er the grassy aisles of the orchard way.
    The mock-bird pipes to the busy jay :
There's a gleam of white on the vines that twine
    Where your casement opes to the golden day,
                O lady mine.

O lady mine with the sunlit hair,
    The rills are glad that the month is May ;
The dawns are bright and the eves are fair
    O'er the grassy aisles of the orchard way.
    The dales have doffed their gowns of grey,
The sending buttercups spill their wine,
    There is joy in the heart of faun and fay,
                O lady mine.

O lady mine with the sunlit hair
    The bees, like ruthless bandits, prey
On the blooms that part their lips in prayer
    O'er the grassy aisles of the orchard way.
    From the sunny shores where the nereids play
The breezes blow o'er the foamy brine,
    And I dream I hear them softly say,
                " O lady mine ! "

Envoy.

O lady mine, wilt thou not stray
O'er the grassy aisles of the orchard way,
And list to Love where the wind-flowers shine,
              O lady mine ?
            CLINTON SCOLLARD.

WHERE ARE THE SHIPS OF TYRE?

Hark, how the surges dash
    On Tyrian beaches hoar !
With far-resounding crash,
    And unremitting roar,
    The white foam squadrons pour
Their ranks with sullen ire
    Along the sandy floor ;
" Where are the ships of Tyre ? "

Within her walls the clash
    Of arms is heard no more ;
No supple bough of ash
    Is hewn for mast or oar ;
    Through no tall temple's door
Now gleams the altar fire,
    But winds and waves deplore,
" Where are the ships of Tyre ? "

By night no torches flash
    From porches as of yore ;
'Neath sword or stinging lash
    No slave now lies in gore :
    No voice that men adore
Lifts song to lute or lyre ;
    With all the freight they bore,
" Where are the ships of Tyre ? "

Envoy.

Prince, with these " gone before,"
    We, whom these days inspire,
Must seek that unknown shore
    " Where are the ships of Tyre ? "

CLINTON SCOLLARD.

BALLADE OF VAIN HOPES.

O ghosts of Bygone Hours, that stand
    Upon the marge of yonder shore
Where by the pale feet-trampled sand
    (Though none is seen to walk that floor)
    The Stygian wave flows evermore :
We fain would buy what ye can tell,
    Speak ! Speak ! And thrill to each heart's core—
Vain Hopes are all we have to sell !

O spectral Hours that throng this land—
    Where no sweet floods of sunshine pour,
But vast, tenebriously grand,
    Dense glooms abide, wind-swept or frore—
    O ye who thus have gone before,
Break silence—break your charmëd spell !
    Heed not our negligence of yore !
Vain Hopes are all we have to sell !

O sombre, sad-eyed, shadowy band,
    Speak, speak, and wave not o'er and o'er
Each wan phantasmal shadow-hand ;
    O say, if when with battling sore
    We cross the flood and hear the roar
O' the world like a sighed farewell,
    What waits beyond the Grave's last door ?
Vain Hopes are all we have to sell !

Envoy.

O coming Hours, O unspent store,
    Your promise breathe—as in sea-shell
Imprison'd Echo sings her lore—
    Vain Hopes are all we have to sell !

William Sharp.

BALLADE OF THE SONG OF THE SEA-WIND.

What is the song the sea-wind sings—
    The old, old song it singeth for aye?
When abroad it stretcheth its mighty wings
    And driveth the white clouds far away,—
    What is the song it sings to-day?
From fire and tumult the white world came,
    Where all was a mist of driven spray
    And the whirling fragments of a frame!

What is the song the sea-wind sings—
    The old, old song it singeth for aye?
It seems to breathe a thousand things
    Ere the world grew sad and old and grey—
    Of the dear gods banished far astray—
Of strange wild rumours of joy and shame!
    The Earth is old, so old, To-day—
    Blind and halt and weary and lame.

What is the song the sea-wind sings—
    The old, old song it singeth for aye?
Like a trumpet blast its voice out-rings,
    The world spins down the darksome way!
    It crieth aloud in wild dismay,
The Earth that from fire and tumult came
    Draws swift to her weary end To-day,
    Her fires are fusing for that last Flame!

Envoy.

What singeth the sea-wind thus for aye—
    From fire and tumult the white world came!
What is the sea-wind's cry To-day—
    Her central fires make one vast flame!
WILLIAM SHARP.

BALLADE OF THE SEA-FOLK.

Where are the creatures of the deep,
    That made the sea-world wondrous fair?
The dolphins that with royal sweep
    Sped Venus of the golden hair
    Through leagues of summer sea and air?
Are they all gone where past things be?
    The merman in his weedy lair?
    O sweet wild creatures of the sea!

O singing syrens, do ye weep
    That now ye hear not anywhere
The swift oars of the seamen leap,
    See their wild, eager eyes a-stare?
    O syrens, that no more ensnare
The souls of men that once were free,
    Are ye not filled with cold despair—
    O sweet wild creatures of the sea!

O Triton, on some coral steep
    In green-gloom depths, dost thou forbear
With wreathèd horn to call thy sheep,
    The wandering sea-waves, to thy care?
    O mermaids, once so debonnair,
Sport ye no more with mirthful glee?
    The ways of lover-folk forswear?—
    O sweet wild creatures of the sea!

Envoy.

Deep down 'mid coral caves, beware!
    They wait a day that yet must be,
When Ocean shall be earth's sole heir—
    O sweet wild creatures of the sea!

WILLIAM SHARP.

TO AUSTIN DOBSON.

From the sunny climes of France,
    Flying to the west,
Came a flock of birds by chance,
    There to sing and rest :
    Of some secrets deep in quest,—
Justice for their wrongs,—
    Seeking one to shield their breast,
One to write their songs.

Melodies of old romance,
    Joy and gentle jest,
Notes that made the dull heart dance
    With a merry zest ;—
    Maids in matchless beauty drest,
Youths in happy throngs ;—
    These they sang to tempt and test
One to write their songs.

In old London's wide expanse
    Built each feathered guest,—
Man's small pleasure to entrance,
    Singing him to rest,—
    Came, and tenderly confessed,
Perched on leafy prongs,
    Life were sweet if they possessed
One to write their songs.

Envoy.

Austin, it was you they blest :
    Fame to you belongs !
Time has proven you're the best
    One to write their songs.

            FRANK DEMPSTER SHERMAN.

BALLADE OF RHYME.

When blossoms born of balmy spring
    Breathe fragrance in the pleasant shade
Of branches where the blue-birds sing,
    Their hearts with music overweighed ;
    When brooks go babbling through the glade,
And over rocks the grasses climb
    To greet the sunshine, half-afraid,—
How easy 'tis to write a rhyme !

When invitations are a-wing
    For gay Terpsichore's parade ;
When dreamy waltzes stir the string
    And jewels flash on rich brocade,
    Where Paris dresses are displayed,
And slippered feet keep careful time ;—
    In winter, when the roses fade,
How easy 'tis to write a rhyme !

When by your side, with graceful swing,
    Some fair-faced, gentle girl has strayed,
Willing and glad to have you bring
    Your claims for love and get them paid
    In kisses, smiles, and words that aid
The bells of bliss to better chime ;—
    When Cupid's rules are first obeyed,
How easy 'tis to write a rhyme !

Envoy.

Reader, forgive me, man or maid,
    Against Calliope this crime ;
And let this brief ballade persuade
    How easy 'tis to write a rhyme !

FRANK DEMPSTER SHERMAN.

A BALLAD OF DREAMLAND.

I hid my heart in a nest of roses,
    Out of the sun's way, hidden apart ;
In a softer bed than the soft white snow's is,
    Under the roses I hid my heart.
    Why would it sleep not ? why should it start,
When never a leaf of the rose-tree stirred ?
    What made sleep flutter his wings and part?
Only the song of a secret bird.

Lie still, I said, for the wind's wing closes,
    And mild leaves muffle the keen sun's dart ;
Lie still, for the wind on the warm seas dozes,
    And the wind is unquieter yet than thou art.
    Does a thought in thee still as a thorn's wound
        smart
Does the fang still fret thee of hope deferred ?
    What bids the lips of thy sleep dispart ?
Only the song of a secret bird.

The green land's name that a charm encloses,
    It never was writ in the traveller's chart,
And sweet on its trees as the fruit that grows is,
    It never was sold in the merchant's mart.
    The swallows of dreams through its dim fields
        dart,
And sleep's are the tunes in its tree-tops heard ;
    No hound's note wakens the wildwood hart,
Only the song of a secret bird.

Envoi.

In the world of dreams I have chosen my part,
    To sleep for a season and hear no word
Of true love's truth or of light love's art,
    Only the song of a secret bird.

           ALGERNON CHARLES SWINBURNE.

A BALLADE OF KINGS.

Where are the mighty kings of yore
　　Whose sword-arm cleft the world in twain ?
And where are they who won and wore
　　The empire of the land and main ?
　　Where's Alexander, Charlemain ?
Alone the sky above them brings
　　Their tombs the tribute of the rain.
Dust in dust are the bones of kings !

Where now is Rome's old emperor,
　　Who gazed on burning Rome full fain ;
And where, at one for evermore,
　　The Liege of France, the Lord of Spain ?
　　What of Napoleon's lightning brain,
Grim Fritz's iron hammerings,
　　Forging the links of Europe's chain ?
Dust in dust are the bones of kings !

Where, 'neath what ravenous curses sore,
　　Hath Well-Loved Louis lapsed and lain ?
Where is the Lion-Heart, who bore
　　The spears toward Zion's gate again ?
　　And can so little space contain,
Quiet from all his wanderings,
　　The world-demanding Tamburlaine ?
Dust in dust are the bones of kings !

Envoy.

O Kings, bethink ye then how vain
　　The pride and pomp of earthly things :
A little pain, a little gain,
　　Then dust in dust are the bones of kings.
ARTHUR SYMONS.

BALLADE OF ACHERON.

Between the Midnight and the Morn,
    The under-world my soul espied ;
I saw the shades of men out-worn,
    The Heroes fallen in their pride ;
    I saw the marsh-lands drear and wide,
And many a ghost that strayed thereon ;
    " Still must I roam," a maiden sighed,
" The sunless marsh of Acheron."

" And is thy fate thus hope-forlorn ? "
    " Yea, even so," the shade replied,
" For one I wronged in life hath sworn
    In hatred ever to abide :
    The lover seeketh not the bride,
But aye, with me, his heart dreams on,
    Asleep in these cold mists that hide
The sunless marsh of Acheron.

" And still for me will Lacon mourn,
    And still my pardon be denied :
Ah, never shall I cross the bourne
    That Dead from Living doth divide ;
    Yet I repent me not ! " she cried,
" Nay—only that mine hour is gone ;
    One memory hath glorified
The sunless marsh of Acheron."

Envoy.

Ah, Princess ! when thy ghost shall glide
    Where never star nor sunlight shone,
See thou she tarry not beside
    The sunless marsh of Acheron.

GRAHAM R. TOMSON.

BALLADE OF ASPHODEL.

Κατ' ἀσφοδελὸν λειμῶνα.

Now who will thread the winding way,
    Afar from fervid summer heat,
Beyond the sunshafts of the day,
    Beyond the blast of winter sleet?
In the green twilight, dimly sweet,
    Of poplar shades, the shadows dwell,
Who found erewhile a fair retreat
    Along the mead of Asphodel.

There death and birth are one, they say;
    Those lowlands bear no yellow wheat;
No sound doth rise of mortal fray,
    Of lowing herds, of flocks that bleat:
Nor wind nor rain doth blow nor beat;
    Nor shrieketh sword, nor tolleth bell;
But lovers one another greet
    Along the mead of Asphodel.

I would that there my soul might stray;
    I would my phantom, fair and fleet,
Might cleave the burden of the clay,
    Might leave the murmur of the street,
Nor with half-hearted prayer entreat
    The half-believed-in Gods; too wel
I know the name I shall repeat
    Along the mead of Asphodel.

Envoy.

Queen Proserpine, at whose white feet
    In life my love I may not tell,
Wilt give me welcome when we meet
    Along the mead of Asphodel?

GRAHAM R. TOMSON.

BALLADE OF THE BOURNE.

What goal remains for pilgrim feet
    Now all our gods are banishèd?
Afar, where sea and sunrise meet,
    Tall portals bathed in gold and red,
    From either door a carven head
Smiles down on men full drowsilie
    'Mid mystic forms of wings outspread
Between the Gates of Ivorie.

Now if beyond lie town or street
    I know not nor hath any said,
Though tongues wag fast and winds are fleet ;
    Some say that there men meet the dead,
    Or filmy phantoms in their stead,
And some " it leads to Arcadie,"
    In sooth I know not, yet would tread
Between the Gates of Ivorie.

For surely there sounds music sweet
    With fair delights and perfumes shed,
And all things broken made complete,
    And found again things forfeited ;
    All this for him who scorning dread
Shall read the wreathen fantasie,
    And pass, where no base soul had sped
Between the Gates of Ivorie.

Envoy.

Ah, Princess ! grasp the golden thread,
    Rise up and follow fearlesslie,
By high desire and longing led
    Between the Gates of Ivorie.

GRAHAM R. TOMSON.

BALLADE OF FAIRY GOLD.

A goblin trapped in netted skein,
　　Did bruise his wings with vain essay ;
" Now who will rend this hempen chain ?
　　Let that man ask me what he may,
　　I shall not, surely, say him nay :
The shadows wane, the day grows old,
　　Meseems this mesh will keep for aye
The sun-bright glint of Fairy Gold ! "

These echoes of the creature's pain,
　　As in the fowler's net he lay,
Drew soon anigh a surly swain
　　Who cut the cords and freed the fay :
　　" Now what fair gift shall well repay
Thy service done ?—for words are cold—
　　Sweet looks or wisdom ! vine or bay ? "
" The sun-bright glint of Fairy Gold."

" Thou choosest ill, but speech is vain,
　　Lo ! here is treasure good and gay : "
The goat-herd grasped his golden gain
　　And bore the shining store away ;
　　He oped his chest, at break of day,
To find—no talents, bright and cold,
　　But soft, dead cowslips—nowhere lay
The sun-bright glint of Fairy Gold !

Envoy.

Take hands, O Prince, for we will stray,
　　We twain, where nought is bought or sold,
And find in every woodland way,
　　The sun-bright glint of Fairy Gold.

Graham R. Tomson.

BALLADE OF MIGHT-BE.

Young Love flies fast, on wavering wing,
    Full fast he flies for woe or weal,
And some do bear his grievous sting
    Too deep for any leech to heal ;
    I scorn to swell their sad appeal,
False phantom, fled from our embrace !
    And yet—I doubt me I might kneel
Should you but chance to turn your face.

Of days long done our praises ring
    Right loud and full, a valorous peal,
For life was then a lusty thing :
    Ah ! then were mighty blows to deal.
    Brave days, my masters !—still, I feel
In sooth I could not deem him base
    Who'd shun your stare, O age of steel !
Should you but chance to turn your face.

" Alas ! " our dainty minstrels sing,
    " That sorrow sets unbroken seal
On saint and sinner, clown and king."
    They beg death's boon with busy zeal.
    They'll do you homage warm and leal,
Death ! while you pass their dwelling-place
    But lips would gape and senses reel,
Should you but chance to turn your face.

Envoy.

Queen Fortune ! of the mystic wheel,
    We bow to find you full of grace,
We would not turn on sullen heel
    Should *you* but chance to turn your face.

GRAHAM R. TOMSON.

BALLADE OF THE OPTIMIST.

Heed not the folk who sing or say
  In sonnet sad or sermon chill,
" Alas, alack, and well-a-day,
  This round world's but a bitter pill.'
Poor porcupines of fretful quill !
  Sometimes we quarrel with our lot :
We, too, are sad and careful ; still
  We'd rather be alive than not.

What though we wish the cats at play
  Would some one else's garden till ;
Though Sophonisba drop the tray
  And all our worshipped Worcester spill,
Though neighbours " practise " loud and shrill,
  Though May be cold and June be hot,
Though April freeze and August grill,
  We'd rather be alive than not.

And, sometimes, on a summer's day
  To self and every mortal ill
We give the slip, we steal away,
  To lie beside some sedgy rill ;
The darkening years, the cares that kill,
  A little while are well forgot ;
Deep in the broom upon the hill
  We'd rather be alive than not.

Pistol, with oaths didst thou fulfil
  The task thy braggart tongue begot.
We eat our leek with better will,
  We'd rather be alive than not.

Graham R. Tomson.

BALLADE OF OLD INSTRUMENTS.

So quaintly sadly mute they hang,
    We ask in vain what fingers played,
What hearts were stirred, what voices sang,
    What songs in life's brief masquerade,—
    What old-world catch or serenade,
What ill-worn mirth, what mock despairs
    Found voice when maid or ruffling blade
Sang long-forgot familiar airs.

We only know that once they rang
    In oaken room and forest glade,
Where yule logs glowed or branches swang ;
    When earth and heaven itself were made
    For roistering off a Spanish raid,
To drown in such life's shallower cares,
    Or trip in ruffs and old brocade,
To long-forgot familiar airs.

Dead all—a pun for every pang
    (So Shakespeare then the race portrayed
That fought and revelled, danced and sprang
    Half-way to meet death undismayed) ;
    About them gather mist and shade,
Yet Time ironically spares
    These strings on which their fingers strayed
To long-forgot familiar airs.

Envoy.

Ah ! child, so soon the colours fade
    From Watteau fêtes and Teniers fairs,
You yet may seek in notes decayed
    Our long-forgot familiar airs.

MORTIMER WHEELER.

BALLADE OF SEA-MUSIC.

Sink, sun, in crimson far away,
　　Float out, pale moon, above the roar,
While brown and silver, flame and grey,
　　Round rock and sand, the waters pour;
　　For night hath clue to all the store,
Of wild wave-harmony that rings,
　　And earth hath not in all her lore,
The legends that sea-music brings.

Here singing silver shallows fray
　　The ruby-tufted golden floor,
Here wondrous twilight forests sway
　　Round coral porch and corridor
　　Where lurk——but ah ; why yet implore
The splendid dream that round them clings? . .
　　Where lie the dead who heard of yore
The legends that sea-music brings.

This is the sea that could not stay,
　　The tides of men that evermore
Rolled westward still and cleft its spray,
　　With hollowed trunk, and dauntless oar.
　　Here Grecian trireme reeled before,
Rome's purple galley ; here sea kings,
　　Left red on wave and blackened shore
The legends that sea-music brings.

Envoy.

Earth keeps not now the face she wore
　　The smoke-trails dusk the wide white wings ;
No longer as of old shall soar,
　　The legends that sea-music brings.

MORTIMER WHEELER.

THE NIGHTINGALE AND THE LARK.

When the fairies are all for their dances drest,
    When day's discords in the distance fail,
When the robin and wren are asleep in the nest,
    Then list to the note of the nightingale !
    But when diamonds glint on the dewy swale,
When star-fires are fading spark by spark,
    And the little birds all the dawning hail,
O hark to the song of the merry lark !

When over the hills the silver crest
    Is pouring enchantment on mere and vale,
And the world lies hushed in a dreamy rest,
    Then list to the note of the nightingale !
    But when the bright sun dight in golden mail
Flames over the tree-tops in the park,
    And the world goes again on its busy trail,
O hark to the song of the merry lark !

When the young heart flutters in Mabel's breast,
    And Algernon's cheek for once only is pale,
As the secret, half guessed, is at last confessed,
    Then list to the note of the nightingale !
    But when Corydon hides in a turn o' the dale,
And Phillis is met where no one may mark,
    And the sudden blush and the kiss tell the tale,
O hark to the song of the merry lark !

Envoi.

If Il Penseroso's mood prevail,
    Then list to the note of the nightingale !
But whenever L'Allegro woos, then hark,
    O hark to the song of the merry lark !

ERNEST WHITNEY.

MY GRANDCHILDREN AT CHURCH.

Bright Dorothy, with eyes of blue,
    And serious Dickie, brave as fair,
Crossing to Church you oft may view
    When no one but myself is there :
    First to the belfry they repair,
And while to the large ropes they cling,
    And make believe to call to prayer,
For angels' ears the bells they ring !

Next seated gravely in a pew,
    A pulpit homily they share,
Meet for my little flock of two,
    Pointed and plain as they can bear :
    Then venture up the pulpit's stair,
Pray at the desk or gaily sing :
    O sweet Child-life without a care—
For angels' ears the bells they ring !

Dear little ones, the early dew
    Of holy infancy they wear,
And lift to Heaven a face as true
    As flowers that breathe the morning air :
    Whate'er they do, where'er they fare,
They can command an angel's wing
    Their voices have a music rare,
For angels' ears the bells they ring !

O parents, of your charge beware :
    Their angels stand before the King :
In work, play, sleep, and everywhere
    For angels' ears the bells they ring !

RICHARD WILTON.

BALLADE MADE IN THE HOT WEATHER.

Fountains that frisk and sprinkle
    The moss they overspill ;
Grass that the breezes crinkle ;
    The wheel beside the mill,
    With its wet, weedy frill ;
Wind-shadows in the wheat ;
A water-cart in the street ;
    The fringe of foam that girds
An islet's ferneries ;
    A green sky's minor thirds—
To live, I think of these !

Of ice and glass the tinkle,
    Pellucid, silver-shrill ;
Peaches without a wrinkle ;
    Cherries and snow, at will
    From china bowls that fill
The senses with a sweet
Incuriousness of heat ;
    A melon's dripping sherds ;
Cream-clotted strawberries ;
    Dusk dairies set with curds—
To live, I think of these !

Vale-lily and periwinkle ;
    Wet stone-crop on the sill ;
The look of leaves a-twinkle
    With windlets clear and still ;
    The feel of a forest rill
That wimples fresh and fleet
About one's naked feet ;
    The muzzles of drinking herds ;
Lush flags and bulrushes ;
    The chirp of rain-bound birds—
To live, I think of these !

Envoy.

Dark aisles, new packs of cards,
  Mermaidens' tails, cool swards,
  Dawn dews and starlit seas,
White marbles, whiter words—
  To live, I think of these !

W. E. HENLEY.

BALLADE OF ASPIRATION.

O to be somewhere by the sea,
  Far from the city's dust and shine,   [shrine,
  From Mammon's priests and from Mammon's
From the stony street, and the grim decree
  That over an inkstand crooks my spine,
From the books that are and the books to be,
  And the need that makes of the sacred Nine
  A school of harridans !—sweetheart mine,
O to be somewhere by the sea !

Under a desk I bend my knee,
  Whether the morn be foul or fine.
  I envy the tramp, in a ditch supine,
Or footing it over the sunlit lea.
  But I struggle and write and make no sign,
For a labouring ox must earn his fee,
  And even a journalist has to dine ;
  But O for a breath of the eglantine !
O to be somewhere by the sea !

Out on the links, where the wind blows free,
  And the surges gush, and the rounding brine
  Wanders and sparkles, an air like wine
Fills the senses with pride and glee.
  In neighbour hedges are flowers to twine,

A white sail glimmers, the foamlines flee :
 Life, love, and laziness are a trine
 Worshipful, wonderful, dear, divine. . . .
O to be somewhere by the sea !

Envoy.

Out and alas for the sweet Lang Syne,
When I was rich in a certain key—
 The key of the fields ; and I hadn't to pine,
 Or to sigh in vain at the sun's decline,
O to be somewhere by the Sea !

W. E. HENLEY.

BALLADE OF TRUISMS.

Gold or silver every day,
    Dies to grey.
There are knots in every skein.
Hours of work and hours of play
    Fade away
Into one immense Inane.
Shadow and substance, chaff and grain,
    Are as vain
As the foam or as the spray.
Life goes crooning, faint and fain,
    One refrain—
" If it could be always May ! "

Though the earth be green and gay,
    Though, they say,
Man the cup of heaven may drain ;
Though his little world to sway.
    He display
Hoard on hoard of pith and brain,
Autumn brings a mist and rain
    That constrain

Him and his to know decay,
Where undimmed the lights that wane
                    Would remain,
If it could be always May.

Yea, alas, must turn to *Nay*,
                    Flesh to clay.
Chance and Time are ever twain.
Men may scoff and men may pray,
                    But they pay
Every pleasure with a pain.
Life may soar and Fortune deign
                    To explain
Where her prizes hide and stay;
But we lack the lusty train
                    We should gain
If it could be always May.

Envoy.
Time the pedagogue his cane
                    Might retain,
But his charges all would stray
Truanting in every lane—
                    Jack with Jane !—
If it could be always May.
                    W. E. HENLEY.

DOUBLE BALLADE OF LIFE AND FATE.

Fools may pine, and sots may swill,
        Cynics jibe and prophets rail,
Moralists may scourge and drill,
        Preachers prose, and faint hearts quail.
        Let them whine, or threat, or wail !
'Till the touch of Circumstance
        Down to darkness sink the scale—
Fate's a fiddler, Life's a dance.

What if skies be wan and chill ?
　　What if winds be harsh and stale ?
Presently the East will thrill,
　　And the sad and shrunken sail,
　　Bellying with a kindly gale,
Bear you sunwards, while your chance
　　Sends you back the hopeful hail—
" Fate's a fiddler, Life's a dance."

Idle shot or coming bill,
　　Hapless love or broken bail,
Gulp it (never chew your pill !)
　　And if Burgundy should fail,
　　Try a humble pot of ale !
Over all is heaven's expanse.
　　Gold exists among the shale.
Fate's a fiddler, Life's a dance.

Dull Sir Joskin sleeps his fill,
　　Good Sir Galahad seeks the Grail,
Proud Sir Pertinax flaunts his frill,
　　Hard Sir Æger dints his mail ;
　　And the while, by hill and dale,
Tristram's braveries gleam and glance,
　　And his blithe horn tells its tale. . . ,
Fate's a fiddler, Life's a dance.

Araminta's grand and shrill,
　　Delia's passionate and frail,
Doris drives an earnest quill,
　　Athanasia takes the veil ;
　　Wiser Phyllis o'er her pail,
At the heart of all romance
　　Reading, sings to Strephon's flail—
Fate's a fiddler, Life's a dance.

Every Jack must have his Jill,
 (Even Johnson had his Thrale !)
Forward, couples—with a will !
 This, the world, is not a jail.
 Hear the music, sprat and whale !
Hands across, retire, advance !
 Though the doomsman's on your trail,
Fate's a Fiddler, Life's a dance.

Envoy.

Boys and girls, at slug and snail
 And their compeers look askance.
Pay your footing on the nail :
 Fate's a fiddler, Life's a dance.

W. E. HENLEY.

DOUBLE BALLADE OF THE NOTHINGNESS OF THINGS.

The big teetotum twirls,
 And epochs wax and wane
As chance subsides or swirls ;
 But of the loss and gain
 The sum is always plain.
Read on the mighty pall,
The weed of funeral
 That covers praise and blame,
The isms and the anities,
 Magnificence and shame,
" O Vanity of Vanities ! "

The Fates are subtile girls !
 They give us chaff for grain :
And Time, the Thunderer, hurls,
 Like bolted death, disdain
 At all that heart and brain
Conceive, or great or small,

Upon this earthly ball.
  Would you be knight and dame?
Or woo the sweet humanities?
  Or illustrate a name?
O Vanity of Vanities!

We sound the sea for pearls,
  Or lose them in the drain;
We flute it with the merles,
  Or tug and sweat and strain;
  We grovel, or we reign;
We saunter, or we brawl;
We answer, or we call;
  We search the stars for Fame,
Or sink her subterranities;
  The legend's still the same:—
"O Vanity of Vanities!"

Here at the wine one birls,
  There someone clanks a chain.
The flag that this man furls
  That man to float is fain.
  Pleasure gives place to pain:--
These in the kennel crawl,
While others take the wall.
  She has a glorious aim,
He lives for the inanities.
  What comes of every claim?
O Vanity of Vanities!

Alike are clods and earls.
  For sot, and seer, and swain,
For emperors and for churls,
  For antidote and bane,
  There is but one refrain:
But one for king and thrall,
For David and for Saul,

For fleet of foot and lame,
For pieties and profanities,
      The picture and the frame—
" O Vanity of Vanities ! "

Life is a smoke that curls—
      Curls in a flickering skein,
That winds and whisks and whirls,
      A figment thin and vain,
      Into the vast Inane.
One end for hut and hall !
One end for cell and stall !
      Burned in one common flame
Are wisdoms and insanities.
      For this alone we came :—
" O Vanity of Vanities ! "

Envoi.

Prince, pride must have a fall.
What is the worth of all
      Your state's supreme urbanities ?
Bad at the best's the game.
Well might the sage exclaim :—
      " O Vanity of Vanities ! "

W. E. HENLEY.

BALLADE OF SLEEP.

The hours are passing slow,
      I hear their weary tread
Clang from the tower, and go
      Back to their kinsfolk dead.
      Sleep ! death's twin brother dread !
Why dost thou scorn me so ?
      The wind's voice overhead
Long wakeful here I know,
      And music from the steep,

Where waters fall and flow.
    Wilt thou not hear me, Sleep ?

All sounds that might bestow
    Rest on the fever'd bed,
All slumb'rous sounds and low
    Are mingled here and wed,
  · And bring no drowsihed.
Shy dreams flit to and fro
    With shadowy hair dispread ;
With wistful eyes that glow,
    And silent robes that sweep.
Thou wilt not hear me ; no ?
    Wilt thou not hear me, Sleep ?

What cause hast thou to show
    Of sacrifice unsped ?
Of all thy slaves below
    I most have labourèd
    With service sung and said ;
Have cull'd such buds as blow,
    Soft poppies white and red
Where thy still gardens grow
    And Lethe's waters weep,
Why, then, art thou my foe ?
    Wilt thou not hear me, Sleep ?

Envoi.

Prince, ere the dark be sped
    By golden shafts, ere low
And long the shadows creep :
Lord of the wand of lead,
    Soft-footed as the snow,
Wilt thou not hear me, Sleep ?

ANDREW LANG.

THE BALLADE OF LOVELACE.

My days for singing and loving are over
    And stark I lie in my narrow bed,
I care not at all if roses cover
    Or if above me the snow is spread ;
    I am weary of dreaming of my sweet dead—
Vera and Lily and Annie and May,
And my soul is set on the present fray,
    Its piercing kisses and subtle snares :
So gallants are conquered, ah wellaway,
    My love was stronger and fiercer than theirs.

O happy moths that now flit and hover
    From the blossom of white to the blossom of red,
Take heed, for I was a lordly lover
    Till the little day of my life had sped ;
    As straight as a pine tree, a golden head,
And eyes as blue as an austral bay.
Ladies when loosing your satin array,
    Reflect, in my years had you lived my prayers
Might have won you from weakly lovers away.
    My love was stronger and fiercer than theirs.

Through the song of the thrush and the pipe of the plover
    Sweet voices come down through the binding lead ;
O queens that every age must discover
    For men, that Man's delight may be fed ;
    Oh, sister queens to the queens I wed
For the space of a year, a month, a day,
No thirst but mine could your thirst allay ;
    And oh, for an hour of life, my dears,
To kiss you, to laugh at your lovers' dismay,—
    My love was stronger and fiercer than theirs.

Envoi.

Prince was I ever of festival gay,
And time never silvered my locks with grey ;
   The love of your lovers is as hope that despairs,
So think of me sometimes dear ladies I pray,
   My love was stronger and fiercer than theirs.
GEORGE MOORE.

BALLAD.

I.

What do we here who, with reverted eyes,
   Turn back our longing from the modern air
To the dim gold of long-evanished skies,
   When other songs in other mouths were fair ?
   Why do we stay the load of life to bear,
To measure still the weary, worldly ways,
   Waiting upon the still recurring sun,
That ushers in another waste of days,
Of roseless Junes and unenchanted Mays ?
   Why, but because our task is yet undone ?

II.

Were it not thus, could but our high emprise
   Be once fulfilled, which of us would forbear
To seek that haven where contentment lies ?
   Who would not doff at once life's load of care,
   To be at peace amid the silence there ?
Ah, who alas ?—Across the heat and haze
   Death beckons to us in the shadow dun—
Favouring and fair—" My rest is sweet," he says ;
But we reluctantly avert our gaze :
   Why, but because our task is yet undone ?

III.

Songs have we sung, and many melodies
    Have from our lips had issue rich and rare ;
But never yet the conquering chant did rise,
    That should ascend the very heaven's stair,
    To rescue life from anguish and despair.
Often and again, drunk with delight of lays,
    "Lo !" have we cried, "this is the golden one
That shall deliver us !"—Alas ! Hope's rays
Die in the distance, and Life's sadness stays.
    Why, but because our task is yet undone?

Envoy.

Great God of Love, thou whom all poets praise,
    Grant that the aim of rest for us be won ;
Let the light shine upon our life that strays
Disconsolate within the desert maze ;
    Why, but because our task is yet undone ?

JOHN PAYNE.

DOUBLE BALLAD.   OF THE SINGERS OF THE TIME.

I.

Why are our songs like the moan of the main,
    When the wild winds buffet it to and fro,
(Our brothers ask us again and again),
    A weary burden of hope laid low?
    Have birds ceased singing or flowers to blow?
Is life cast down from its fair estate ?
    This I answer them, nothing mo',
Songs and singers are out of date.

II.

What shall we sing of? Our hearts are fain,
    Our bosoms burn with a sterile glow.
Shall we sing of the sordid strife for gain
    For shameful honour, for wealth and woe,
    Hunger and luxury—weeds that throw
Up from one seeding their flowers of hate?
    Can we tune our lute to these themes? ah no!
Songs and singers are out of date.

III.

Our songs should be of faith without stain,
    Of haughty honour and deaths that sow
The seeds of life on the battle-plain,
    Of loves unsullied and eyes that show
    The fair white soul in the deeps below.
Where are they, these that our songs await,
    To wake to joyance?   Doth any know?
Songs and singers are out of date.

IV.

What have we done with meadow and lane?
    Where are the flowers and the hawthorn snow?
Acres of brick in the pitiless rain,——
    These are our gardens for thorpe and stow!
    Summer has left us long ago,
Gone to the lands where the turtles mate
    And the crickets chirp in the wild rose row;
Songs and singers are out of date.

V.

We sit and sing to a world in pain,
    Our heartstrings quiver sadly and slow;
But, aye and anon, the murmurous strain
    Swells up to a clangour of strife and throe,

And the folks that hearken, or friend or foe,
Are ware that the stress of the time is great
    ·And say to themselves, as they come and go,
Songs and singers are out of date.

VI.

Winter holds us, body and brain :
    Ice is over our being's flow ;
Song is a flower that will droop and wane,
    If it have no heaven toward which to grow.
    Faith and beauty are dead, I trow
Nothing is left but fear and fate :
    Men are weary of hope ; and so
Songs and singers are out of date.

JOHN PAYNE.

A BALLAD OF LOST LOVERS.

Beyond the end of Paradise
    Where never mortal may repair,
A phantom-haunted forest lies
    With twisted branches always bare,
    And here unhappy lovers fare
And ever more complain their lot,
    Ah ! pity them that wander there,
Half-remembered and half-forgot.

There Orpheus leaves his lute and cries
    No more on Eurydice the fair,
There silent Sappho sits and sighs,
    Sad as the violets in her hair,
    And pale Francesca's heart-strings stir
(She knows not why) if Launcelot
    Look round, and dead days call to her
Half-remembered and half-forgot.

There Jason walks with coward eyes
    Bent down yet seeing everywhere
How fiery vested Glaucé dies,
    And white Medea's wild despair,
    Fair Rosamond and French Heaulmière,
And he who sang the queenly Scot,
    Meet many another wanderer,
Half-remembered and half-forgot.

Alas ! they never shall arise
    Nor leave this lonely limbo where
They share not in our common skies,
    And know not of our sunlit air ;
    They had their time for work and prayer,
For hope and help, but used them not,
    Or if they dreamed that such things were,
Half-remembered and half-forgot.

Envoy.

Lovers, I pray ye mind whene'er
    Your youth is proud and passion-hot,
How Love itself may turn a care
    Half-remembered and half-forgot.

A Mary F. Robinson.

A BALLAD OF HEROES.

O conquerors and heroes, say—
    Great Kings and Captains tell me this,
Now that you rest beneath the clay
    What profit lies in victories ?
    Do softer flower-roots twine and kiss
The whiter bones of Charlemain ?
    Our crownless heads sleep sweet as his,
Now all your victories are in vain.

All ye who fell that summer's day
    When Athens lost Amphipolis,
Who blinded by the briny spray
    Fell dead i' the sea at Salamis,
    You captors of Thyreatis,
Who bear yourselves a heavier chain,
    With your young brother, Bozzaris,
Now all your victories are in vain.

And never Roman armies may
    Rouse Hannibal where now he is,
When Cæsar makes no king obey,
    And fast asleep lies Lascaris;
    Who fears the Goths or Khan-Yenghiz?
Not one of all the paynim train
    Can taunt us with Nicopolis,
Now all your victories are in vain.

What reck you Spartan heroes, pray,
    Of Arcady or Argolis?
When one barbarian boy to-day
    Would fain be king of all of Greece.
    Brave knights, you would not stir I wis,
Altho' the very Cross were ta'en;
    Not Rome itself doth Cæsar miss,
Now all your victories are in vain.

Envoy.

O kings, bethink how little is
    The good of battles or the gain—
Death conquers all things with his peace
    Now all your victories are in vain.

A. MARY F. ROBINSON.

A BALLAD OF FRANÇOIS VILLON,

PRINCE OF ALL BALLAD-MAKERS.

Bird of the bitter bright grey golden morn
    Scarce risen upon the dusk of dolorous years,
First of us all and sweetest singer born
      Whose far shrill note the world of new men hears
      Cleave the cold shuddering shade as twilight clears ;
When song new-born put off the old world's attire
And felt its tune on her changed lips expire,
      Writ foremost on the roll of them that came
Fresh girt for service of the latter lyre,
      Villon, our sad bad glad mad brother's name !

Alas the joy, the sorrow, and the scorn,
    That clothed thy life with hopes and sins and fears,
And gave thee stones for bread and tares for corn
      And plume-plucked gaol-birds for thy starveling peers
      Till death clipt close their flight with shameful shears ;
Till shifts came short and loves were hard to hire,
When lilt of song nor twitch of twangling wire
      Could buy thee bread or kisses ; when light fame
Spurned like a ball and haled through brake and briar,
      Villon, our sad bad glad mad brother's name !

Poor splendid wings so frayed and soiled and torn !
    Poor kind wild eyes so dashed with light quick tears!
Poor perfect voice, most blithe when most forlorn,
      That rings athwart the sea whence no man steers
      Like joy-bells crossed with death-bells in our ears !
What far delight has cooled the fierce desire
      That like some ravenous bird was strong to tire
      On that frail flesh and soul consumed with flame,
But left more sweet than roses to respire,
      Villon, our sad bad glad mad brother's name ?

Envoi.

Prince of sweet songs made out of tears and fire,
A harlot was thy nurse, a God thy sire ;
    Shame soiled thy song, and song assoiled thy shame.
But from thy feet now death has washed the mire,
Love reads out first at head of all our quire,
    Villon, our sad bad glad mad brother's name.

ALGERNON CHARLES SWINBURNE.

THE EPITAPH IN FORM OF A BALLAD

Which Villon made for himself and his comrades, expecting to
be hanged along with them.

Men, brother men, that after us yet live,
    Let not your hearts too hard against us be ;
For if some pity of us poor men ye give,
    The sooner God shall take of you pity.
    Here are we five or six strung up, you see,
And here the flesh that all too well we fed
Bit by bit eaten and rotten, rent and shred,
    And we the bones grow dust and ash withal ;
Let no man laugh at us discomforted,
    But pray to God that he forgive us all.

If we call on you, brothers, to forgive,   [we
    Ye should not hold our prayer in scorn, though
Were slain by law ; ye know that all alive
    Have not wit alway to walk righteously ;
    Make therefore intercession heartily
With him that of a virgin's womb was bred,
That his grace be not as a dry well-head
    For us, nor let hell's thunder on us fall ;
We are dead, let no man harry or vex us dead,
    But pray to God that he forgive us all.

The rain has washed and laundered us all five,
    And the sun dried and blackened ; yea, per die,
Ravens and pies with beaks that rend and rive,
Have dug our eyes out, and plucked off for fee
    Our beards and eyebrows ; never are we free,
    Not once, to rest ; but here and there still sped,
Drive at its wild will by the wind's change led,
    More pecked of birds than fruits on garden-wall.
Men, for God's love, let no gibe here be said,
    But pray to God that he forgive us all.

Prince Jesus, that of all art lord and head,
Keep us, that hell be not our bitter bed ;
    We have nought to do in such a master's hall.
Be not ye therefore of our fellowhead,
    But pray to God that he forgive us all.

ALGERNON CHARLES SWINBURNE.

A BALLAD OF BATH.

Like a queen enchanted who may not laugh or weep,
    Glad at heart and guarded from change and care like
        ours,
Girt about with beauty by days and nights that creep
Soft as breathless ripples that softly shoreward sweep,
    Lies the lovely city whose grace no grief deflowers.
Age and grey forgetfulness, time that shifts and veers,
Touch thee not, our fairest, whose charm no rival nears,
    Hailed as England's Florence of one whose praise
        gives grace,
Landor, once thy lover, a name that love reveres :
    Dawn and noon and sunset are one before thy face.

Dawn whereof we know not, and noon whose fruit we
    reap,
    Garnered up in record of years that fell like flowers,
Sunset liker sunrise along the shining steep
Whence thy fair face lightens, and where thy soft springs
    leap,
    Crown at once and gird thee with grace of guardian
    powers.
Loved of men beloved of us, souls that fame inspheres,
All thine air hath music for him who dreams and hears ;
    Voices mixed of multitudes, feet of friends that pace,
Witness why for ever, if heaven's face clouds or clears,
    Dawn and noon and sunset are one before thy face.

Peace hath here found harbourage mild as very sleep :
    Not the hills and waters, the fields and wildwood
    bowers,
Smile or speak more tenderly, clothed with peace more
    deep,
Here than memory whispers of days our memories keep
    Fast with love and laughter and dreams of withered
    hours.
Bright were these as blossom of old, and thought endears
Still the fair soft phantoms that pass with smiles or tears,
    Sweet as roseleaves hoarded and dried wherein we
    trace
Still the soul and spirit of sense that lives and cheers :
    Dawn and noon and sunset are one before thy face.

City lulled asleep by the chime of passing years,
Sweeter smiles thy rest than the radiance round thy peers ;
    Only love and lovely remembrance here have place.
Time on thee lies lighter than music on men's ears ;
    Dawn and noon and sunset are one before thy face.

ALGERNON CHARLES SWINBURNE.

A BALLAD OF SARK.

High beyond the granite portal arched across,
    Like the gateway of some godlike giant's hold
Sweep and swell the billowy breasts of moor and moss
    East and westward, and the dell their slopes enfold.
    Basks in purple, glows in green, exults in gold.
Glens that know the dove and fells that hear the lark
Fill with joy the rapturous island, as an ark   [tree,
    Full of spicery wrought from herb and flower and
None would dream that grief even here may disembark
    On the wrathful woful marge of earth and sea.

Rocks emblazoned like the mid shield's royal boss
    Take the sun with all their blossom broad and bold.
None would dream that all this moorland's glow and gloss
    Could be dark as tombs that strike the spirit acold,
    Even in eyes that opened here, and here behold
Now no sun relume from hope's belated spark,
Any comfort, nor may ears of mourners hark
    Though the ripe woods ring with golden-throated
       glee,
While the soul lies shattered, like a stranded bark
    On the wrathful woful marge of earth and sea.

Death and doom are they whose crested triumphs toss
    On the proud plumed waves whence mourning notes
       are tolled.
Wail of perfect woe and moan for utter loss
    Raise the bride-song through the graveyard on the
       wold
    Where the bride-bed keeps the bridegroom fast in
       mould,
Where the bride, with death for priest and doom for clerk,

Hears for choir the throats of waves like wolves that bark,
  Sore anhungered, off the drear Eperquerie,
Fain to spoil the strongholds of the strength of Sark
  On the wrathful woful marge of earth and sea.

Prince of storm and tempest, lord whose ways are dark,
Wind whose wings are spread for flight that none may
     mark,
  Lightly dies the joy that lives by grace of thee.
Love through thee lies bleeding, hope lies cold and stark,
  On the wrathful woful marge of earth and sea.

ALGERNON CHARLES SWINBURNE.

THE DANCE OF DEATH.

(Chant Royal, after Holbein.)

" Contra vim MORTIS
Non est medicamen in hortis."

He is the despots' Despot.   All must bide,
  Later or soon, the message of his might ;
Princes and potentates their heads must hide,
  Touched by the awful sigil of his right ;
Beside the Kaiser he at eve doth wait
And pours a potion in his cup of state ;
  The stately Queen his bidding must obey ;
  No keen-eyed Cardinal shall him affray ;
And to the Dame that wantoneth he saith—
  " Let be, Sweetheart, to junket and to play. . ."
There is no king more terrible than Death.

The lusty Lord, rejoicing in his pride,
  He draweth down ; before the armèd Knight
With jingling bridle-rein he still doth ride ;
  He crosseth the strong Captain in the fight ;

He beckons the grave Elder from debate,
He hales the Abbot by his shaven pate,
  Nor for the Abbess' wailing will delay ;
  No bawling Mendicant shall say him nay ;
E'en to the pyx the Priest he followeth,
  Nor can the Leech his chilling finger stay. .
There is no king more terrible than Death.

All things must bow to him.   And woe betide
  The Wine-bibber,—the Roisterer by night ;
Him the feast-master, many bouts defied,
  Him 'twixt the pledging and the cup shall smite ;
Woe to the Lender at usurious rate,
The hard Rich Man, the hireling Advocate ;
  Woe to the Judge that selleth right for pay ;
  Woe to the Thief that like a beast of prey
With creeping tread the traveller hurryeth :—
  These, in their sin, the sudden sword shall slay. .
There is no king more terrible than Death.

He hath no pity,—nor will be denied.
  When the low hearth is garnishèd and bright,
Grimly he flingeth the dim portal wide,
  And steals the Infant in the Mother's sight :
He hath no pity for the scorned of fate :—
He spares not Lazarus lying at the gate,
  Nay, nor the Blind that stumbleth as he may ;
  Nay, the tired Ploughman,—at the sinking ray,—
In the last furrow,—feels an icy breath,
  And knows a hand hath turned the team astray.
There is no king more terrible than Death.

He hath no pity.   For the new-made Bride,
  Blithe with the promise of her life's delight,
That wanders gladly by her Husband's side,
  He with the clatter of his drum doth fright ;

He scares the Virgin at the convent grate ;
The maid half-won, the Lover passionate ;
  He hath no grace for weakness or decay :
  The tender Wife, the Widow bent and grey,—
The feeble Sire whose footstep faltereth,—
  All these he leadeth by the lonely way. . .
There is no king more terrible than Death.

Envoy.

YOUTH, for whose ear and monishing of late,
I sang of Prodigals and lost estate,
  Have thou thy joy of living and be gay ;
But know not less that there must come a day,—
Aye, and perchance e'en now it hasteneth,—
  When thine own heart shall speak to thee and say,—
There is no king more terrible than Death.

AUSTIN DOBSON.

THE PRAISE OF DIONYSUS.

(Chant Royal.)

Behold, above the mountains there is light,
  A streak of gold, a line of gathering fire,
And the dim East hath suddenly grown bright
  With pale aerial flame, that drives up higher
The lurid mists that, of the night aware,
Breasted the dark ravines and coverts bare ;
  Behold, behold ! the granite gates unclose,
  And down the vales a lyric people flows,
Who dance to music, and in dancing fling
  Their frantic robes to every wind that blows,
And deathless praises to the vine-god sing.

Nearer they press, and nearer still in sight,
  Still dancing blithely in a seemly choir ;
Tossing on high the symbol of their rite,
  The cone-tipped thyrsus of a god's desire ;
Nearer they come, tall damsels flushed and fair,
With ivy circling their abundant hair,
    Onward, with even pace, in stately rows,
    With eye that flashes, and with cheek that glows,
And all the while their tribute songs they bring,
    And newer glories of the past disclose,
And deathless praises to their vine-god sing.

The pure luxuriance of their limbs is white,
    And flashes clearer as they draw the nigher,
Bathed in an air of infinite delight,
    Smooth without wound of thorn or fleck of mire,
Born up by song as by a trumpet's blare,
Leading the van to conquest, on they fare ;
    Fearless and bold, whoever comes or goes,
    These shining cohorts of Bacchantes close,
Shouting and shouting till the mountains ring,
    And forests grim forget their ancient woes,
And deathless praises to the vine-god sing.

And youths are there for whom full many a night
    Brought dreams of bliss, vague dreams that
        haunt and tire,
Who rose in their own ecstasy bedight,   [briar,
    And wandered forth through many a scourging
And waited shivering in the icy air,
And wrapped their leopard-skins about them there.
    Knowing, for all the bitter air that froze,
    The time must come, that every poet knows,
When he shall rise and feel himself a king,
    And follow, follow where the ivy grows,
And deathless praises to the vine-god sing.

But oh ! within the heart of this great flight,
    What ivory arms held up the golden lyre?
What form is this of more than mortal height
    What matchless beauty, what inspirèd ire ?
The brindled panthers know the prize they bear,
And harmonise their steps with stately care ;
    Bent to the morning like a living rose,
    The immortal splendour of his face he shows,
And where he glances, leaf and flower and wing
    Tremble with rapture, stirred in their repose,
And deathless praises to the vine-god sing.

Envoi.

    Prince of the flute and ivy, all thy foes
Record the bounty that thy grace bestows,
But we, thy servants, to thy glory cling ;
    And with no frigid lips our songs compose,
And deathless praises to the vine-god sing.

Edmund Gosse.

THE GOD OF LOVE.

(Chant Royal.)

I.

O most fair God. O Love both new and old,
    That wast before the flowers of morning blew,
Before the glad sun in his mail of gold
    Leapt into light across the first day's dew ;
That art the first and last of our delight,
That in the blue day and the purple night
    Holdest the hearts of servant and of king.
    Lord of liesse, sovran of sorrowing,
That in thy hand hast heaven's golden key
    And Hell beneath the shadow of thy wing.
Thou art my Lord to whom I bend the knee.

II.

What thing rejects thy mastery? who so bold
    But at thine altars in the dusk they sue?
Even the strait pale goddess, silver-stoled,
    That kissed Endymion when the Spring was new,
To thee did homage in her own despite,
When in the shadow of her wings of white
    She slid down trembling from her moonèd ring
    To where the Latmian boy lay slumbering,
And in that kiss put off cold chastity.
    Who but acclaim with voice and pipe and string,
" Thou art my Lord to whom I bend the knee?"

III.

Master of men and gods, in every fold
    Of thy wide vans the sorceries that renew
The labouring earth, tranced with the winter's cold,
    Lie hid—the quintessential charms that woo
The souls of flowers, slain with the sullen might
Of the dead year, and draw them to the light.
    Balsam and blessing to thy garments cling;
    Skyward and seaward, when thy white hands fling
Their spells of healing over land and sea,
    One shout of homage makes the welkin ring,
" Thou art my Lord to whom I bend the knee!"

IV.

I see thee throned aloft; thy fair hands hold
    Myrtles for joy, and euphrasy and rue:
Laurels and roses round thy white brows rolled,
    And in thine eyes the royal heaven's hue:
But in thy lips' clear colour, ruddy bright,
The heart's blood shines of many a hapless wight.
    Thou are not only fair and sweet as spring;

Terror and beauty, fear and wondering
Meet on thy brow, amazing all that see :
    All men do praise thee, ay, and everything ;
Thou art my Lord to whom I bend the knee.

v.

I fear thee, though I love. Who can behold
    The sheer sun burning in the orbèd blue,
What while the noontide over hill and wold
    Flames like a fire, except his mazèd view
Wither and tremble ? So thy splendid sight
Fills me with mingled gladness and affright.
    Thy visage haunts me in the wavering
    Of dreams, and in the dawn awakening,
I feel thy radiance streaming full on me.
    Both fear and joy unto thy feet I bring ;
Thou art my Lord to whom I bend the knee !

Envoy.

God above Gods, High and Eternal King,
To whom the spheral symphonies do sing,
    I find no whither from thy power to flee,
Save in thy pinions vast o'ershadowing.
    Thou art my Lord to whom I bend the knee.

JOHN PAYNE.

THE CHANT OF THE CHILDREN OF THE MIST.

(Chant Royal.)

I waited on a mountain's midmost side,
    The lifting of a cloud, and standing there,
Keeping my soul in patience far and wide
    Beheld faint shadows wandering, felt the air
Stirred as with voices which in passing by
Still dulled its weary weight with many a sigh.

No band of pilgrims or of soldiers they—
These children of the mist—who took their way,
    Each one aloof, perplexed and pondering
With steps untimed to music grave or gay ;—
    This was a people that had lost its king.

In happier days of old it was their pride
    To serve him on their knee and some were 'ware
E'en of his voice or presence as they plied
    Their daily task, or ate their simple fare.
Now in new glory shrouded, far and nigh
He had withdrawn himself from ear and eye ;
    Scorning such service as they knew to pay,
    His ministers were as the golden ray [spring,—
        Shot from the sun when he would wake the
Swift to perform and pliant to obey—
    This was a people that had lost its king.

Single as beasts, or if allied, allied
    But as the wolf who leaves his dusky lair
To hound for common need, which scarce supplied,
    He lone returns with his disputed share,—
Even so sole, so scornful, or so shy,
Each man of these pursued his way on high,
    Still high and higher, seeking through the grey
    Gloom of the mist, the lord of yesterday.
        Dim, serviceless, bereft and sorrowing
Shadows continuing never in one stay ;—
    This was a people that had lost its king.

Then as the day wore on, and none descried
    The longed-for presence, as the way grew bare,
As strength declined, and hope within them died
    A sad new birth,—the fruit of their despair,—
Stirred in their midst, and with a human cry
Awoke a human love, and flushed a dry

Sweet spring of tears, whose fertilising play
 Broke up the hard cold barriers of their clay,
Till hands were stretched in help, or seen to
  cling
In fealty that was only joined to pray ;
 This was a people that had lost its king.

So blent in heart and hand, so myriad-eyed,
 With gathering power and ever lessening care,
The veiled beguilements of the way defied   [fair ;
 They cleave the cloud, and climb that mountain
Till lo upon its crown at last they vie
In songs of rapture as they hail the sky,
 And trace their lost one through the vast array
 Of tuneful suns, which keep not now at bay
 Their questing love, but help to waft and wing ;
And over all a voice which seems to say,
 This is a people that has found its king !

Envoy.

Lord of our lives ! Thou scorned us that day
 When at thy feet a scattered host we lay.
Behold us ONE ! One mighty heart we bring,
Strong for thy tasks, and level to thy sway.
 This was the people that had lost its king !

EMILY PFEIFFER.

KING BOREAS.

(Chant Royal.)

I sit enthroned 'mid icy wastes afar,
 Beyond the level land of endless snow,
For months I see the brilliant polar star
 Shine on a shore, the lonelier none may know.
Supreme I rule in monarchy of might,—
My realms are boundless as the realms of Night.

Proud court I hold, and tremblingly obey
    My many minions from the isles of Day ;
And when my heralds sound aloud, behold
    My slaves appear with suppliant heads alway !
I am great Boreas, King of wind and cold.

I am the god of the winds that are !
    I blow where'er I list,—I come, I go.
Athwart the sky upon my cloud-capped car
    I rein my steeds, swift-prancing to and fro.
The dreary woodlands shudder in affright
To hear my clarion on the mountain height.
    The sobbing sea doth moan in pain, and pray,
    "Is there no refuge from the storm-king's sway ?"
I am as aged as the earth is old,
    Yet strong am I although my locks are grey ;
I am great Boreas, King of wind and cold.

I loose my chains, and then with awful jar
    And presage of disaster and dire woe,
Out rush the storms and sound the clash of war
    'Gainst all the earth, and shrill their bugles blow.
I bid them haste ; they bound in eager flight
Toward far fair lands, where'er the sun's warm light
    Makes mirth and joyance; there, in rude affray,
    They trample down, despoil, and crush and slay.
They turn green meadows to a desert wold,
    And naught for rulers of the earth care they ;—
I am great Boreas, King of wind and cold.

When in the sky, a lambent scimitar,
    In early eve Endymion's bride doth glow,
When night is perfect, and no cloud doth mar
    The peace of nature, when the rivers flow
Is soft and musical, and when the sprite
Whispers to lovers on each breeze bedight

With fragrance, then I steal forth, as I may,
   And seize upon whate'er I will for prey.
I see the billows high as hilltops rolled,
   And clutch and flaunt aloft the snowy spray !
I am great Boreas, King of wind and cold.

I am in league with Death.   When I unbar
   My triple-guarded doors, and there bestow
Upon my frost-fiends freedom, bid them scar
   The brightest dales with summer blooms a-row,
They breathe on every bower a deadly blight,
And all is sere and withered in their sight.
   Unheeded now, Apollo's warming ray
   Wakes not the flower, for my chill breezes play
Where once soft zephyrs swayed the marigold,
   And where his jargon piped the noisy jay,—
I am great Boreas, King of wind and cold.

Envoy.

O Princes, hearken what my trumpets say !—
" Man's life is naught, no mortal lives for aye ;
   His might hath empire only of the mold,"
Boast not yourselves, ye fragile forms of clay !
   I am great Boreas, King of wind and cold.

CLINTON SCOLLARD.

THE NEW EPIPHANY.

(Chant Royal.)

Awake, awake, nay, slumber not, nor sleep !
   Forth from the dreamland and black dome of night,
From chaos and thick darkness, from the deep
   Of formless being, comes a gracious light,
Gilding the crystal seas, and casting round
A golden glory on the enchanted ground ;—

Awake, O souls of harmony, and ye
  That greet the dayspring with your jubilee
Of lute and harp ! Awake, awake, and bring
  Your well-tuned cymbals, and go forth with glee,
Go forth, and welcome the eternal king.

Far o'er the hills have not the watchful sheep
  Espied their shepherd, and with eager flight
Gone forth to meet him on the craggy steep ;
  Hasting the while his summoning notes invite
Where riper grasses and green herbs abound :—
But ye ! your shepherd calls, thrice happy sound !
  He comes, he comes, your shepherd king, 'tis he !
  Oh, quit these close-cropped meads, and gladly flee
To him who makes once more new growths upspring ;
  Oh, quit your ancient glebes,—oh, joyfully
Go forth, and welcome the eternal king.

Too long ye till exhausted lands and reap
  Thin crops that ne'er your weary toil requite :
Too long your laggard oxen labouring creep
  Up the wide furrows, and full idly smite
The weed-encircled ridge, the rocky mound :
Will ye not quit these fields now barren found ?
  Ah ! ye are old, yet not too old to be
  Brave travellers o'er bald custom's boundary ;—
Then each, let each his robe around him fling,
  And with his little one, his child, set free,
Go forth, and welcome the eternal king.

See, on the strand, watching the waves that sweep
  Their creamy ripples up the sandy bight,
Your child waits, leaping as the wavelets leap,
  The faery infant of the infinite !
Ah ! happy child, with what new wonders crowned
He'll turn to thee to fathom and expound ;

Asking, enquiring, looking unto thee
  To solve the universe, its destiny ;—
And still unto thy vestment's hem will cling,
  Asking, enquiring,—whispering, may not we
Go forth, and welcome the eternal king.

Oh, linger not, no longer vainly weep
  O'er vanished hopes, but with new strength unite ;
Oh, linger not !   But let your glad eyes keep
  Watch on this guiding star that beams so bright
Around your brows be this phylacter bound,—
Let Truth be king and let his praise resound !
  Oh, linger not !   Let earth, and sky, and sea,
  To sound his praises let all hearts agree ;
Still loud, and louder, let your pæans ring,
  Go forth, go forth, in glad exultancy
Go forth, and welcome the eternal king.

Envoy.

Thou art the king, O Truth ! we bend the knee
  To thee ; we own thy wondrous sovranty ;
And still thy praises in our songs we'll sing,
  Bidding all people with blithe minstrelsy
Go forth, and welcome the eternal king.

SAMUEL WADDINGTON.

THE GLORY OF THE YEAR.

When Spring came softly breathing o'er the land,
  With warmer sunshine and sweet April shower ;
Bidding the silken willow leaves expand ;
  Calling to hill and meadow, bee and flower,
Bright with new life and beauty ; on light wing
Bringing the birds again to love and sing ;

And waking in the heart its joy amain,
  With old fond hopes and memories in its train ;
Childishly glad mid universal cheer,
  How oft we sang the half-forgotten strain :
" *Now* we behold the glory of the year ! "

When Summer by her fervid breezes fanned,
  With footstep free and proud in restless power,
With plump, round cheek to ruddy beauty tanned,
  In blooming loveliness came to her bower,
Her golden tresses loosely wandering
In wild luxuriance,—then pretty Spring
  Seemed but a playful sister, pettish, vain.
  How well we loved the passionate Summer's reign !
How day by day our empress grew more dear !
  " Beyond," we asked, " what fairer can remain ?
Now we behold the glory of the year ! "

But when grave Autumn's ever bounteous hand
  Poured round our feet the riches of her dower :
The pulpy fruit, the nut's sweet ripened gland,
  The largess free to gleaner and to plower,
And all the Summer sought in vain to bring ;
When stood the hills in glorious garmenting ;
  Shadowed by low-hung skies of sober grain,
  No more could our ennobled thoughts sustain
Regretful memory of Summer sere,—
  " What of the past ! " we cried in quick disdain :
" *Now* we behold the glory of the year ! "

Then before mighty Winter, stern and grand,
  We saw defenceless Autumn shivering, cower,
Changed to Duessa by his potent wand,
  Shorn of her loveliness, in Fortune's lower
Naked for Winter's scourge to smite and sting.
How godlike came the world's new sceptered King !

He fettered fast her torrents with his chain,
  Bound with his manacles the moaning main,
Yea, wrought his will with all things far and near.
  "At last," we said, "what more can Time attain?
Now we behold the glory of the year!"

Neglected Spring, despised, insulted, banned!
  Poor weakling! came again one April hour,
The tyrant struck his tent at her command;
  She laughed,—down tumbling fell his frosty tower;
At one light finger-touch his captives fling
Their shackles off and make the valleys ring
  With praises to the conqueror of pain.
  All the lost lives that languishing have lain,
Leaves, grasses, buds, and birds again appear,
  "O now!" we cried again and yet again,
" *Now* we behold the glory of the year!"

Prince, while Spring sports with sunbeam, flower, and
    rain,—
While wanton Summer riots on the plain,—
  'Neath Autumn's calm, or Winter's frown severe,
Change only clearer chants the old refrain,
" *Now* we behold the glory of the year!"

ERNEST WHITNEY.

The Kyrielle, Pantoum, and Rondeau Redoublé.

*Qui voudra sçavoir la pratique
De cette rime juridique,
Je dis que bien mise en effet
La Kyrielle ainsi se fait.
De plante de sillabes huit
Usez en donc si bien vous duit ;
Pour faire le couplet parfait
La Kirielle ainsi si fait.*

—THEODORE DE BANVILLE.

KYRIELLE.

A lark in the mesh of the tangled vine,
A bee that drowns in the flower-cup's wine,
A fly in the sunshine,—such is man.
All things must end, as all began.

A little pain, a little pleasure,
A little heaping up of treasure;
Then no more gazing upon the sun.
All things must end that have begun.

Where is the time for hope or doubt?
A puff of the wind, and life is out;
A turn of the wheel, and rest is won.
All things must end that have begun.

Golden morning and purple night,
Life that fails with the failing light;
Death is the only deathless one.
All things must end that have begun.

Ending waits on the brief beginning;
Is the prize worth the stress of winning?
E'en in the dawning the day is done.
All things must end that have begun.

Weary waiting and weary striving,
Glad outsetting and sad arriving;
What is it worth when the goal is won?
All things must end that have begun.

Speedily fades the morning glitter;
Love grows irksome and wine grows bitter.
Two are parted from what was one.
All things must end that have begun.

Toil and pain and the evening rest ;
Joy is weary and sleep is best ;
Fair and softly the day is done.
All things must end that have begun.

JOHN PAYNE.

THE PAVILION.

In the tent the lamps were bright ;
Out beyond the summer night
Thrilled and quivered like a star :
We beneath were left so far.

From the depths of blue profound
Never any sight or sound
Came our loneliness to mar :
We beneath were left so far.

But against the summer sky
Only you stood out and I ;
From all other things that are
We beneath were left so far.

A. MARY F. ROBINSON.

KYRIELLE.

In spring Love came, a welcome guest,
And tarried long at my behest ;
Now autumn wanes, the skies are grey
But loyal Love flees not away.

I charmed him with melodious lays
Through long rose-scented summer days ;
My songs no more are clear and gay
But loyal Love flees not away.

We plucked and twined the myrtle flowers,
Made joyance in the sylvan bowers ;
The blooms have died, wild winds hold sway,
But loyal Love flees not away.

Gone are the fifing crickets, gone
The feathered harbingers of dawn,
And gone the woodland's bright display,
But loyal Love flees not away.

With intermingled light and shade
The shifting seasons come and fade ;
Our fond hopes fail, false friends betray,
But loyal Love flees not away !

CLINTON SCOLLARD.

IN TOWN.

"The blue fly sung in the pane."—*Tennyson.*

Toiling in Town now is "horrid"
  (There is that woman again !)—
June in the zenith is torrid,
  Thought gets dry in the brain.

There is that woman again :
  "Strawberries ! fourpence a pottle !"
Thought gets dry in the brain ;
  Ink gets dry in the bottle.

"Strawberries ! fourpence a pottle !"
  Oh for the green of a lane !—
Ink gets dry in the bottle ;
  "Buzz" goes a fly in the pane !

Oh for the green of a lane,
　　Where one might lie and be lazy!
"Buzz" goes a fly in the pane;
　　Bluebottles drive me crazy!

Where one might lie and be lazy,
　　Careless of Town and all in it!—
Bluebottles drive me crazy:
　　I shall go mad in a minute!

Careless of Town and all in it,
　　With some one to soothe and to still you;
I shall go mad in a minute,
　　Bluebottle, then I shall kill you!

With some one to soothe and to still you,
　　As only one's feminine kin do,—
Bluebottle, then I shall kill you:
　　There now! I've broken the window!

As only one's feminine kin do,—
　　Some muslin-clad Mabel or May!—
There now! I've broken the window!
　　Bluebottle's off and away!

Some muslin-clad Mabel or May,
　　To dash one with eau de Cologne;—
Bluebottle's off and away,
　　And why should I stay here alone?

To dash one with eau de Cologne,
　　All over one's eminent forehead;
And why should I stay here alone?
　　Toiling in Town now is "horrid."

AUSTIN DOBSON.

MONOLOGUE D'OUTRE TOMBE.

(Pantoum.)

Morn and noon and night,
    Here I lie in the ground ;
No faintest glimmer of light,
    No lightest whisper of sound.

Here I lie in the ground ;
    The worms glide out and in ;
No lightest whisper of sound,
    After a life-long din.

The worms glide out and in ;
    They are fruitful and multiply ;
After a life-long din,
    I watch them quietly.

They are fruitful and multiply,
    My body dwindles the while ;
I watch them quietly ;
    I can scarce forbear a smile.

My body dwindles the while,
    I shall soon be a skeleton ;
I can scarce forbear a smile
    They have had such glorious fun.

I shall soon be a skeleton,
    The worms are wriggling away ;
They have had such glorious fun,
    They will fertilise my clay.

The worms are wriggling away,
    They are what I have been,
They will fertilise my clay.
    The grass will grow more green.

They are what I have been.
    I shall change, but what of that ?
The grass will grow more green,
    The parson's sheep grow fat.

I shall change, but what of that ?
    All flesh is grass, one says,
The parson's sheep grow fat,
    The parson grows in grace.

All flesh is grass, one says,
    Grass becomes flesh, one knows,
The parson grows in grace ;
    I am the grace he grows.

Grass becomes flesh, one knows,
    He grows like a bull of Bashan.
I am the grace he grows ;
    I startle his congregation.

He grows like a bull of Bashan,
    One day he'll be Bishop or Dean,
I startle his congregation :
    One day I shall preach to the Q—n.

One day he'll be Bishop or Dean,
    One of those science-haters ;
One day I shall preach to the Q—n.
    To think of my going in gaiters !

One of those science-haters,
    Blind as a mole or bat ;
To think of my going in gaiters,
    And wearing a shovel hat !

Blind as a mole or bat,
    No faintest glimmer of light,
And wearing a shovel hat,
    Morning and noon and night.
            "Love in Idleness."

PANTOUM.

(Song in the Malay manner.)

The wind brings up the hawthorn's breath.
    The sweet airs ripple up the lake :
My soul, my soul is sick to death,
    My heart, my heart is like to break.

The sweet airs ripple up the lake,
    I hear the thin woods' fluttering :
My heart, my heart is like to break ;
    What part have I, alas ! in spring?

I hear the thin woods' fluttering ;
    The brake is brimmed with linnet-song :
What part have I, alas ! in spring?
    For me, heart's winter is life-long.

The brake is brimmed with linnet song ;
    Clear carols flutter through the trees ;
For me heart's winter is life-long ;
    I cast my sighs on every breeze.

Clear carols flutter through the trees ;
    The new year hovers like a dove :
I cast my sighs on every breeze ;
    Spring is no spring, forlorn of love.

The new year hovers like a dove
    Above the breast of the green earth :
Spring is no spring, forlorn of love ;
    Alike to me are death and birth.

Above the breast of the green earth
    The soft sky flutters like a flower :
Alike to me are death and birth ;
    I dig Love's grave in every hour.

The soft sky flutters like a flower
    Along the glory of the hills :
I dig Love's grave in every hour,
    I hear Love's dirge in all the rills.

Along the glory of the hills
    Flowers slope into a rim of gold :
I hear Love's dirge in all the rills ;
    Sad singings haunt me as of old.

Flowers slope into a rim of gold
    Along the marges of the sky :
Sad singings haunt me as of old ;
    Shall Love come back to me to die ?

Along the marges of the sky
    The birds wing homeward from the East :
Shall Love come back to me to die ?
    Shall Hope relive, once having ceas'd ?

The birds wing homeward from the East ;
    I smell spice-breaths upon the air :
Shall Hope relive, once having ceas'd ?
    It would lie black on my despair.

I smell spice-breaths upon the air ;
    The golden Orient savours pass :
Hope would lie black on my despair.
    Like a moon-shadow on the grass.

The golden Orient savours pass :
    The full spring throbs in all the shade :
Like a moon-shadow on the grass,
    My hope into the dusk would fade.

The full spring throbs in all the shade ;
    We shall have roses soon, I trow ;
My hope into the dusk would fade ;
    Bring lilies on Love's grave to strow.

We shall have roses soon I trow ;
    Soon will the rich red poppies burn :
Bring lilies on Love's grave to strow :
    My hope is fled beyond return.

Soon will the rich red poppies burn ;
    Soon will blue iris star the stream :
My hope is fled beyond return ;
    Have my eyes tears for my waste dream ?

Soon will blue iris star the stream ;
    Summer will turn the air to wine :
Have my eyes tears for my waste dream ?
    Can songs come from these lips of mine ?

Summer will turn the air to wine,
    So full and sweet the mid-spring flowers :
Can songs come from those lips of mine ?
    My thoughts are grey as winter hours.

So full and sweet the mid-spring flowers.
    The wind brings up the hawthorn's breath ;
My thoughts are grey as winter hours ;
    My soul, my soul is sick to death.

JOHN PAYNE.

EN ROUTE.

(Pantoum.)

Here we are riding the rail,
    Gliding from out of the station ;
Man though I am, I am pale,
    Certain of heat and vexation.

Gliding from out of the station,
    Out from the city we thrust ;
Certain of heat and vexation,
    Sure to be covered with dust.

Out from the city we thrust :
    Rattling we run o'er the bridges :
Sure to be covered with dust,
    Stung by a thousand of midges.

Rattling we dash o'er the bridges,
    Rushing we dash o'er the plain ;
Stung by a thousand of midges,
    Certain precursors of rain.

Rushing we dash o'er the plain,
    Watching the clouds darkly lowering,
Certain precursors of rain :
    Fields about here need a showering.

Watching the clouds darkly lowering,—
    Track here is high on a bank—
Fields about here need a showering,
    Boy with the books needs a spank.

Track here is high on a bank,
    Just by a wretched old hovel :
Boy with the books needs a spank—
    "No ! I don't want a new novel !"

Just by a wretched old hovel,
    Small speck of dust in my eye.
" No ! I don't want a new novel !"
    —Babies beginning to cry.—

Small speck of dust in my eye,
    " I will not buy papers or candy ! "
—Babies beginning to cry—.
    Oh, for a tomahawk handy !

" I will not buy papers or candy ! "
    Train boys deserve to be slain ;
Oh, for a tomahawk handy !
    Oh, for the cool of the rain !

Train boys deserve to be slain,
    Heat and the dust—they are choking,
Oh, for the cool of the rain !
    —" Gent " just behind me is joking.

Heat and the dust, they are choking,
    Clogging and filling my pores ;
—" Gent " just behind me is joking,
    " Gent " just in front of me snores.

Clogging and filling my pores,
    Ears are on edge at the rattle ;
"Gent" just in front of me snores,
    Sounds like the noise of a battle.

Ears are on edge at the rattle,
    Man tho' I am, I am pale,
Sounds like the noise of a battle,
    Here we are riding the rail.

BRANDER MATTHEWS.

IN THE SULTAN'S GARDEN.

(Pantoum.)

She oped the portal of the palace,
    She stole into the garden's gloom ;
From every spotless snowy chalice
    The lilies breathed a sweet perfume.

She stole into the garden's gloom,
    She thought that no one would discover ;
The lilies breathed a sweet perfume,
    She swiftly ran to meet her lover.

She thought that no one would discover,
    But footsteps followed ever near ;
She swiftly ran to meet her lover
    Beside the fountain crystal clear.

But footsteps followed ever near ;
    Ah, who is that she sees before her
Beside the fountain crystal clear ?
    'Tis not her hazel-eyed adorer.

Ah, who is that she sees before her,
    His hand upon his scimitar ?
'Tis not her hazel-eyed adorer,
    It is her lord of Candahar !

His hand upon his scimitar—
    Alas, what brought such dread disaster !
It is her lord of Candahar,
    The fierce Sultan, her lord and master.

Alas, what brought such dread disaster !
    " Your pretty lover's dead ! " he cries—
The fierce Sultan, her lord and master—
    " 'Neath yonder tree his body lies."

" Your pretty lover's dead ! " he cries—
    (A sudden, ringing voice behind him) ;
" 'Neath yonder tree his body lies—"
    " Die, lying dog ! go thou and find him ! "

A sudden, ringing voice behind him,
    A deadly blow, a moan of hate,
" Die, lying dog ! go thou and find him !
    Come, love, our steeds are at the gate ! "

A deadly blow, a moan of hate,
    His blood ran red as wine in chalice ;
" Come, love, our steeds are at the gate ! "
    She oped the portal of the palace.

Clinton Scollard.

RONDEAU REDOUBLÉ.

My soul is sick of nightingale and rose,
The perfume and the darkness of the grove ;
I weary of the fevers and the throes,
And all the enervating dreams of love.

At morn I love to hear the lark, and rove
The meadows, where the simple daisy shows
Her guiltless bosom to the skies above—
My soul is sick of nightingale and rose.

The afternoon is sweet, and sweet repose,
But let me lie where breeze-blown branches move.
I hate the stillness where the sunbeams doze,
The perfume and the darkness of the grove.

I love to hear at eve the gentle dove
Contented coo the day's delightful close.
She sings of love and all the calm thereof,—
I weary of the fevers and the throes.

I love the night, who like a mother throws
Her arms round hearts that throbbed and limbs
   that strove,
As kind as Death, that puts an end to woes
And all the enervating dreams of love.

Because my soul is sick of fancies wove
Of fervid ecstasies and crimson glows ;
Because the taste of cinnamon and clove
Palls on my palate—let no man suppose
   My soul is sick.
COSMO MONKHOUSE.

RONDEAU REDOUBLÉ.

My day and night are in my lady's hand ;
I have no other sunrise than her sight ;
For me her favour glorifies the land ;
Her anger darkens all the cheerful light.

Her face is fairer than the hawthorn white,
When all a-flower in May the hedgerows stand ;
While she is kind, I know of no affright ;
My day and night are in my lady's hand.

All heaven in her glorious eyes is spanned ;
Her smile is softer than the summer's night,
Gladder than daybreak on the Faery strand ;
I have no other sunrise than her sight.

Her silver speech is like the singing flight
Of runnels rippling o'er the jewelled sand ;
Her kiss a dream of delicate delight ;
For me her favour glorifies the land.

What if the Winter chase the Summer bland !
The gold sun in her hair burns ever bright.
If she be sad, straightway all joy is banned ;
Her anger darkens all the cheerful light.

Come weal or woe, I am my lady's knight
And in her service every ill withstand ;
Love is my Lord in all the world's despite
And holdeth in the hollow of his hand
    My day and night.

JOHN PAYNE.

THE PRAYER OF DRYOPE.

(Rondeau Redoublé.)

O goddess sweet, give ear unto my prayer.
    Come with thy doves across the briny sea,
Leave thy tall fanes and thy rose gardens rare,
    From cruel bondage set thy vot'ress free !

Ah how my heart would joy again to be
    Like chirming bird that cleaves the sunny air,
Like wildwood roe that bounds in ecstasy ;
    O goddess sweet, give ear unto my prayer !

That I am innocent hast thou no care
    Of crime against celestial deity ?
Must I the fate of lovely Lotis share ?—
    Come with thy doves across the briny sea !

I hear no waters' silvern melody,
    And yet the rippling water once was there,
And on its bloomy banks I worshipped thee ;—
    Leave thy tall fanes and thy rose gardens rare !

Could I but feel my boy's hands on my hair,
    Could I but kiss my sister Iole,
Then bravely would I cast forth chill despair.
    From cruel bondage set thy vot'ress free !

I, who was once the blithesome Dryope,
    Am now a tree bole, cold and brown and bare ;
Pity, I pray, my ceaseless agony,
    Or grant forgetfulness of all things fair,
        O goddess sweet.

CLINTON SCOLLARD.

RONDEAU REDOUBLÉ.

I will go hence, and seek her, my old Love ;
    All bramble-laced, and moss-grown is the way,
There is no sun, nor broad, red moon above,
    The year is old, he said, and skies are grey.

The rose-wreaths fade, the viols are not gay,
    That which seemed sweet doth passing bitter prove ;
So sweet *she* was, she will not say me nay—
    I will go hence and seek her, my old Love.

Low, labouring sighs stirred coldly through the grove,
    Where buds unblossomed on the mosses lay ;
His upraised hands the dusky tangle clove,
    " All bramble-laced and moss-grown is the way ! "

With grievous eyes, and lips that smiled alway,
    Strange, flitting shapes, wreathed round him as he
        strove
Their spectral arms, and filmy green array ;
    There was no sun, nor broad red moon above.

Here lies her lute—and here her slender glove ;
    (Her bower well won, sweet joy shall crown the
        day) ;
But her he saw not, vanished was his Love,
    The year is old, he said, and skies are grey.

The wrong was mine ! he cried.   I left my dove
    (He flung him down upon the weeping clay),
And now I find her flown—ah wellaway !
    The house is desolate that held my Love,
                I will go hence.

GRAHAM R. TOMSON.

THE SICILIAN OCTAVE DESCRIBED AND EXEMPLIFIED.

To thee, fair Isle, Italia's satellite,
   Italian harps their native measures lend ;
Yet, wooing sweet diversity, not quite
   Thy octaves with Italia's octaves blend.
Six streaming lines amass the arrowy might
   In hers, one cataract couplet doth expend ;
Thine lake-wise widens, level in the light,
   And like to its beginning is its end.

To thee 'tis pleasure, haply to have brought
   Home precious ware from China or Japan ;
And thine, when keen and long pursuit hath caught
   Strange bird, or Psyche gay with veinèd fan—
And thine, to spell some sentence wisdom-fraught
   In palimpest or Arab alcoran ;
And mine, to seize some rare and coloured thought
   And cage it in my verse Sicilian.

RICHARD GARNETT, LL.D.

Although this shape is not actually akin to the group of forms in this book, yet for examples of another variety of strict verse, the author has kindly allowed two specimens to be quoted.

The
Rondel, Rondeau, and Roundel.

RONDEL.

Allez-vous en, allez, allez,
Soussy, soing et merencolie :
Me cuidez-vous toute ma vie
Gouverner, comme fait avez ?
Je vous promets que non ferez
Rayson aura sur vous maistrie
Allez-vous en, allez, allez,
Soussy, soing et merencolie.

Si jamais plus vous retournez
Avecques vostre compaignie
Je prye à Dieu qu' il vous mauldie
Et le jour que vous reviendrez :
Allez-vous en, allez, allez,
Soussy, soing et merencolie.

—CHARLES D'ORLÉANS.

RONDEAU.

Ma foi, c'est fait de moi, car Isabeau
M' a conjuré de lui faire un rondeau.
Cela me met en peine extrême
Quoi ! treize vers, huit en eau, cinq en ême !
Je lui ferais aussitôt un bateau.

En voilà cinq pourtant en un monceau.
Faisons-en huit en invoquant Brodeau,
Et puis mettons, par quelque stratagème :
Ma foi, c'est fait.

Si je pouvais encor de mon cerveau
Tirer cinq vers l'ouvrage serait beau ;
Mais cependant je suis dedans l'onzième :
Et si je crois que je fais le douzième ;
En voilà treize ajustés au niveau.
Ma foi, c'est fait.

—VOITURE.

O HONEY OF HYMETTUS HILL.

O honey of Hymettus Hill,
    Gold-brown, and cloying sweet to taste,
Wert here for the soft amorous bill
    Of Aphrodite's courser placed ?

    Thy musky scent what virginal chaste
Blossom was ravished to distil,
O honey of Hymettus Hill,
    Gold-brown, and cloying sweet to taste ?

What upturned calyx drank its fill
    When ran the draught divine to waste,
That her white hands were doomed to spill—
    Sweet Hebe, fallen and disgraced—
O honey of Hymettus Hill,
    Gold-brown, and cloying sweet to taste?
H. C. BUNNER.

READY FOR THE RIDE—1795.

Through the fresh fairness of the Spring to ride,
    As in the old days when he rode with her,
With joy of Love that had fond Hope to bride,
    One year ago had made her pulses stir.

    Now shall no wish with any day recur
(For Love and Death part year and year full wide),
Through the fresh fairness of the Spring to ride,
    As in the old days when he rode with her.

No ghost there lingers of the smile that died
    On the sweet pale lip where his kisses were—
. . . Yet still she turns her delicate head aside,
    If she may hear him come with jingling spur—
Through the fresh fairness of the Spring to ride,
    As in the old days when he rode with her.
H. C. BUNNER.

RONDEL.

This book of hours Love wrought
    With burnished letters gold ;
Each page with art and thought,
    And colours manifold.

His calendar he taught
    To youths and virgins cold :
This book of hours Love wrought
    With burnished letters gold.

This priceless book is bought
    With sighs and tears untold,
Of votaries who sought
    His countenance of old—
This book of hours Love wrought
    With burnished letters gold.
               WALTER CRANE.

RONDEL.

When time upon the wing
    A swallow heedless flies,
Love-birds forget to sing
    Beneath the lucent skies.

For now belated spring
    With her last blossom hies,
When time upon the wing
    A swallow heedless flies.

What summer hope shall bring
    To wistful dreaming eyes?
What fateful forecast fling
    Before life's last surprise?
When time upon the wing
    A swallow heedless flies.
               WALTER CRANE.

THE WANDERER.

(Rondel.)

Love comes back to his vacant dwelling,—
  The old, old Love that we knew of yore !
We see him stand by the open door,
With his great eyes sad, and his bosom swelling.

He makes as though in our arms repelling,
  He fain would lie as he lay before ;—
Love comes back to his vacant dwelling,—
  The old, old Love that we knew of yore !

Ah ! who shall help us from over-spelling,
  That sweet forgotten, forbidden lore !
  E'en as we doubt in our hearts once more,
With a rush of tears to our eyelids welling,
Love comes back to his vacant dwelling.

AUSTIN DOBSON.

RONDEL.

When love is in her eyes
    What need of Spring for me ?
A brighter emerald lies
    On hill and vale and lea.

The azure of the skies
    Holds nought so sweet to me ;
When love is in her eyes
    What need of spring for me ?

Her bloom the rose outvies,
    The lily dares no plea,
The violet's glory dies,
    No flower so sweet can be ;
When love is in her eyes
    What need of spring for me ?

ANNA MARIA FAY.

RONDEL.

[After Anyte of Tegea.]

Underneath this tablet rest,
  Grasshopper by autumn slain,
Since thine airy summer nest
  Shivers under storm and rain.

Freely let it be confessed
  Death and slumber bring thee gain
  Spared from winter's fret and pain,
Underneath this tablet rest.

  Myro found thee on the plain,
Bore thee in her lawny breast,
  Reared this marble tomb amain
To receive so small a guest !
Underneath this tablet rest,
  Grasshopper by autumn slain.

EDMUND GOSSE.

RONDEL.

How is it you and I
  Are always meeting so?
I see you passing by
  Whichever way I go.

  I cannot say I know
The spell that draws us nigh.
How is it you and I
  Are always meeting so?

Still thoughts to thoughts reply,
  And whispers ebb and flow ;
I say it with a sigh
  But half confessed and low,
How is it you and I
  Are always meeting so?

JOHN CAMERON GRANT.

VARIATIONS.

I.

" Alons au bois le may cueillir."—CHARLES D'ORLÉANS.

We'll to the woods and gather may
    Fresh from the footprints of the rain;
    We'll to the woods, at every vein
To drink the spirit of the day.

The winds of spring are out at play,
    The needs of spring in heart and brain.
We'll to the woods and gather may
    Fresh from the footprints of the rain.

The world's too near her end, you say ?—
    Hark to the blackbird's mad refrain !
    It waits for her, the vast Inane ?—
Then, girls, to help her on the way
We'll to the woods and gather may.

W. E. HENLEY.

II.

" Ainsi qu' aux fleurs la vieillesse,
    Fera ternir votre beauté."—RONSARD.

And lightly, like the flowers,
    Your beauties Age will dim,
    Who makes the song a hymn,
And turns the sweets to sours !

Alas ! the chubby Hours
    Grow lank and grey and grim,
And lightly, like the flowers,
    Your beauties Age will dim.

Still rosy are the bowers,
    The walks yet green and trim.
    Among them let your whim
Pass sweetly, like the showers,
And lightly, like the flowers.

W. E. HENLEY.

III.

"Hic habitat Felicitas."

"Felicity.   Enquire within.
    The genial goddess is at home!"
    So read and thought the rakes of Rome,
Some frail one's lintel fain to win.

And now it blares thro' bronze and tin,
    Thro' clarion, organ, catcall, comb:—
"Felicity.   Enquire within.
    The genial goddess is at home!"

For, tent or studio, bank or bin,
    Platonic porch, Petræan dome,
    Where'er our hobbies champ and foam,
Thero'er the brave old sign we pin—
"Felicity.   Enquire within."

W. E. HENLEY.

IV.

"And sweet girl graduates in their golden hair."—TENNYSON.

Sweet girl graduates, golden-haired,
You for whom has been prepared
        Love's fair university,
        Dons and double-firsts to be—
Why are you so quickly scared?

When the prudes their worst have glared,
        When the dowagers have stared,
        What has passed they might not see,
Sweet girl-graduates, golden-haired,
You for whom has been prepared
        Love's fair university?

Most is won when most is dared.
Let your dainty lore be aired.
        Love and thought and fun are free.
        All must flirt in their degree.
Books alone have never reared
Sweet girl-graduates, golden-haired.

W. E. HENLEY.

141

RONDEL.

The ways of Death are soothing and serene,
　　And all the words of Death are grave and sweet.
　　From camp and church, the fireside and the street,
She signs to come, and strife and song have been.

A summer night descending, cool and green
　　And dark, on daytime's dust and stress and heat,
The ways of Death are soothing and serene,
　　And all the words of Death are grave and sweet.

O glad and sorrowful, with triumphant mien
　　And hopeful faces look upon and greet
　　This last of all your lovers, and to meet
Her kiss, the Comforter's, your spirit lean. . . .
The ways of Death are soothing and serene.
W. E. HENLEY.

RONDEL.

I love you dearly, O my sweet !
　　Although you pass me lightly by,
　　Although you weave my life awry,
And tread my heart beneath your feet.

　　I tremble at your touch ; I sigh
To see you passing down the street ;
I love you dearly, O my sweet !
　　Although you pass me lightly by.

You say in scorn that love's a cheat,
　　Passion a blunder, youth a lie.
I know not.   Only when we meet
　　I long to kiss your hand and cry,
" I love you dearly, O my sweet,
　　Although you pass me lightly by."
JUSTIN HUNTLY McCARTHY.

TWO RONDELS.

I.

When on the mid sea of the night,
    I waken at thy call, O Lord.
    The first that troop my bark aboard
Are darksome imps that hate the light,
Whose tongues are arrows, eyes a blight—
    Of wraths and cares a pirate horde—
Though on the mid sea of the night
    It was thy call that waked me, Lord.

Then I must to my arms and fight—
    Catch up my shield and two-edged sword,
    The words of him who is thy word :
Nor cease till they are put to flight :—
Then in the mid sea of the night
    I turn and listen for thee, Lord.

II.

There comes no voice from thee, O Lord,
    Across the mid sea of the night !
    I lift my voice and cry with might :
If thou keep silent, soon a horde
Of imps again will swarm aboard,
    And I shall be in sorry plight
If no voice come from thee, O Lord,
    Across the mid sea of the night.

There comes no voice ; I hear no word !
    But in my soul dawns something bright :—
    There is no sea, no foe to fight !
Thy heart and mine beat one accord :
I need no voice from thee, O Lord,
    Across the mid sea of the night.

GEORGE MacDonald.

RONDELS.

I.

The lilacs are in bloom,
  All is that ever was,
  And Cupids peep and pass
Through the curtains of the room.

Season of light perfume,
  Hide all beneath thy grass.
The lilacs are in bloom,
  All is that ever was.

Dead hopes new shapes assume ;
  Town belle and country lass
  Forget the word " Alas,"
For over every tomb
The lilacs are in bloom.

II.

Summer has seen decay
  Of roses white and red,
  And Love with wings outspread
Speeds after yesterday.

Blue skies have changed to grey,
  And joy has sorrow wed :
Summer has seen decay
  Of roses white and red.

May's flowers outlast not May ;
  And when the hour has fled,
  Around the roses dead
The mournful echoes say---
Summer has seen decay.

GEORGE MOORE.

TO A BLANK SHEET OF PAPER.

Paper, inviolate, white,
    Shall it be joy or pain?
    Shall I of fate complain,
Or shall I laugh to-night?

Shall it be hopes that are bright?
    Shall it be hopes that are vain?
Paper, inviolate, white,
    Shall it be joy or pain?

A dear little hand so light,
    A moment in mine hath lain;
    Kind was its pressure again—
Ah, but it was so slight!

Paper, inviolate, white,
Shall it be joy or pain?
COSMO MONKHOUSE.

RONDEL.

Kiss me, sweetheart; the Spring is here
    And Love is Lord of you and me.
    The blue-bells beckon each passing bee;
The wild wood laughs to the flowered year:
There is no bird in brake or brere,
    But to his little mate sings he,
" Kiss me, sweetheart; the Spring is here,
    And Love is Lord of you and me!

The blue sky laughs out sweet and clear,
    The missel-thrush upon the tree
    Pipes for sheer gladness loud and free;
And I go singing to my dear,
    " Kiss me, sweetheart; the Spring is here,
And Love is Lord of you and me."
JOHN PAYNE.

"BEFORE THE DAWN."

Before the dawn begins to glow,
    A ghostly company I keep;
    Across the silent room they creep,
The buried forms of friend and foe.
Amid the throng that come and go,
    There are two eyes that make me weep;
Before the dawn begins to glow,
    A ghostly company I keep.

Two dear dead eyes.   I love them so!
    They shine like starlight on the deep;
    And often when I am asleep
They stoop and kiss me, bending low,
    Before the dawn begins to glow.

SAMUEL MINTURN PECK.

RONDEL.

Oh, say not ye that summer's over
    When birds within the wood stop singing!
    While hands still touch in desperate clinging,
Some ghost of hope in hearts must hover;
Though died the dream of loved and lover,
    While yet the marriage bells were ringing.
Oh, say not ye that summer's over
    When birds within the wood stop singing!

Their vanished hopes may none recover
    In some new day, new morrow bringing?
    And shall we see no buds fresh springing
Upon the stalks of last year's clover?
Oh, say not ye that summer's over
    When birds within the wood stop singing!

MAY PROBYN.

FROM THEODORE DE BANVILLE.

I.

NIGHT.

We bless the coming of the Night,
    Whose cool sweet kiss has set us free,
    Life's clamour and anxiety
Her mantle covers out of sight.
All eating cares have taken flight,
    The scented air is wine to me;
We bless the coming of the Night,
    Whose cool sweet kiss has set us free.
Rest now, O reader, worn and white,
    Driven by some divinity,
    Aloft, like sparkling hoar frost see,
A starry ocean throb in light,
We bless the coming of the Night.

II.

THE MOON.

The moon, with all her tricksy ways,
    Is like a careless young coquette,
    Who smiles, and then her eyes are wet,
And flies or follows or delays.
By night, along the sand-hills' maze,
    She leads and mocks you till you fret.
The moon with all her tricksy ways,
    Is like a careless young coquette.
As oft she veils herself in haze,
    A cloak before her splendour set;
    She is a silly charming pet,
We needs must give her love and praise,
The moon with all her tricksy ways.

ARTHUR REED ROPES.

RONDEL.

Oh, modern singers ! ye who vote
    Our times for song unfit,
Your Pegasus is smooth of coat,
    And patient of the bit ;

But lost the freedom of his throat,
    And dulled his prairie wit,
Oh, modern singers, ye who vote
    Our times for song unfit,

If kin, fame, critics, age, you quote
    As fain to thwart and twit,
Just try to feel your wings, and float
    Above the scornful kit :—
Oh, modern singers, ye who vote
    Our times for song unfit !

EMILY PFEIFFER.

COME, LOVE, ACROSS THE SUNLIT LAND.
(Rondel.)

Come, Love, across the sunlit land,
    As blithe as dryad dancing free,
While time slips by like silvery sand
    Within the glass of memory.

Ere Winter, in his reckless glee,
    Blights all the bloom with ruthless hand,
Come, Love, across the sunlit land,
    As blithe as dryad dancing free.

And all the years of life shall be
    Like peaceful vales that wide expand
To meet a bright, untroubled sea
    By radiant azure arches spanned ;
    Come, Love, across the sunlit land
As blithe as dryad dancing free.

CLINTON SCOLLARD.

UPON THE STAIR I SEE MY LADY STAND.
(Rondel.)

Upon the stair I see my lady stand,
　　Her hair is like the gleaming gold of dawn,
　　And, like the laughing sunbeam on the lawn,
The radiant smile by which her lips are spanned.

A chiselled marvel seems her slender hand
　　What time she waves it ere my steps are gone ;
Upon the stair I see my lady stand,
　　Her hair is like the gleaming gold of dawn.

Through the green covert that the breeze has fanned
　　She fleets as graceful as the flexile fawn ;
　　She is the star to which my soul is drawn
When shadows drive the daylight from the land.
Upon the stair I see my lady stand,
　　Her hair is like the gleaming gold of dawn.
CLINTON SCOLLARD.

I HEARD A MAID WITH HER GUITAR.
(Rondel.)

I heard a maid with her guitar
　　Who played, like Orpheus, to the wind,
And sent forth rhythmic notes afar
　　From out an arbor vine-entwined.

She knew the God of love was blind,
　　And left her white heart-gates ajar—
I heard a maid with her guitar
　　Who played, like Orpheus, to the wind.

But ah ! Love's ears are keen as are
　　The ears of shy, pool-haunting hind,
And when she closed her bosom's bar
　　She found the god was there enshrined ;
I heard a maid with her guitar
　　Who played, like Orpheus, to the wind.
CLINTON SCOLLARD.

VALENTINE.

Awake, awake, O gracious heart,
　　There's some one knocking at the door ;
The chilling breezes make him smart ;
　　His little feet are tired and sore.

Arise, and welcome him before
　　Adown his cheeks the big tears start :
　　Awake, awake, O gracious heart,
There's some one knocking at the door.

'Tis Cupid come with loving art
　　To honour, worship, and implore ;
And lest, unwelcomed, he depart
　　With all his wise mysterious lore,
Awake, awake, O gracious heart,
　　There's some one knocking at the door !
　　　　　　　　FRANK DEMPSTER SHERMAN.

LOVE'S CAPTIVE.

I hide her in my heart, my May,
　　And keep my darling captive there !
But not because she'd fly away
　　To seek for liberty elsewhere,
For love is ever free as air !
　　And as with me her love will stay,
I hide her in my heart, my May,
　　And keep my darling captive there.

Our love is love that lives for aye
　　Enchained in fetters strong and fair,
So evermore, by night and day,
　　That we our prisoned home may share,
I hide her in my heart, my May,
　　And keep my darling captive there.
　　　　　　　　C. H. WARING.

LOVE.

Looks that love not are silver-cold—
　　Gold the glory of love-sweet eyes !
　　Hearts are wide as the boundless skies
Full of loves—like the stars—untold !

Love by love should be bought and sold.
　　Other payments are shams and lies !
Looks that love not are silver-cold—
　　Gold the glory of love-sweet eyes !

Many loves will a great heart hold—
　　Foolish often, but often wise ;
Some of silver, but *one* of gold,—
　　Life's great treasure, and crowning prize.
Looks that love not are silver-cold—
　　Gold the glory of love-sweet eyes—
　　　　　　　　　　C. H. WARING.

RONDEL.

The larch has donned its rosy plumes,
　　And hastes its emerald beads to string :
　　The warblers now are on the wing.
Across the pathless ocean-glooms,
Through tender grass and violet blooms,
　　I move along and gaily sing.
The larch has donned its rosy plumes,
　　And hastes its emerald beads to string.

Nature with beauteous tints illumes
　　The fields and groves of budding Spring,
　　Loud voices from afar to bring ;
And my glad Muse its song resumes—
The larch has donned its rosy plumes,
　　And hastes its emerald beads to string.
　　　　　　　　　　RICHARD WILTON.

BENEDICITE.

O all ye Green Things on the Earth,
    Bless ye the Lord in sun and shade ;
    To whisper praises ye were made,
Or wave to Him in solemn mirth.
For this the towering pine had birth,
    For this sprang forth each grassy blade ;
O all ye Green Things on the Earth,
    Bless ye the Lord in sun and shade.

Ye wayside weeds of little worth,
    Ye ferns that fringe the woodland glade,
    Ye dainty flowers that quickly fade,
Ye steadfast yews of mighty girth :
O all ye Green Things on the Earth,
    Bless ye the Lord in sun and shade !

RICHARD WILTON.

RONDELETS.

    " Which way he went ? "
I know not—how should I go spy
    Which way he went ?
I only know him gone.   " Relent ? "
He never will—unless I die !
And then, what will it signify
    Which way he went ?

    Say what you please,
But know, I shall not change my mind !
    Say what you please,
Even, if you wish it, on your knees—
And, when you hear me next defined
As something lighter than the wind,
    Say what you please !

MAY PROBYN.

MIGHT LOVE BE BOUGHT.

Might Love be bought, I were full fain
My all to give thy love to gain.
    Yet would such getting profit naught;
    Possession with keen fears were fraught,
Would make even love's blisses vain.

For who could tell what god might deign
His golden treasures round thee rain,
    Till ruin on my hopes were brought,
        Might Love be bought.

Better a pensioner remain
On thy dear grace, since to attain
    To worthiness in vain I sought.
    Thy kindness hath assurance wrought
Could never be between us twain
        Might Love be bought.

ARLO BATES.

IN THY CLEAR EYES.

In thy clear eyes, fairest, I see
    Sometimes of love a transient glow;
But ere my heart assured may be,
With cold disdain thou mockest me :
    Hope fades as songs to silence flow.

Ah ! most bewitching, mocking she,
    Fairer than poet's dream may show,
The glance of scorn how can I dree
        In thy clear eyes?

    Life is so brief, and to and fro,
Like thistledown above the lea,
    Fly on poor days; why then so slow
    To bend from pride?   Let us bliss know
Ere age the light dims ruthlessly
        In thy clear eyes.

ARLO BATES.

THE SWEET, SAD YEARS.

The sweet sad years ; the sun, the rain,
Alas ! too quickly did they wane,
    For each some boon, some blessing bore ;
    Of smiles and tears each had its store,
Its chequered lot of bliss and pain.

Although it idle be and vain,
Yet cannot I the wish restrain
    That I had held them evermore,
        The sweet sad years !

Like echo of an old refrain
That long within the mind has lain,
    I keep repeating o'er and o'er,
    " Nothing can e'er the past restore,
Nothing bring back the years again,
        The sweet sad years ! "
        Rev. Charles D. Bell, D.D.

A WISH.

Fain would I pass from all the pain,
The aching heart and weary brain,
    From gnawing grief and withering care,
    And passion rising to despair,
From love dissatisfied and vain.

From tears that burn the cheeks they stain,
And hopes that droop like flowers in rain,
    From sorrows that turn grey the hair,
        Fain would I pass !

Beyond the silent, soundless main,
Where the long lost are found again,
    Where summer smiles for ever fair,
    Where skies are pure, divine the air,
Where love and joy eternal reign,
        Fain would I pass !
        Rev. Charles D. Bell, D.D.

TO A DOLEFUL POET.

Why are you sad when the sky is blue?
Why, when the sun shines bright for you,
    And the birds are singing, and all the air
    So sweet with the flowers everywhere?
If life hath thorns, it has roses too.

Be wise and be merry.   'Tis half untrue
Your doleful song.   You have work to do.
    If the work be good, and the world so fair,
                Why are you sad?

Life's sorrows are many, its joys so few!
Ah! sing of the joys!   Let the dismal crew
    Of black thoughts bide in their doleful lair,
    Give us glad songs ; sing us free from care.
Gladness maketh the world anew,
                Why are you sad?

An Answer.

Why am I sad when the sky is blue,
You ask, O friend, and I answer you—
    I love the sun and balmy air,
    The flowers and glad things everywhere.
But if life is merry, 'tis earnest too.

And the earnest hour, if hope be true,
Must be solemn or sad ; for the work we do
    Is little and weak.   Ask the world so fair
                Why I am sad.

For me glad hours are nowise few,
But life is so serious—ship and crew
    Bound such a voyage to death's dark lair.
    My work is my happy song : but care
Still steals on the quiet hour anew
                And makes it sad.
            H. Courthope Bowen.

"HIS POISONED SHAFTS."

His poisoned shafts, that fresh he dips
In juice of plants that no bee sips,
    He takes, and with his bow renown'd
    Goes out upon his hunting ground,
Hanging his quiver at his hips.

He draws them one by one, and clips
Their heads between his finger tips,
    And looses with a twanging sound
        His poisoned shafts.
But if a maiden with her lips
Suck from his wound the blood that drips,
    And drink the poison from the wound,
    The simple remedy is found
That of their deadly terror strips
        His poisoned shafts.
              ROBERT BRIDGES.

TO HOMER.

All down the years thy tale has rolled—
A brilliant streak of burnished gold
    Old Homer, near we seem to thee,
    As roving over vale and sea
Thou tellest of thy hero bold !

For we too wonder, as of old
Thy hero did.   The fates are doled
    To us the same, both serf and free,
        All down the years.

None other yet has ever told
So sweet a tale ; as we unfold
    Thy mystic page we find the key
    Of human sorrow, guilt and glee,
Which ever comes our souls to mould
        All down the years.
        JOHN MALCOLM BULLOCH.

SEPTEMBER.

The Summer's gone—how did it go?
And where has gone the dogwood's show?
   The air is sharp upon the hill,
   And with a tinkle sharp and chill
The icy little brooklets flow.

What is it in the season, though,
Brings back the days of old, and so
     Sets memory recalling still
          The Summer's gone?

Why are my days so dark? for lo!
The maples with fresh glory glow,
   Fair shimmering mists the valleys fill,
   The keen air sets the blood a-thrill—
Ah! now that *you* are gone, I know
         The Summer's gone.

H. C. BUNNER.

LES MORTS VONT VITE.

Les morts vont vite! Ay for a little space
We miss and mourn them, fallen from their place;
   To take our portion in their rest are fain;
   But by-and-by, having wept, press on again,
Perchance to win their laurels in the race.

What man would find the old in the new love's face?
Seek on the fresher lips the old kisses' trace,
   For withered roses newer blooms disdain?
         Les morts vont vite!

But when disease brings thee in piteous case,
Thou shalt thy dead recall, and thy ill grace
   To them for whom remembrance plead in vain.
   Then, shuddering, think, while thy bedfellow Pain
Clasp thee with arms that cling like Death's embrace:
         Les morts vont vite!

H. C. BUNNER.

"IN LOVE'S DISPORT."

In love's disport, gay bubbles blown
On summer winds light-freighted flown :
    A child intent upon delight
    The painted spheres would keep in sight,
Dissolved too soon in worlds unknown.

Lo ! from the furnace mouth hath grown
Fair shapes, as frail ; with jewelled zone,
    Clear globes where fate may read aright
        In love's disport.

O frail as fair ! though in the white
Of flameful heat with force to fight,
    Art thou by careless hands cast down
    Or killed, when frozen hearts disown
The children born of love and light
        In love's disport.
          WALTER CRANE.

"WHAT MAKES THE WORLD?"

What makes the world, Sweetheart, reply?
A space of lawn, a strip of sky,
    The bread and wine of fellowship,
    The cup of life for love to sip,
A glass of dreams in Hope's blue eye

So let the days and hours go by,
Let Fortune flout, and Fame deny,
    With feathered heel shall fancy trip—
        What makes the world ?

The wealth that never in the grip
Of blighting greed shall heedless slip,—
    When bought and sold is liberty,
    With worth of life and love gone by—
        What makes the world ?
          WALTER CRANE.

"O FONS BANDUSIÆ."

O babbling Spring, than glass more clear,
Worthy of wreath and cup sincere,
    To-morrow shall a kid be thine
    With swelled and sprouting brows for sign,—
Sure sign !—of loves and battles near.

Child of the race that butt and rear !
Not less, alas ! his life-blood dear
    Must tinge thy cold wave crystalline,
        O babbling Spring !

Thee Sirius knows not.   Thou dost cheer
With pleasant cool the plough-worn steer,—
    The wandering flock.   This verse of mine
    Will rank thee one with founts divine ;
Men shall thy rock and tree revere,
        O babbling Spring !
          AUSTIN DOBSON.

"ON LONDON STONES."

On London stones I sometimes sigh
For wider green and bluer sky ;—
    Too oft the trembling note is drowned
    In this huge city's varied sound ;—
" Pure song is country-born,"—I cry.

Then comes the spring,—the months go by,
The last stray swallows seaward fly ;
    And I—I too !—no more am found
        On London stones !

In vain ! the woods, the fields deny
That clearer strain I fain would try ;
    Mine is an urban Muse, and bound
    By some strange law to paven ground ;
Abroad she pouts ;—she is not shy
        On London stones !
          AUSTIN DOBSON.

A RONDEAU TO ETHEL.

"In teacup-times!"   The style of dress
Would suit your beauty, I confess;
    BELINDA-like, the patch you'd wear:
    I picture you with powdered hair,--
You'd make a charming Shepherdess!

And I—no doubt—could well express
SIR PLUME'S complete conceitedness,—
    Could poise a clouded cane with care
        "In teacup-times!"

The parts would fit precisely—yes:
We should achieve a huge success!
    You should disdain and I despair,
    With quite the true Augustan air;
But . . . . could I love you more, or less,—
        "In teacup-times?"

AUSTIN DOBSON.

TO A JUNE ROSE.

O royal Rose! the Roman dress'd
His feast with thee; thy petals press'd
    Augustan brows; thine odour fine,
    Mix'd with the three-times-mingled wine,
Lent the long Thracian draught its zest.

What marvel then, if host and guest
By Song, by Joy, by Thee caress'd,
    Half-trembled on the half-divine,
        O royal Rose!

And yet—and yet—I love thee best
In our old gardens of the West,
    Whether about my thatch thou twine,
    Or Her's, that brown-eyed maid of mine,
Who lulls thee on her lawny breast,
        O royal Rose!

AUSTIN DOBSON.

"WITH PIPE AND FLUTE."

With pipe and flute the rustic Pan
Of old made music sweet for man;
    And wonder hushed the warbling bird,
    And closer drew the calm-eyed herd,—
The rolling river slowlier ran.

Ah! would,—ah! would, a little span,
Some air of Arcady could fan
    This age of ours, too seldom stirred
        With pipe and flute!

But now for gold we plot and plan;
And from Beersheba unto Dan,
    Apollo's self might pass unheard,
    Or find the night-jar's note preferred . . .
Not so it fared, when time began
        With pipe and flute!

AUSTIN DOBSON.

"IN AFTER DAYS."

In after days, when grasses high
O'er-top the stone where I shall lie,
    Though ill or well the world adjust
    My slender claim to honoured dust,
I shall not question nor reply.

I shall not see the morning sky,
I shall not hear the night-wind sigh,
    I shall be mute, as all men must
        In after days!

But yet, now living, fain were I
That some one then should testify,
    Saying—*He held his pen in trust*
    To Art, not serving shame or lust.
Will none? . . Then let my memory die
        In after days!

AUSTIN DOBSON.

"IN VAIN TO-DAY."

In vain to-day I scrape and blot :
  The nimble words, the phrases neat,
  Decline to mingle and to meet ;
My skill is all forgone, forgot.

He will not canter, walk, or trot,
  My Pegasus ; I spur, I beat
      In vain to-day.

And yet 'twere sure the saddest lot
  That I should fail to leave complete
'One poor .. the rhyme suggests "conceit !"
Alas ! 'tis all too clear I'm not
      In vein to-day.

AUSTIN DOBSON.

"WHEN BURBADGE PLAYED."

When Burbadge played, the stage was bare
Of fount and temple, tower and stair ;
  Two backswords eked a battle out ;
  Two supers made a rabble rout ;
The Throne of Denmark was a chair !

And yet, no less, the audience there
Thrilled through all changes of Despair,
    Hope, Anger, Fear, Delight, and Doubt,
        When Burbadge played !

This is the Actor's gift ; to share
All moods, all passions, nor to care
    One whit for scene, so he without
    Can lead men's minds the roundabout,
Stirred as of old those hearers were,
        When Burbadge played !

AUSTIN DOBSON.

OLD BOOKS ARE BEST.

(To J. H. P.)

Old books are best !   With what delight
Does " Faithorne fecit " greet our sight ;
On frontispiece or title-page
Of that old time, when on the stage
" Sweet Nell " set " Rowley's " heart alight !
And you, O friend, to whom I write,
Must not deny, e'en though you might,
Through fear of modern pirates' rage,
Old books are best.
What though the print be not so bright,
The paper dark, the binding slight ?
Our author, be he dull or sage,
Returning from that distant age
So lives again, we say of right :
Old books are best.

BEVERLY CHEW.

A COWARD STILL.

A coward still : I've longed to fling
My arms about you, and to bring
My beating heart so near to thine,
That it might learn all thought of mine,
And closer to me cling.
But ere I dared do anything,
My trembling courage took to wing,
And left its bold design,
A coward still.
Poor heart : these words for ever ring,
Fair dame wins not the faint fearing ;
Tho' secretly it may repine
The loss that would make life divine,
Yet it must be content to sing,
A coward still.

JOHN CAMERON GRANT.

RONDEAUX OF CITIES.

I.

(Rondeau à la Boston.)

A cultured mind !   Before I speak
The words, sweet maid, to tinge thy cheek
    With blushes of the nodding rose
    That on thy breast in beauty blows,
I prithee satisfy my freak.

Canst thou read Latin and eke Greek?
Dost thou for knowledge pine and peak?
    Hast thou, in short, as I suppose,
        A cultured mind.

Some men require a maiden meek
Enough to eat at need the leek ;
    Some lovers crave a classic nose,
    A liquid eye, or faultless pose ;
I none of these, I only seek
        A cultured mind.

II.

(Rondeau à la New York.)

A pot of gold ! O mistress fair,
With eyes of brown that pass compare,
    Ere I on bended knee express
    The love which you already guess,
I fain would ask a small affair.

Hast thou, my dear, an ample share
Of this world's goods?   Wilt thy papa*
    Disgorge, to gild our blessedness,
        A pot of gold?

Some swains for mental graces care ;
Some fall a prey to golden hair ;
   I am not blind, I will confess,
   To intellect or comeliness ;
Still let these go beside, *ma chère,*
        A pot of gold.

    * Pronounced *papaire.*

III.

(Rondeau à la Philadelphia.)

A pedigree !   Ah, lovely jade !
Whose tresses mock the raven's shade,
       Before I free this aching breast,
       I want to set my mind at rest ;
'Tis best to call a spade a spade.

What was thy father ere he made
His fortune ? Was he smeared with trade,
          Or does he boast an ancient crest—
                    A pedigree ?

Brains and bright eyes are overweighed,
For wits grow dull and beauties fade ;
          And riches, though a welcome guest,
          Oft jar the matrimonial nest ;
I kiss her lips who holds displayed
                    A pedigree.

IV.

(Rondeau à la Baltimore.)

A pretty face !   O maid divine,
Whose vowels flow as soft as wine,
          Before I say upon the rack
          The words I never can take back,
A moment meet my glance with thine.

Say, art thou fair ?   Is the incline
Of that sweet nose an aquiline ?
          Hast thou, despite unkind attack,
                    A pretty face ?

Some sigh for wisdom ; Three, not nine,
The Graces were.   I won't repine
          For want of pedigree, or lack
          Of gold to banish Care the black,
If I can call forever mine
                    A pretty face.

ROBERT GRANT.

COULD SHE HAVE GUESSED.

Could she have guessed my coward care?
I knew her foot upon the stair,
    Her figure chained my inmost eye;
    I only looked a lover's lie,—
I feigned indifference, felt despair.

My very blood leaped up, aware
Of her free step and morning air;
She raised her head, she caught my eye—
              Could she have guessed?

I faced her with a chilly stare,
With words so common and so bare!
    Her whispering skirts, as she went by,
    Swept every sense—a thrilling sigh!
Ah, would her heart have heard my prayer
              Could she have guessed?
               ELAINE GOODALE.

FIRST SIGHT.

When first we met the nether world was white,
    And on the steel-blue ice before her bower
    I skated in the sunrise for an hour,
Till all the grey horizon, gulphed in light,
Was red against the bare boughs black as night;
    Then suddenly her sweet face, like a flower
    Enclosed in sables from the frost's dim power,
Shone at her casement, and flashed burning bright
             When first we met!

My skating being done, I loitered home,
    And sought that day to lose her face again;
But love was weaving in his golden loom
    My story up with hers, and all in vain
    I strove to loose the threads he spun amain
            When first we met!
              EDMUND GOSSE.

EXPECTATION.

When flower-time comes and all the woods are gay,
    When linnets chirrup and the soft winds blow,
    Adown the winding river I will row,
And watch the merry maidens tossing hay,
And troops of children shouting in their play,
    And with my thin oars flout the fallen snow
    Of heavy hawthorn blossom as I go:
And shall I see my love at fall of day
                When flower-time comes?

Ah, yes! for by the border of the stream
    She binds red roses to a trim alcove,
And I shall fade into her summer-dream
Of musing upon love,—nay, even seem
    To be myself the very god of love,
                When flower-time comes!

                        EDMUND GOSSE.

IN THE GRASS.

Oh! flame of grass, shot upward from the earth,
    Keen with a thousand quivering sunlit fires,
    Green with the sap of satisfied desires
And sweet fulfilment of your pale sad birth,
Behold! I clasp you as a lover might,
    Roll on you, bathing in the noonday sun,
    And, if it might be, I would fain be one
With all your odour, mystery, and light,
                Oh flame of grass!

For here, to chasten my untimely gloom,
    My lady took my hand and spoke my name;
    The sun was on her gold hair like a flame;
The bright wind smote her forehead like perfume;
    The daisies darkened at her feet; she came,
As spring comes, scattering incense on your bloom
              Oh flame of grass!
                        EDMUND GOSSE.

BY THE WELL.

Hot hands that yearn to touch her flower-like face,
    With fingers spread, I set you like a weir
    To stem this ice-cold stream in its career,—
And chill your pulses there a little space ;
Brown hands, what right have you to claim the grace
    To touch her head so infinitely dear ?
    Learn courteously to wait and to revere,
Lest haply ye be found in sorry case,
                Hot hands that yearn !

But if ye pluck her flowers at my behest,
    And bring her crystal water from the well,
And bend a bough for shade when she will rest,
    And if she find you fain and teachable,
    That flower-like face, perchance, ah ! who can tell?
In your embrace may some sweet day be found,
                Hot hands that yearn !
                      EDMUND GOSSE.

A GARDEN PIECE.

Among the flowers of summer-time she stood,
    And underneath the films and blossoms shone
    Her face, like some pomegranate strangely grown
To ripe magnificence in solitude ;
The wanton winds, deft whisperers, had strewed
    Her shoulders with her shining hair outblown,
    And dyed her robe with many a changing tone
Of silvery green, and all the hues that brood
                Among the flowers ;

She raised her arm up for her dove to know
    That he might perch him on her lovely head ;
Then I, unseen, and rising on tip-toe,
Bowed over the rose-barrier, and lo,
    Touched not her arm, but kissed her lips instead
                Among the flowers !
                      EDMUND GOSSE.

LOVERS' QUARREL.

Beside the stream and in the alder-shade,
    Love sat with us one dreamy afternoon,
    When nightingales and roses made up June,
And saw the red light and the amber fade
Under the canopy the willows made,
    And watched the rising of the hollow moon,
    And listened to the water's gentle tune,
And was as silent as she was, sweet maid,
                Beside the stream ;

Till with " Farewell ! " he vanished from our sight,
    And in the moonlight down the glade afar
    His light wings glimmered like a falling star ;
Then ah ! she took the left path, I the right,
And now no more we sit by noon or night
                Beside the stream !
                    EDMUND GOSSE.

IF LOVE SHOULD FAINT.

If Love should faint, and half decline
Below the fit meridian sign,
    And shorn of all his golden dress,
    His royal state and loveliness,
Be no more worth a heart like thine,
Let not thy nobler passion pine,
But with a charity divine,
    Let Memory ply her soft address
                If Love should faint ;

And oh ! this laggard heart of mine,
Like some halt pilgrim stirred with wine,
    Shall ache in pity's dear distress,
    Until the balm of thy caress
To work the finished cure combine,
              If Love should faint.
                  EDMUND GOSSE.

MY LOVE TO ME.

My love to me is always kind :
She neither storms, nor is she pined ;
    She does not plead with tears or sighs,
    But gentle words and soft replies—
Dear earnests of the thought behind.

They say the little god is blind,
    They do not count him quite too wise;
Yet he, somehow, could bring and bind
        My love to me.

And sweetest nut hath sourest rind ?
    It may be so ; but she I prize
    Is even lovelier in mine eyes
Than good and gracious to my mind.
I bless the fortune that consigned
        My love to me.
            W. E. HENLEY.

WITH STRAWBERRIES.

With strawberries we filled a tray,
And then we drove away, away
    Along the links beside the sea,
    Where wave and wind were light and free,
And August felt as fresh as May.

And where the springy turf was gay
With thyme and balm and many a spray
    Of wild roses, you tempted me
        With strawberries !

A shadowy sail, silent and grey,
Stole like a ghost across the bay ;
    But none could hear me ask my fee,
    And none could know what came to be.
Can sweethearts *all* their thirst allay
        With strawberries ?
            W. E. HENLEY.

A FLIRTED FAN.

A flirted fan of blade and gold
Is wondrous winsome to behold :
    It seems an armoured shard to bear
    The Emperor-Scarab—strange and rare,
Metallic, lustrous, jewel-cold.

Fawning and fluttering fold on fold
And scale on scale, its charm unrolled,
    Lures, dazzles, slays.   It thrills the air,
    A flirted fan !

Ah me, that night . . . . I cannot scold—
Ich grolle nicht ! My grief untold
    Shall still remain, but I will swear
    Some Spanish grace, dissembled there,
Stood by her stall, she so controlled
    A flirted fan.

W. E. HENLEY.

IN ROTTEN ROW.

In Rotten Row a cigarette
I sat and smoked, with no regret
    For all the tumult that had been.
    The distances were still and green,
And streaked with shadows cool and wet.

Two sweethearts on a bench were set,
Two birds among the boughs were met ;
    So love and song were heard and seen
    In Rotten Row.

A horse or two there was to fret
The soundless sand ; but work and debt,
    Fair flowers and falling leaves between,
    While clocks are chiming clear and keen,
A man may very well forget
    In Rotten Row.

W. E. HENLEY.

THE LEAVES ARE SERE.

The leaves are sere, and on the ground
They rustle with an eerie sound,
    A sound half-whisper and half-sigh—
    The plaint of sweet things fain to die,
Poor things for which no ruth is found.

With summer once the land was crowned ;
But now that autumn scatters round
    Decay, and summer fancies die,
        The leaves are sere.

Once, too, my thought within the bound
Of summer frolicked, like a hound
    In meadows jocund with July.
    And now I sit and wonder why,
With all my waste of plack and pound,
        The leaves are sere !
               W. E. HENLEY.

WITH A FAN FROM RIMMEL'S.

Go, happy Fan, in all the land
The happiest . . seek my lady's hand,
    And, swinging at her winsome waist,
    Forget for aye, so greatly graced,
The House of Odours in the Strand.

Ivory, with lilac silk outspanned,
With ruffling black sedately grand,
    With bloom of eglantine o'ertraced,
        Go, happy Fan.

Her kindly heart will understand,
Her gentle eyes will grow more bland
    At sight of you.   Away in haste,
    Dear New Year's gift !   Such perfect taste
As yours her praises *may* command. . .
        Go, happy Fan !
               W. E. HENLEY.

IF I WERE KING.

If I were king, my pipe should be premier.
The skies of time and chance are seldom clear,
    We would inform them all with bland blue weather.
Delight alone would need to shed a tear,
    For dream and deed should war no more together.

Art should aspire, yet ugliness be dear ;
    Beauty, the shaft, should speed with wit for feather ;
And love, sweet love, should never fall to sere,
        If I were king.
But politics should find no harbour near ;
    The Philistine should fear to slip his tether ;
Tobacco should be duty free, and beer ;
    In fact, in room of this, the age of leather,
An age of gold all radiant should appear,
        If I were king.

                W. E. HENLEY.

THE GODS ARE DEAD.

The gods are dead?   Perhaps they are !   Who knows ?
    Living at least in Lempriere undeleted,
The wise, the fair, the awful, the jocose,
    Are one and all, I like to think, retreated
In some still land of lilacs and the rose.

Once high they sat, and high o'er earthly shows
    With sacrificial dance and song were greeted.
Once . . . long ago : but now the story goes,
        The gods are dead.

It must be true. The world a world of prose, [sheeted,
    Full-crammed with facts, in science swathed and
Nods in a stertorous after-dinner doze.
Plangent and sad, in every wind that blows
    Who will may hear the sorry words repeated—
        The gods are dead.

                W. E. HENLEY.

HER LITTLE FEET.

Her little feet ! . . . Beneath us ranged the sea,
   She sat, from sun and wind umbrella-shaded,
One shoe above the other danglingly,
   And lo ! a Something exquisitely graded,
Brown rings and white, distracting—to the knee !

The band was loud. A wild waltz melody
   Flowed rhythmic forth. The nobodies paraded.
And thro' my dream went pulsing fast and free :
         Her little feet.

Till she made room for some one. It was He !
   A port-wine-flavoured He, a He who traded,
Rich, rosy, round, obese to a degree !
A sense of injury overmastered me.
   Quite bulbously his ample boots upbraided
         Her little feet.
                  W. E. HENLEY.

WHEN YOU ARE OLD.

When you are old, and I am passed away—
Passed, and your face, your golden face, is grey—
   I think, whate'er the end, this dream of mine,
   Comforting you, a friendly star will shine
Down the dim slope where still you stumble and stray.

So may it be ; that so dead Yesterday,
   No sad-eyed ghost, but generous and gay,
May serve your memories like almighty wine,
       When you are old.

Dear Heart, it shall be so. Under the sway
Of death the past's enormous disarray   [sign,
   Lies hushed and dark. Yet though there come no
   Live on well pleased ! Immortal and divine,
Love shall still tend you, as God's angels may,
       When you are old.
                  W. E. HENLEY.

MY BOOKS.

These are my books—a Burton old,
A Lamb arrayed against the cold
    In polished dress of red and blue,
    A rare old Elzevir or two,
And Johnson clothed in green and gold.

A Pope in gilded calf I sold,
To buy a Sterne of worth untold,
    To cry, as bibliomaniacs do,
    " These are my books ! "

What though a Fate unkind hath doled
But favours few to me, yet bold
    My little wealth abroad I strew,
    To purchase acquisitions new,
And say by love of them controlled,
    These are my books.

Nathan M. Levy.

MOST SWEET OF ALL.

Most sweet of all the flowers memorial
    That autumn tends beneath his wasted trees,
    Where wearily the unremembering breeze
Whirls the brown leaves against the blackening wall
More sweet than those that summer fed so tall
    And glad with soft wind blowing overseas ;
    Through all incalculable distances
Of many shades that swerve and sands that crawl,
            Most sweet of all !

When comes the fulness of the time to me
    As yours is full to-day, O flower of mine ?
Touched by her hand who evermore shall be,
    While the slow planets circle for a sign,
Till periods flag and constellations fall,
            Most sweet of all !

" *Love in Idleness.*"

THE REDBREAST.

In country lanes the robins sing,
Clear-throated, joyous, swift of wing,
From misty dawn to dewy eve
(Though cares of nesting vex and grieve)
Their little heart-bells ring and ring.

And when the roses say to Spring:
" Your reign is o'er " when breezes bring
The scent of spray that lovers weave
In country lanes,

The redbreast still is heard to fling
His music forth ; and he will cling
To Autumn till the winds bereave
Her yellowing trees, nor will he leave
Till Winter finds him shivering
In country lanes.

C. H. LÜDERS.

TO Q(UINTUS) H(ORATIUS) F(LACCUS).

To Q. H. F. the idle band
Of poetasters oft has planned
Tributes of praise—and penned them, too—
For love of verse that keeps its hue
Though dead its language and its land.

True, Pegasus has ever fanned
The ether at a bard's command,
But ah ! how eagerly he flew
To Q. H. F.

Not oversweet or overgrand
Your poems, Horace, hence your stand
Firm in the hearts of men : and few
Have gained a place so clearly due,
Since Death with unrelenting hand.
Took you, H. F.

C. H. LÜDERS.

LOVE IN LONDON.

In London town men love and hate,
And find Death tragic soon or late,
  Just in the old unreasoning way,
  As if they breathed the warmer day
In Athens when the gods were great.

Mine is the town by Thames's spate,
And so it chanced I found my fate,
  One of my fates, that is to say—
      In London town.

The whole world comes to those who wait ;
Mine came and went with one year's date.
  Pity it made so short a stay !
  The sweetest face, the sweetest sway
That ever Love did consecrate
      In London town.
          JUSTIN HUNTLY McCARTHY.

SLEEP.

O happy sleep ! that bear'st upon thy breast
The blood-red poppy of enchanting rest,
  Draw near me through the stillness of this place
  And let thy low breath move across my face,
As faint winds move above a poplar's crest.

The broad seas darken slowly in the west ;
The wheeling sea-birds call from nest to nest ;
  Draw near and touch me, leaning out of space,
      O happy Sleep !

There is no sorrow hidden or confess'd,
There is no passion uttered or suppress'd,
  Thou can'st not for a little while efface ;
  Enfold me in thy mystical embrace,
Thou sovereign gift of God, most sweet, most blest,
      O happy Sleep !
          ADA LOUISE MARTIN.

TO TAMARIS.

It is enough to love you.   Let me be
Only an influence, as the wandering sea
     Answers the moon that yet foregoes to shine ;
     Only a sacrifice, as in a shrine
The lamp burns on where dead eyes cannot see ;
Only a hope unknown, withheld from thee,
Yet ever like a petrel plaintively,
     Just following on to life's far twilight line,
                         It is enough.

Go where you will, I follow.   *You* are free.
Alone, unloved, to all eternity
     I track that chance no virtue can divine,
     When pitiful, loving, with fond hands in mine,
You say : " True heart, here take your will of me,
                         It is enough."
                                   THEO. MARZIALS.

WHEN I SEE YOU.

When I see you my heart sings
     Deep within me for deep love ;
     In my deep heart's dreamiest grove,
Your bright image comes like Spring's,
     Bringing back the murmured dove
To the wan dim watersprings.
Would my tongue could tell the things
     Love seems but one echo of
                 When I see you !

     Hope lies dying, Time's disproof
Strips love's roses to the stings ;
But the bird that knows its wings
     Bear it where it will aloof,
Sings not, Love, as my heart sings
                 When I see you.
                         THEO. MARZIALS.

CARPE DIEM.

To-day, what is there in the air
That makes December seem sweet May?
    There are no swallows anywhere,
    Nor crocuses to crown your hair,
And hail you down my garden way.

Last night the full moon's frozen stare
    Struck me, perhaps ; or did you say
Really,—you'd come, sweet friend and fair !
               To-day ?

To-day is here :—come ! crown to-day
    With Spring's delight or Spring's despair,
Love cannot bide old Time's delay :—
Down my glad gardens light winds play,
    And my whole life shall bloom and bear
            To-day.
            THEO. MARZIALS.

THE OLD AND THE NEW.

The Old Year goes down-hill so slow
And silent that he seems to know
    The mighty march of time, foretelling
    His passing : into his eyelids welling
Come tears of bitter pain and woe.

The lusty blast can scarce forego
His cape about his ears to blow,
    As feebly to his final dwelling
        The Old Year goes.

Within the belfry, row on row,
The bells are swinging to and fro ;
    Now joyfully the chimes are swelling—
    Now solemn and few the notes are knelling—
For here the New Year comes :—and lo !
        The Old Year goes !
          BRANDER MATTHEWS.

SUB ROSA.

Under the rows of gas-jets bright,
Bathed in a blazing river of light,
    A regal beauty sits ; above her
    The butterflies of fashion hover,
And burn their wings, and take to flight.

Mark you her pure complexion,—white
Though flush may follow flush ? Despite
    Her blush, the lily I discover
        Under the rose.

All compliments to her are trite ;
She has adorers left and right ;
    And I confess, here, under cover
    Of secrecy, I too—I love her !
Say naught ; she knows it not.   'Tis quite
        Under the rose.
               BRANDER MATTHEWS.

"VIOLET."

Violet, delicate, sweet,
    Down in the deep of the wood,
Hid in thy still retreat,
Far from the sound of the street,
    Man and his merciless mood :—

Safe from the storm and the heat,
    Breathing of beauty and good
    Fragrantly, under thy hood
        Violet.

Beautiful maid, discreet,
Where is the mate that is meet,
    Meet for thee—strive as he could—
Yet will I kneel at thy feet,
    Fearing another one should,
        Violet !
               COSMO MONKHOUSE.

O SCORN ME NOT.

O scorn me not, although my worth be slight,
Although the stars alone can match thy light,
    Although the wind alone can mock thy grace,
    And thy glass only show so fair a face—
Yet—let me find some favour in thy sight.

The proud stars will not bend from their chill height,
Nor will the wind thy faithfulness requite.
    Thy mirror gives thee but a cold embrace.
        O scorn me not.

My lamp is feeble, but by day or night
It shall not wane, and, but for thy delight,
    My footsteps shall not for a little space
    Forego the echo of thy tender pace,—
I would so serve and guard thee if I might.
        O scorn me not.
            Cosmo Monkhouse.

TEN THOUSAND POUNDS.

Ten thousand Pounds (a-year), no more
Nor less will suit.   A man is poor
    Without his horses and his cows,
    His city and his country house,
His salmon river and his moor ;

And many things unmissed before
Would be desired and swell the score ;
    But 'tis enough when fate allows
        Ten thousand Pounds.

But O, my babies on the floor ;
My wife's blithe welcome at the door ;
    My bread well-earned with sweat of brows ;
    My garden flowerful, green of boughs ;
Friends, books ;—I would not change ye for
        Ten thousand Pounds.
            Cosmo Monkhouse.

ONE OF THESE DAYS.

One of these days, my lady whispereth,
    A day made beautiful with summer's breath,
    Our feet shall cease from these divided ways,
    Our lives shall leave the distance and the haze
And flower together in a mingling wreath.

    No pain shall part us then, no grief amaze,
    No doubt dissolve the glory of our gaze ;
Earth shall be heaven for us twain, she saith,
            One of these days.

    Ah love, my love !   Athwart how many Mays
    The old hope lures us with its long delays !
How many winters waste our fainting faith !
I wonder, will it come this side of death,
    With any of the old sun in its rays,
            One of these days ?

JOHN PAYNE.

LIFE LAPSES BY.

Life lapses by for you and me ;
    Our sweet days pass us by and flee
And evermore death draws us nigh ;
The blue fades fast out of our sky,
    The ripple ceases from our sea.
What would we not give, you and I,
The early sweet of life to buy ?
    Alas ! sweetheart, that cannot we ;
    Life lapses by.

But though our young days buried lie,
Shall love with Spring and Summer die ?
    What if the roses faded be ?
    We in each other's eyes will see
New Springs, nor question how or why
    Life lapses by.

JOHN PAYNE.

BEYOND THE NIGHT.

Beyond the night no withered rose
Shall mock the later bud that blows,
 Nor lily blossom e'er shall blight,
 But all shall gleam more pure and white
Than starlight on the Arctic snows.

Sigh not when daylight dimmer grows,
And life a turbid river flows,
 For all is sweetness—all is light
    Beyond the night.

Oh, haste, sweet hour that no man knows ;
Uplift us from our cumbering woes
 Where joy and peace shall crown the right,
 And perished hopes shall blossom bright—
To aching hearts bring sweet repose
    Beyond the night.
      Samuel Minturn Peck.

AMONG MY BOOKS.

Among my books—what rest is there
From wasting woes ! what balm for care !
 If ills appal or clouds hang low,
 And drooping dim the fleeting show,
I revel still in visions rare.

At will I breathe the classic air,
The wanderings of Ulysses share ;
 Or see the plume of Bayard flow
    Among my books.

Whatever face the world may wear—
If Lilian has no smile to spare,
 For others let her beauty blow,
 Such favours I can well forgo ;
Perchance forget the frowning fair
    Among my books.
      Samuel Minturn Peck.

I GO MY GAIT.

I go my gait, and if my way
Is cheered by song and roundelay,
    Or if I bear upon my road,
    Like Issachar, a double load,
I sing and bear as best I may.

But lo a rondeau ! Can I say,
While halting thus my toll to pay
Before a stile now *a la mode*,
        I go my gate ?

Ah truly ; if for once I stray
Into the treadmill,—'tis in play.
    I will not own its narrow code,
    It shall not be my cramped abode.
Free of the fields, in open day
        I go my gait !
            EMILY PFEIFFER.

(TO LOUIS HONORE FRÉCHETTE.)

Laurels for song !   And nobler bays,
In old Olympian golden days
    Of clamour thro' the clear-eyed morn,
    No bowed triumphant head hath borne
Victorious in all Hellas' gaze !

They watched his glowing axles graze
The goal, and rent the heavens with praise ;—
    Yet the supremer heads have worn
        Laurels for song.

So thee, from no palaestra-plays
A conqueror, to the gods we raise,
    Whose brows of all our singers born
    The sacred fillets chief adorn,—
Who first of all our choice displays
        Laurels for song.
        CHARLES G. D. ROBERTS.

"WITHOUT ONE KISS."

Without one kiss she's gone away,
And stol'n the brightness out of day ;
  With scornful lips and haughty brow
  She's left me melancholy now,
In spite of all that I could say.

And so, to guess as best I may
What angered her, awhile I stay
  Beneath this blown acacia bough,
    Without one kiss;

Yet all my wildered brain can pay
My questioning, is but to pray
  Persuasion may my speech endow,
  And Love may never more allow
My injured sweet to sail away
    Without one kiss.

CHARLES G. D. ROBERTS.

VIS EROTIS.

Love that holdeth firm in fee
    Many a lord of many a land,
From thy thraldom few would flee ;
Wide the wondrous potency
    Of thy heart-enchanting hand.

Since on shining Cyprian sand
Did thy mother, Venus, stand,
    Man and maid have worshipped thee,
        Love.

They that scorn thy slaves to be,
    Oft before thy throne, unmanned,
Grant thy great supremacy ;
    Hear my prayer, O Monarch, and
Let my lady smile on me,
        Love.

CLINTON SCOLLARD.

WHEN SIRIUS SHINES.

When Sirius shines, a fulgent fire,
And locusts in a drowsy choir
    At noon within the maples drone,
    And pines at nightfall make sad moan
Like waves upon the rocks of Tyre,

Then strike the softly sounding lyre,
And let the soaring song rise higher,
    Or fall to minor monotone,
        When Sirius shines.

But should the chiming voices tire,
And thoughts of past and vain desire
    Refill the mind, as doves once flown
    Return to cotes aforetime known,
Then let the soul to heaven aspire,
        When Sirius shines.
            CLINTON SCOLLARD.

AT PEEP OF DAWN.

At peep of dawn the daffodil
That slumbers 'neath the grassy hill
    Greets smilingly, with lifted head,
    The rosy morn's oncoming tread,
The thrush sings matins by the rill.

The swallows from the ruined mill
Go coursing through the air, and fill
    The sky with songs till then unsaid
        At peep of dawn.

No harbinger of day is still.
With pipe new tuned and merry trill,
    The lark uprises from her bed
    'Mong grasses wet with dews unshed,
And puts to shame the whip-poor-will
        At peep of dawn.
            CLINTON SCOLLARD.

IN GREENWOOD GLEN.

In greenwood glen, where greedy bees
Drain fragrant flower-cups to the lees,
    When summer's shining lances smite
    The grain-fields gleaming golden bright,
I hear Æolian melodies.

The music bounds along the breeze
In ever-changing symphonies,
    And lulls my soul with calm delight
        In Greenwood glen.

Elusively it faints and flees,
Retreats, returns,—but no one sees
    The piper; for, as in affright,
    He skilfully eludes the sight;
'Tis Pan who hides amid the trees,
        In Greenwood glen.
            CLINTON SCOLLARD,

HER CHINA CUP.

Her china cup is white and thin;
A thousand times her heart has been
    Made merry at its scalloped brink;
    And in the bottom, painted pink,
A dragon greets her with a grin.

The brim her kisses loves to win;
The handle is a manikin,
    Who spies the foes that chip or chink
        Her china cup.

Muse, tell me if it be a sin:
I watch her lift it past her chin
    Up to the scarlet lips and drink
    The Oolong draught, somehow I think
I'd like to be the dragon in
        Her china cup.
            FRANK DEMPSTER SHERMAN.

BEHIND HER FAN.

Behind her fan of downy fluff,
Sewed on soft saffron satin stuff,
    With peacock feathers, purple-eyed,
    Caught daintily on either side,
The gay coquette displays a puff :
Two blue eyes peep above the buff :
Two pinky pouting lips . . enough !
      That cough means surely come and hide
          Behind her fan.

The barque of Hope is trim and tough,
So out I venture on the rough,
    Uncertain sea of girlish pride.
    A breeze ! I tack against the tide,—
Capture a kiss and catch a cuff,—
          Behind her fan.
        Frank Dempster Sherman.

AN ACROSTICAL VALENTINE.
(A. S. R.)

Fast in your heart, O rondeau rare,
    Rich with the wealth of love, I dare,
Alas ! to send, but not to sign,
Nestles my name.   The fetters fine
    Kissed by her lips may break,—beware
Delight is dizzy with despair.
Suppose she fain would answer,—there !
    How shall she find this name of mine
      Fast in your heart ?

Enough if secrecy you swear :
Red lips can't solve the subtile snare
My tricksy muse weaves with her line :
And I am caught, vain Valentine !
    N.B.—Say,—should she ask you where ?
      " Fast in your heart."
      Frank Dempster Sherman.

WHEN TWILIGHT COMES.

When twilight comes and nature stills
The hum that haunts the dales and hills,
   Dim shadows deepen and combine,
   And Heaven with its crystal wine
The cups of thirsty roses fills.
Blithe birds with music-burdened bills
Hush for a space their tender trills,
   And seek their homes in tree or vine
         When twilight comes.
Soft melody the silence thrills,
Played by the nymphs along the rills ;
   And where the dew-kist grasses twine,
   The toads and crickets tatoo fine
Drums to the fife of whip-poor-wills,
         When twilight comes.
        FRANK DEMPSTER SHERMAN.

COME, PAN, AND PIPE.

Come, Pan, and pipe upon the reed,
And make the mellow music bleed,
   As once it did in days of yore,
   Along the brook's leaf-tangled shore,
Through sylvan shade and fragrant mead.

On Hybla honey come and feed,—
To tempt the Fauns in dance to lead
   The Dryads on the mossy floor,—
        Come, Pan, and pipe !

To-day the ghosts,—Gold, Gain, and Greed,
The world pursues with savage speed :
   Forgotten is your magic lore.
   Oh, bring it back to us once more !
For simple, rustic song we plead :
   Come, Pan, and pipe !
        FRANK DEMPSTER SHERMAN.

AN OLD RONDO.

Her scuttle Hatt is wondrous wide,
All furrie, too, on every side,
    Soe out she trippeth daintylie,
    To let ye Youth full well to see
How fayre ye mayde is for ye Bryde.

A lyttle puffed, may be, bye Pryde,
She yett soe lovelye ys thatt I'd
    A Shyllynge gyve to tye, perdie,
        Her scuttle Hatt.

Ye Coales unto ye Scuttle slide,
Soe yn her Hatt wolde I, and hide
    To steale some Kisses—two or three :
    But synce She never asketh me,
Ye scornful Cynick doth deride
        Her scuttle Hatt !
           FRANK DEMPSTER SHERMAN.

A STREET SKETCH.

Upon the Kerb, a maiden neat—
Her hazel eyes are passing sweet—
    There stands and waits in dire distress :
    The muddy road is pitiless,
And 'busses thunder down the street !

A snowy skirt, all frills and pleat ;
Two tiny, well-shod, dainty feet
    Peep out, beneath her kilted dress,
        Upon the Kerb.

She'll first advance and then retreat,
Half-frightened by a hansom fleet.
    She looks around, I must confess,
    With marvellous coquettishness !—
Then droops her eyes and looks discreet,
        Upon the Kerb !
           J. ASHBY STERRY.

DOVER.

On Dover Pier, brisk blew the wind,
The Fates against me were combined
    For when I noticed standing there,
    Sweet Some-one with the sunny hair—
To start I felt not much inclined.

Too late ! I cannot change my mind,
The paddles move ! I am resigned—
    I only know I would I were
              On Dover Pier.

I wonder—will the Fates be kind?
On my return, and shall I find
    That grey-eyed damsel passing fair,
    So bonny, blithe, and debonair,
The pretty girl I left behind?
              On Dover Pier?
                J. ASHBY STERRY.

HOMESICK.

'Mid Autumn Leaves, now thickly shed,
We wander where our paths o'erspread,
    With yellow russet, red and sere :
    The country's looking dull and drear,
The sky is gloomy overhead.

The equinoctial gales we dread,
The summer's gone, the sunshine's fled ;
    We've rambled far enough this year—
           'Mid Autumn Leaves.

Though fast our travel-time has sped,
On London's flags we long to tread ;
    The latest laugh and chaff to hear,
    To find the Club grown doubly dear ;
Its gas burns bright, its fire glows red—
           'Mid Autumn Leaves.
                J. ASHBY STERRY.

IN BEECHEN SHADE.

In beechen shade the hours are sweet,
By mist-veiled morn or noonday heat
    (And sweeter still when daylight dies)
    So soft the wandering streamlet sighs
In passage musical and fleet.

Full drowsily the white lambs bleat,
And tinkling bell-notes faintly beat
    The languid air where Lacon lies
        In beechen shade.

And still, when day and even meet ;
Selene strays with golden feet,
    That gleam along the low blue skies
    And paceth slow, with dreaming eyes
That seek the shepherds' dim retreat
        'Mid beechen shade.
GRAHAM R. TOMSON.

THE GATES OF HORN.

The Gates of Horn are dull of hue
(If all our wise men tell us true).
    No songs, they say, nor perfumed air
    Shall greet the wistful pilgrim there,
No leaves are green, no skies are blue.

Yet he who will may find a clue
(Mid shadows steeped in opal dew)
    To seek, and see them passing fair,
        The Gates of Horn.

The man that goes not wreathed with rue,
Right lovely shapes his smile shall sue,
    With red rose-garlands in their hair
    And garments gay with gold and vair,
Full fain to meet him trooping through
        The Gates of Horn.
GRAHAM R. TOMSON.

IF LOVE BE TRUE.

If love be true—not bought at mart—
  Though night and darkness hide from view,
What harshest of harsh things can part
The loved-one from the lover's heart,
  Or stay the dreams that flit thereto?
If love be true dreams need no chart
  To gain the goal to which they're due ;
For love will guide them with love's dart,
      If love be true.

If love be true, if thou be true,
  Sweet love, as fair thou surely art,
Night shall not hide your eyes of blue
From my heart's eyes the long night through ;
  Though in sweet sadness tears may start,
      If love be true.
          SAMUEL WADDINGTON.

THE COQUETTE.

This pirate bold upon love's sea
Will let no passing heart go free ;
  No barque by those bright eyes espied
  May sail away o'er life's blue tide
Till all its treasure yielded be.

Her craft, the *Conquest*, waits for thee,
Where her swift rapine none may see ;
  From shadowing coves on thee will glide
    This pirate bold.

Yet thou, if thou her power wouldst flee,
Go, feign thyself love's refugee,
  And crave sweet shelter ;—she'll deride
  Thy piteous suit with scornful pride ;
And thou, thou shalt escape in glee
    This pirate bold.
          SAMUEL WADDINGTON.

YES OR NO?

A Good man's love ! Oh, prithee, stay,
Before you turn such gift away,
    And write no unconsidered " No "
    To him who proves he loves you so,
And humbly owns your regal sway.

For hearts may change, the wise folk say,
And as full oft the brightest ray
    Fades in an hour, so too may go
        A Good man's love.

Then pause awhile.   This short delay
May gladden many an after-day.
    Search well your heart, and if it show
    True signs of love, bid pride bend low,
And take this great gift while you may—
        A Good man's love !

G. WEATHERLY.

MY WINDOW BIRDS.

My window birds, I love to strew
With punctual hands the crumb for you,
    Flying for comfort day by day
    From frozen woodland and highway,
And bringing Christmas bills now due !

Fair creditors of every hue
Crimson and yellow, brown and blue,
    Whate'er your thoughts, your coats are gay,
        My window birds.

Your claims are neither small nor few,
Dated, when May-flowers drank the dew,
    And on sweet pipes ye used to play,
    Scattering full many a golden lay ;
Now ye for wages mutely sue,
        My window birds.

REV. RICHARD WILTON, M.A.

SNOWDROPS AND ACONITES.

Silver and gold ! The snowdrop white
And yellow blossomed aconite,
    Waking from Winter's slumber cold,
    Their hoarded treasures now unfold,
And scatter them to left and right.

Ah, with how much more rare delight
Upon my sense their colours smite
    Than if my fingers were to hold
        Silver and gold.

They bear the superscription bright
Of the great King of love and might,
    Who stamped such beauty there of old
    That men might learn, as ages rolled,
To trust in God, nor worship quite
        Silver and gold.
        REV. RICHARD WILTON, M.A.

THE CHIFF-CHAFF'S MESSAGE, HEARD IN MARCH.

" Cheer up, cheer up ! " it seems to say,
As lighting on some leafless spray,
    It shakes its dissyllabic song,
    And with small beak, but courage strong,
Charges the East-wind all the day.

" Soon will the Swallow round you play,
The Nightingale be on its way,
    Blue skies and gladness come ere long,
        Cheer up, cheer up ! "

Such happy voice be mine, I pray,
Bleak hours to bless with sunny ray,
    A comfort life's rough path among ;
    Be mine to lighten pain and wrong,
Still letting fall a hopeful lay—
        Cheer up, cheer up !
        REV. RICHARD WILTON, M.A.

"WHEN SUMMER DIES."

When Summer dies, the leaves are falling fast
In fitful eddies on the chilly blast,
    And fields lie blank upon the bare hillside
    Where erst the poppy flaunted in its pride,
And woodbine on the breeze its fragrance cast.

And where the hawthorn scattered far and wide
Its creamy petals in the sweet Springtide
    Red berries hang, for birds a glad repast
        When summer dies.

Gone are the cowslips and the daisies pied ;
The swallow to a warmer clime hath hied ;
    The beech has shed its store of bitter mast,
    And days are drear and skies are overcast,
But Love will warm our hearts whate'er betide
        When summer dies.
ARTHUR G. WRIGHT.

MY LITTLE SWEETHEART.

Across the pew, with complaisance
And eyes that with Love's sunshine dance,
    My little sweetheart smiles at me—
    She is the only saint I see ;
The sermon passes in a trance.

The painted figures gaze askance,
Down from their glassy vigilance,
    On this our tender heresy
        Across the pew.

Ah ! little sweetheart, the romance
Of Life, with all its change and chance,
    Is but a sealèd book to thee —
    When opened, may its pages be
As fair and sweet as thy bright glance
        Across the pew !
ARTHUR G. WRIGHT.

THREE ROUNDELS.

I.

Love, though I die, and dying lave
My soul in Lethe endlessly,
Losing all else, I still would save
—Love, though I die—

Thy living presence, touch and sigh,
All that the golden moments gave
To vanished hours of ecstasy.

Then make thou great and wide my grave,
So wide we two therein may lie;
For sense of thee my soul will crave,
Love, though I die.

II.

My lips refuse to take farewell of bliss,
Sweet Love! so sweet and false, I can but choose
To leave thee, only parting word and kiss
My lips refuse.

Fancy wears livery of a thousand hues,
So love in idleness may come to this!
And I must bring the thought to common use

That ever—save in memory—I shall miss
Thy short-lived tenderness—ever lose
All that has taught how dear a thing it is
My lips refuse.

III.

Other lips than yours intreat
Those I vowed in vanished hours,
Never Fate should force to greet
Other lips than yours.

Memory dulls, perchance, or sours
What was once so keenly sweet,
Being ours and only ours.

All the life and heart and heat,
All the soul that love outpours,
Dies upon the lips that meet
Other lips than yours.

D. F. BLOMFIELD.

A SINGING LESSON.

Far-fetched and dear bought, as the proverb rehearses,
Is good, or was held so, for ladies : but nought
In a song can be good if the turn of the verse is
Far-fetched and dear bought.

As the turn of a wave should it sound, and the thought
Ring smooth, and as light as the spray that disperses
Be the gleam of the words for the garb thereof wrought.

Let the soul in it shine through the sound as it pierces
Men's hearts with possession of music unsought;
For the bounties of song are no jealous god's mercies,
Far-fetched and dear bought.

ALGERNON CHARLES SWINBURNE.

IN GUERNSEY.

(To Theodore Watts.)

I.

The heavenly bay, ringed round with cliffs and moors,
Storm-stained ravines, and crags that lawns inlay,
Soothes as with love the rocks whose guard secures
        The heavenly bay.

O friend, shall time take even this away,
This blessing given of beauty that endures,
This glory shown us, not to pass but stay?

Though sight be changed for memory, love ensures
What memory, changed by love to sight, would say—
The word that seals for ever mine and yours,
        The heavenly bay.

II.

My mother sea, my fortress, what new strand,
What new delight of waters, may this be,
The fairest found since time's first breezes fanned
        My mother sea?

Once more I give me body and soul to thee,
Who hast my soul for ever : cliff and sand
Recede, and heart to heart once more are we.

My heart springs first and plunges, ere my hand
Strike out from shore : more close it brings to me,
More near and dear than seems my fatherland,
        My mother sea.

III.

Across and along, as the bay's breadth opens, and o'er us
Wild autumn exults in the wind, swift rapture and strong
Impels us, and broader the wide waves brighten before us
    Across and along.

The whole world's heart is uplifted, and knows not
    wrong ;
The whole world's life is a chant to the sea-tide's chorus ;
Are we not as waves of the water, as notes of the song ?

Like children unworn of the passions and toils that wore
    us,
We breast for a season the breadth of the seas that throng,
Rejoicing as they, to be borne as of old they bore us
    Across and along.
ALGERNON CHARLES SWINBURNE.

THE ROUNDEL.

A Roundel is wrought as a ring or a starbright sphere,
With craft of delight and with cunning of sound unsought,
That the heart of the hearer may smile if to pleasure his
    ear
    A roundel is wrought.

Its jewel of music is carven of all or of aught—
Love, laughter, or mourning—remembrance of rapture or
    fear—
That fancy may fashion to hang in the ear of thought.

As a bird's quick song runs round, and the hearts in us
    hear—
Pause answers to pause, and again the same strain caught,
So moves the device whence, round as a pearl or tear,
    A roundel is wrought.
ALGERNON CHARLES SWINBURNE.

NOTHING SO SWEET.

Nothing so sweet in all the world there is
    Than this—to stand apart in Love's retreat
And gaze at Love.   There is as that, ywis,
    Nothing so sweet.

    Yet surely God hath placed before our feet
Some sweeter sweetness and completer bliss,
    And something that shall prove more truly meet.

Soothly I know not :—when the live lips kiss
    There is no more that our prayers shall entreat,
Save only Death.   Perhaps there is as this
    Nothing so sweet.

CHARLES SAYLE.

THE TRYSTING-TREE.

Meet me, love, where the woodbines grow
 And where the wild rose smells most sweet ;
And the breezes, as they softliest blow,
    Meet ;

Passing along through the field of wheat,
 By the hedge where in spring the violets glow,
And the blue-bells blossom around one's feet ;

Where latest lingers the drifted snow,
 And the fir-tree grows o'er our trysting-seat,
Come—and your love, as long ago,
    Meet.

CHARLES SAYLE.

A ROUNDEL OF REST.

If rest is sweet at shut of day
    For tired hands and tired feet,
How sweet at last to rest for aye,
      If rest is sweet !

We work or work not through the heat :
    Death bids us soon our labours lay
In lands where night and twilight meet.

When the last dawns are fallen on grey
    And all life's toils and ease complete,
They know who work, not they who play,
      If rest is sweet.

ARTHUR SYMONS.

MORS ET VITA.

We know not yet what life shall be,
    What shore beyond earth's shore be set ;
What grief awaits us, or what glee,
      We know not yet.

Still, somewhere in sweet converse met,
    Old friends, we say, beyond death's sea
Shall meet and greet us, nor forget

Those days of yore, those years when we
    Were loved and true,—but will death let
Our eyes the longed-for vision see?
      We know not yet.

SAMUEL WADDINGTON.

RONDELS OF CHILDHOOD.

I.—WHEN CLARICE DIED.

When Clarice died, and it was told to me,
  I only covered up my face, and sighed
To lose the world and cease to breathe or see,
      When Clarice died.

She was my playmate, sweet, and thoughtful-eyed,
  With curls, gold curls, that fluttered wild and
      free ;
My child companion and most tender guide.

When Clarice died I wandered wearily
  Down the mute grove where she was wont to
      hide,
And cast myself beneath her favourite tree,
      When Clarice died.

BERNARD WELLER.

II.—IN A FAIRY BOAT.

In a fairy boat on a fairy sea,
  All amber and gold, I used to float
When never a wind rose stormily ;
      In a fairy boat.

And sweet and sad like a white dove's note
  Strange voices wakened my soul to glee,
And soft scents strayed from the violets' throat.

In a fairy boat I shall no more be,
  For gloom has fallen on creek and moat,
And my tired soul's too heavy to flee
      In a fairy boat.

BERNARD WELLER.

The Sestina.

" La sextine en général sera l'expression d'une rêverie, dans laquelle la même idée, les mêmes objets se représenteront succes- sivement à l'esprit avec des nuances diverses jouant et se transformant par d' harmonieuses gradations."

—De Gramont.

SESTINA.

When from the portals of her paradise
Sweet Eve went forth an exile with sad heart,
She lingered at the thrice-barred gate in tears,
And to the guardian of that Eden fair,
As on her cheeks there came and went the rose,
She weeping mourned the harshness of her fate.

" O angel," cried she, " bitter is the fate
That drives me from this fairest paradise,
And bids me wear life's rue and not its rose !
Give me one flower to lay upon my heart
Before I wander through far lands less fair,
And drown all visions of my past in tears."

She ceased, but still flowed fast her silent tears
At memory of the waywardness of fate.
" Ah," thought she, " young I am, 'tis true, and fair,
But shall I find another paradise ? "
Then turning once again with trembling heart,
She spake : " O angel, but a rose—one rose ! "

Within the angel's breast compassion rose
At sight of her sad face and falling tears,
The while her beauty touched his tender heart,
And knowing well the misery of her fate,
He gave the flower, a rose of paradise,
Because she was so very young and fair.

And since that time there may be flowers as fair,
But they must all yield fealty to the rose,
The red, red rose that bloomed in paradise,
That Eve in exile watered with her tears,
The only blossom in her cheerless fate,
The one flower in the desert of her heart.

And into every mortal's life and heart
There come some time, in cloudy days or fair,
It matters not, to bless and light his fate
For one short space, the perfume of the rose ;
And though the after years may bring but tears,
That moment's pleasure is of paradise.

O wondrous rose of love most passing fair,
Whate'er our fate in earthly paradise,
Grant that our tears be dewdrops in thy heart.

FLORENCE M. BYRNE.

LOVE'S GOING.

(Sestina.)

Love lies a-sleeping : maiden, softly sing,
    Lest he should waken ; pluck the falling rose
    A-brushing 'gainst his cheek, her glowing heart
Ope'd to the sun's hot kisses—foolish thing,
    To list the tale oft told !—but summer goes,
    And all the roses' petals fall apart.

Love lies a-sleeping : let the curtains part
    So that the breeze may lightly to him sing
        A lullaby—the changeful breeze that goes
        A-whispering through the grass, where'er it rose,
    Where'er it listeth bound, a wilful thing,
Low murmuring sweets from an inconstant heart.

Love lies a-sleeping : press the pulsing heart
That beats against thy bosom : stand apart
    And stay thine eager breath, lest anything
    Should mar his rest—the songs that lovers sing,
The tale the butterfly tells to the rose,
The low wind to the grass, and onward goes.

Love lies a-sleeping : ah, how swiftly goes
    The sweet delusion he hath taught thy heart,
Fair maiden, pressing to thy breast the rose
    Whose sun-kiss'd petals sadly fall apart
With thy quick breath ! That rhyme wouldst hear him
    sing
Which yesterday seem'd such a foolish thing ?

Love lies a-sleeping : nay, for such a thing
    Break not his slumber. See how sweetly goes
That smile across his lips, that will not sing
    For very wilfulness. Love hath no heart !
    If he should wake, these red-ripe lips would part
In laughter low to see this ravish'd rose.

Love lies a-sleeping : so the full-blown rose
    Falls to the earth a dead unpitied thing ;
        The grasses 'neath the breeze deep-sighing part
And sway ; and as thy warm breath comes and goes
        In motion with the red tides of thy heart,
The song is hush'd which Love was wont to sing.

Love lies a-sleeping : thus in dreams he goes ;
    Strive not to waken him, but tell thy heart,
      " Love lies a-sleeping, and he may not sing.
        CHARLES W. COLEMAN, JUN.

SESTINA.

To F. H.

" ' Fra tutte il primo Arnoldo Daniello
Grand maestro d'amor.' "—PETRARCH.

In fair Provence, the land of lute and rose,
Arnaut, great master of the lore of love,
First wrought sestines to win his lady's heart ;
For she was deaf when simpler staves he sang,
And for her sake he broke the bonds of rhyme,
And in this subtler measure hid his woe.

'Harsh be my lines,' cried Arnaut, 'harsh the woe,
My lady, that enthron'd and cruel rose,
Inflicts on him that made her live in rhyme !'
But through the metre spake the voice of Love,
And like a wild-wood nightingale he sang
Who thought in crabbed lays to ease his heart.

It is not told if her untoward heart
Was melted by her poet's lyric woe,
Or if in vain so amorously he sang.
Perchance through crowd of dark conceits he rose
To nobler heights of philosophic love,
And crowned his later years with sterner rhyme.

This thing alone we know : the triple rhyme,
Of him who bared his vast and passionate heart
To all the crossing flames of hate and love,
Wears in the midst of all its storm of woe,—
As some loud morn of March may bear a rose,—
The impress of a song that Arnaut sang.

'Smith of his mother-tongue,' the Frenchman sang
Of Lancelot and of Galahad, the rhyme
That beat so bloodlike at its core of rose,
It stirred the sweet Francesca's gentle heart
To take that kiss that brought her so much woe,
And sealed in fire her martyrdom of love.

And Dante, full of her immortal love,
Stayed his drear song, and softly, fondly sang
As though his voice broke with that weight of woe;
And to this day we think of Arnaut's rhyme
Whenever pity at the labouring heart
On fair Francesca's memory drops the rose.

Ah ! sovereign Love, forgive this weaker rhyme !
The men of old who sang were great at heart,
Yet have we too known woe, and worn thy rose.
EDMUND GOSSE.

PULVIS ET UMBRA.

(A Sestina.)

Along the crowded streets I walk and think
How I, a shadow, pace among the shades,
For I and all men seem to me unreal:
Foam that the seas of God which cover all
Cast on the air a moment, shadows thrown
In moving westward by the Moon of Death.

Oh, shall it set at last, that orb of Death?
May any morning follow?   As I think,
From one surmise upon another thrown,
My very thoughts appear to me as shades—
Shades, like the prisoning self that bounds them all,
Shades, like the transient world, and as unreal.

But other hours there be when I, unreal,
When only I, vague in a conscious Death,
Move through the mass of men unseen by all;
I move along their ways, I feel and think,
Yet am more light than echoes, or the shades
That hide me, from their stronger bodies thrown.

And better moments come, when, overthrown
All round me, lie the ruins of the unreal
And momentary world, as thin as shades;
When I alone, triumphant over Death,
Eternal, vast, fill with the thoughts I think,
And with my single soul the frame of all.

Ah, for a moment could I grasp it all!
Ah, could but I (poor wrestler often thrown)
Once grapple with the truth, oh then, I think,
Assured of which is living, which unreal,
I would not murmur, though among the shades
My lot were cast, among the shades and Death.

"One thing is true," I said, "and that is Death,"
And yet it may be God disproves it all ;
And Death may be a passage from the shades,
And films on our beclouded senses thrown ;
And Death may be a step beyond the Unreal
Towards the Thought that answers all I think.

In vain I think.   O moon-like thought of Death,
All is unreal beneath thee, uncertain all,
Dim moon-ray thrown along a world of shades.

A. MARY F. ROBINSON.

CUPID AND THE SHEPHERD.

(Sestina.)

One merry morn when all the earth was bright,
    And flushed with dewy dawn's encrimsoning ray
A shepherd youth, o'er whose fair face the light
    Of rosy smiles was ever wont to stray,
Roamed through a level grassy mead, bedight
    With springtime blossoms, fragrant, fresh and gay.

But now, alas ! his mood was far from gay ;
    And musing how the dark world would be bright
Could he but win his maiden's love, and stray
    With her forever, basking in its light,
He saw afar, in morn's bright beaming ray,
    A lissome boy with archer's arms bedight.

The boy shot arrows at a tree bedight
    With red-winged songsters warbling sweet and gay
Amid the leaves and blossoms blooming bright.
    He seemed an aimless, wandering waif astray,
And so the shepherd caught him, stealing light,
    While from his eyes he flashed an angry ray.

The fair boy plead until a kindly ray
   Shone o'er the shepherd's clouded brow, bedight
With clustering locks, and he said, smiling gay,
   "I prithee promise, by thy face so bright,
To ne'er again, where'er thou mayest stray,
   Slay the sweet birds that make so glad the light."

While yet he spake, from out those eyes a light
   Divine shot forth, before whose glowing ray
The shepherd quailed, it was so wondrous bright ;
   Then well he knew 'twas Cupid coy and gay,
With all his arts and subtle wiles bedight,
   And knelt in homage lest the boy should stray.

"Rise," said the God, "and e'er thy footsteps stray
   Know that within her eyes where beamed no light
Of love for thee, I will implant a ray.
   She shall be thine with all her charms bedight."
The shepherd kissèd Love's hand and bounded gay
   To gain his bliss,—and all the world was bright.

When naught is bright to these that sadly stray,
   Oftimes a single ray of Eros' light
Will make all earth bedight with radiance gay.

CLINTON SCOLLARD.

SESTINA.

I saw my soul at rest upon a day
   As a bird sleeping in the nest of night,
Among soft leaves that give the starlight way
   To touch its wings but not its eyes with light ;
So that it knew as one in visions may,
   And knew not as men waking, of delight.

This was the measure of my soul's delight;
    It had no power of joy to fly by day,
Nor part in the large lordship of the light;
    But in a secret moon-beholden way
Had all its will of dreams and pleasant night,
    And all the love and life that sleepers may.

But such life's triumph as men waking may
    It might not have to feed its faint delight
Between the stars by night and sun by day,
    Shut up with green leaves and a little light;
Because its way was as a lost star's way,
    A world's not wholly known of day or night.

All loves and dreams and sounds and gleams of night
    Made it all music that such minstrels may,
And all they had they gave it of delight;
    But in the full face of the fire of day
What place shall be for any starry light,
    What part of heaven in all the wide sun's way?

Yet the soul woke not, sleeping by the way,
    Watched as a nursling of the large eyed night,
And sought no strength nor knowledge of the day,
    Nor closer touch conclusive of delight,
Nor mightier joy nor truer than dreamers may,
    Nor more of song than they, nor more of light.

For who sleeps once and sees the secret light
    Whereby sleep shows the soul a fairer way
Between the rise and rest of day and night,
    Shall care no more to fare as all men may,
But be his place of pain or of delight,
    There shall he dwell, beholding night as day.
Song, have thy day and take thy fill of light
    Before the night be fallen across thy way;
Sing while he may, man hath no long delight.

ALGERNON CHARLES SWINBURNE.

The Triolet,

TRIOLET.

Le premier jour du mois de mai
Fut le plus heureux de ma vie :
Le beau dessein que je formai,
Le premier jour du mois de mai !
Je vous vis et je vous aimai.
Si ce dessein vous plut, Sylvie,
Le premier jour du mois de mai
Fut le plus heureux de ma vie.

—RANCHIN.

LECON DE CHANT.

Moi, je regardais ce cou-là.
Maintenant chantez, me dit Paule.
Avec des mines d'Attila
Moi, je regardais ce cou-là.
Puis, un peu de temps s'écoula. . .
Moi, je regardais ce cou-là ;
Maintenant chantez, me dit Paule.

—THEODORE DE BANVILLE.

" Mon fils, Absalon
Absalon, mon fils,
Las ! perdu l'avon
Mon fils Absalon ;
Il faut que soyon
En grief deuil confis
Mon fils Absalon
Absalon, mon fils !"

—OLD FRENCH PLAY.

MY SWEETHEART.

She's neither scholarly nor wise,
    But, oh, her heart is wondrous tender,
And love lies laughing in her eyes.
She's neither scholarly nor wise,
And yet above all else I prize
    The right from evil to defend her.
She's neither scholarly nor wise,
    But, oh, her heart is wondrous tender.

GRIFFITH ALEXANDER.

When first we met, we did not guess
    That Love would prove so hard a master;
Of more than common friendliness
When first we met we did not guess.
Who could foretell the sore distress,
    This irretrievable disaster,
When first we met?—we did not guess
    That Love would prove so hard a master.

ROBERT BRIDGES.

All women born are so perverse,
    No man need boast their love possessing,
If nought seem better, nothing's worse;
All women born are so perverse,
From Adam's wife that proved a curse,
    Though God had made her for a blessing.
All women born are so perverse
    No man need boast their love possessing.

ROBERT BRIDGES.

A ROSE.

'Twas a Jacqueminot rose
    That she gave me at parting ;
Sweetest flower that blows,
'Twas a Jacqueminot rose.
In the love garden close,
    With the swift blushes starting,
'Twas a Jacqueminot rose
    That she gave me at parting.

If she kissed it, who knows—
    Since I will not discover,
And love is that close,
If she kissed it, who knows?
Or if not the red rose
    Perhaps then the lover !
If she kissed it, who knows,
    Since I will not discover.

Yet at least with the rose
    Went a kiss that I'm wearing !
More I will not disclose,
Yet at least with the rose
Went *whose* kiss no one knows,—
    Since I'm only declaring,
"Yet at least with the rose
    Went a kiss that I'm wearing."

ARLO BATES.

Wee Rose is but three,
    Yet coquettes she already.
I can scarcely agree
Wee Rose is but three,
When her archness I see !
    Are the sex born unsteady ?—
Wee Rose is but three,
    Yet coquettes she already.

ARLO BATES.

A pitcher of mignonette
    In a tenement's highest casement ;
Queer sort of a flower-pot—yet
That pitcher of mignonette
Is a garden in heaven set
    To the little sick child in the basement,—
The pitcher of mignonette
    In the tenement's highest casement.

H. C. BUNNER.

In the light, in the shade,
    This is time and life's measure:
With a heart unafraid,
In the light, in the shade,
Hope is born and not made,
    And the heart finds its treasure
In the light, in the shade ;
    This is time and life's measure.

WALTER CRANE.

TRIOLETS FOR "THE TWELFTH."

Away from city chafe and care,
  At forty miles an hour flying,
Nor let the train me, *blasé*, bear
Away from city chafe and care.
To breezy braes, from street and square,
  Who would not, an he could, be hieing;
Away from city chafe and care,
  At forty miles an hour flying?

How nice a month on moors to pass
  Mid purling becks and purpling heather,
To give the grouse their *coup de grâce*,
How nice a month on moors to pass!
If Fortune prove a liberal lass,
  If but auspicious be the weather,
How nice a month on moors to pass,
  Mid purling brooks and purpling heather.

Plague take the rain! upon my word,
  These mountain mists, how they do hover!
I wish from town I'd never stirred.
Plague take the rain! upon my word,
'Tis just my luck, and not a bird
  My guileless gun contrives to cover.
Plague take the rain! upon my word,
  These mountain mists, how they *do* hover.

COTSFORD DICK.

ROSE-LEAVES.

(Triolets.)

A. KISS.

Rose kissed me to-day,
    Will she kiss me to-morrow?
Let it be as it may,
Rose kissed me to-day.
But the pleasure gives way
    To a savour of sorrow ;—
Rose kissed me to-day,—
    Will she kiss me to-morrow?

CIRCE.

In the School of Coquettes
    Madam Rose is a scholar :—
O, they fish with all nets,
In the School of Coquettes !
When her brooch she forgets,
    'Tis to show her new collar ;
In the School of Coquettes
    Madam Rose is a scholar !

A TEAR.

There's a tear in her eye,—
    Such a clear little jewel !
What *can* make her cry ?
There's a tear in her eye.
" Puck has killed a big fly,—
    And it's *horribly* cruel ; "
There's a tear in her eye,—
    Such a clear little jewel !

A GREEK GIFT.

Here's a present for Rose,
    How pleased she is looking !
Is it verse?   Is it prose?
Here's a present for Rose !
" *Plats,*" "*Entrees*" and " *Rôts,*"—
    Why, its " Gouffé on Cooking ! "
Here's a present for Rose,
    How *pleased* she is looking !

" URCEUS EXIT."

I intended an Ode,
    And it turned to a Sonnet,
It began *à la mode,*
I intended an Ode ;
But Rose crossed the road
    In her latest new bonnet.
I intended an Ode,
    And it turned to a Sonnet.

———

Oh, Love's but a dance,
    Where Time plays the fiddle !
See the couples advance,—
Oh ! Love's but a dance !
A whisper, a glance,—
    ' Shall we twirl down the middle ? '
Oh, Love's but a dance,
    Where Time plays the fiddle !

AUSTIN DOBSON.

TRIOLET, AFTER CATULLUS.

"Jucundum, mea vita."

Happy, my Life, the love you proffer,
    Eternal as the gods above ;
With such a wealth within my coffer,
Happy my life.   The love you proffer, --
If your true heart sustains the offer,—
    Will prove the Koh-i-noor of love ;
Happy my life !   The love you proffer,
    Eternal as the gods above !

EDMUND GOSSE.

Easy is the Triolet,
    If you really learn to make it !
Once a neat refrain you get,
Easy is the Triolet.
As you see !—I pay my debt
    With another rhyme.   Deuce take it,
Easy is the Triolet,
    If you really learn to make it !

W. E. HENLEY.

Out from the leaves of my " Lucille "
    Falls a faded violet.
Sweet and faint as its fragrance, steal
Out from the leaves of my " Lucille "
Tender memories, and I feel
    A sense of longing and regret.
Out from the leaves of my " Lucille "
    Falls a faded violet.

WALTER LEARNED.

TRIOLETS.

In the days of my youth
    I wooed woman with sonnets.
My ideas were uncouth
In the days of my youth.
Now I know that her ruth
    Is best reached by new bonnets ;
In the days of my youth
    I wooed woman with sonnets.

———

Here's a flower for your grave,
    Little love of last year ;
Since I once was your slave,
Here's a flower for your grave ;
Since I once used to rave
    In the praise of my dear.
Here's a flower for your grave,
    Little love of last year.

———

Lo, my heart, so sound asleep,
    Lady ! will you wake it ?
For lost love I used to weep,
Now my heart is sound asleep,
If it once were yours to keep,
    I fear you'd break it.
Lo ! my heart, so sound asleep,
    Lady, will you wake it ?

JUSTIN HUNTLY MCCARTHY.

TRIOLETS.

A CORSAGE BOUQUET.

Myrtilla, to-night,
  Wears Jacqueminot roses,
She's the loveliest sight !
  Myrtilla, to-night :—
Correspondingly light
  My pocket-book closes.
Myrtilla, to-night
  Wears Jacqueminot roses.

TO AN AUTUMN LEAF.

Wee shallop of shimmering gold !
  Slip down from your ways in the branches.
Some fairy will loosen your hold—
Wee shallop of shimmering gold
Spill dew on your bows and unfold
  Silk sails for the fairest of launches !
Wee shallop of shimmering gold,
  Slip down from your ways in the branches.

A KISS.

You ask me what's a kiss?
  'Tis Cupid's keenest arrow !
A thing to take a " miss "—
(You ask me what's a kiss?)
The brink of an abyss !
A lover's pathway, narrow.
You ask me what's a *kiss?*
  'Tis Cupid's *keenest* arrow !

C. H. Lüders.

You know it is late,
    And the night's growing colder,
Still you lean o'er the gate.
You know it is late,
There's a fire in the grate,
    Ah ! sweetheart, be bolder.
You know it is late,
    And the night's growing colder.
                    The " Century."

Under the sun
    There's nothing new ;
Poem or pun,
Under the sun,
Said Solomon,
    And he said true.
Under the sun
    There's nothing new.
                    " Love in Idleness."

SERENADE TRIOLET.

Why is the moon
    Awake when thou sleepest ?
To the nightingale's tune
Why is the moon
Making a noon
    When night is the deepest ?
Why is the moon
    Awake when thou sleepest ?
                    GEORGE MACDONALD.

TRIOLETS.

Few in joy's sweet riot
    Able are to listen :
Thou, to make me quiet,
Quenchest the sweet riot,
Tak'st away my diet,
    Puttest me in prison—
Quenchest joy's sweet riot
    That the heart may listen.

Spring sits on her nest,
    Daisies and white clover ;
And young love lies at rest
In the Spring's white nest,
For she loves me best,
    And the cold is over ;
Spring sits on her nest,
    Daisies and white clover.

In his arms thy silly lamb
    Lo ! he gathers to his breast !
See, thou sadly bleating dam,
See him lift thy silly lamb !
Hear it cry, " How blest I am !—
    Here is love and love is rest,"
In his arms thy silly lamb
    See him gather to his breast !

GEORGE MACDONALD.

SONG.

I.

I was very cold
    In the summer weather ;
The sun shone all his gold,
But I was very cold—
Alone, we were grown old,
    Love and I together !—
Oh, but I was cold
    In the summer weather !

II.

Sudden I grew warmer,
    When the brooks were frozen :—
" To be angry is to harm her,"
I said, and straight grew warmer.
" Better men, the charmer
    Knows at least a dozen ! "—
I said, and straight grew warmer,
    Though the brooks were frozen.

III.

Spring sits on her nest—
    Daisies and white clover ;
And my heart at rest
Lies in the spring's young nest :
My love she loves me best,
    And the frost is over !
Spring sits on her nest—
    Daisies and white clover !

GEORGE MACDONALD.

UNDER THE ROSE.

HE (*aside*).

If I should steal a little kiss,
   Oh, would she weep, I wonder?
I tremble at the thought of bliss,—
If I should steal a little kiss !
Such pouting lips would never miss
   The dainty bit of plunder ;
If I should steal a little kiss,
   Oh, would she weep, I wonder?

SHE (*aside*).

He longs to steal a kiss of mine—
   He may, if he'll return it :
If I can read the tender sign,
He longs to steal a kiss of mine ;
" In love and war "—you know the line
   Why cannot he discern it ?
He longs to steal a kiss of mine—
   He may if he'll return it.

BOTH (*five minutes later*).

A little kiss when no one sees,
   Where is the impropriety?
How sweet amid the birds and bees
A little kiss when no one sees !
Nor is it wrong, the world agrees,
   If taken with sobriety.
A little kiss when no one sees,
   Where is the impropriety?

SAMUEL MINTURN PECK.

Warm from the wall she chose a peach,
    She took the wasps for councillors ;
She said, " Such little things can teach ; "
Warm from the wall she chose a peach ;
She waved the fruit within my reach,
    Then passed it to a friend of hers :—
Warm from the wall she chose a peach,
    She took the wasps for councillors.

EMILY PFEIFFER.

TWO TRIOLETS.

I.

What he said.

This kiss upon your fan I press,
    Ah ! Saint Nitouche, you don't refuse it,
And may it from its soft recess,
This kiss upon your fan I press
Be blown to you a shy caress
    By this white down whene'er you use it ;
This kiss upon your fan I press,
    Ah ! Saint Nitouche, you don't refuse it.

II.

What she thought.

    To kiss a fan !
        What a poky poet !
    The stupid man
    To kiss a fan,
    When he knows that—he—can,
        Or ought to know it.
    To kiss a fan !
        What a poky poet !

HARRISON ROBERTSON.

SIX TRIOLETS.

DEAR READER.

If you never write verses yourself,
    Dear reader, I leave it with you,
You will grant a half-inch of your shelf,
If you never write verses yourself.
It was praised by some lenient elf,
    It was damned by a heavy review ;
If you never write verses yourself,
    Dear reader, I leave it with you.

TRANSPONTINE.

Ices—Programmes—Lemonade !
    'E thinks 'e's a Hirving, my eye !
Why, Pussy, you're crying : afraid ?
Ices—Programmes—Lemonade !
It's the first time you've seen a piece played ?
    Its pretty, but, Pussy, don't cry.
Ices—Programmes—Lemonade !
    'E thinks 'e's a Hirving, my eye !

OUT.

I killed her ?   Ah, why do they cheer ?
    Are those twenty years gone to-day ?
Why, she was my wife, sir, dear—so dear.
I killed her ?   Ah, why do they cheer ?
    . . . Ah hound !   He was shaking with fear,
And I rushed—with a knife, they say. . . .
I killed her ?   Ah, why do they cheer ?
    Are those twenty years gone to-day ?

[*v.* Police Reports of the release of George Hall from Birmingham prison.]

A HUPROAR.

Down 'Ob'n, sir?   Circus, Bank, Bank!
   'Ere's a huproar, my bloomin', hoff side!
A flower, miss?   Ah, thankee, miss, thank—
Down 'Ob'n, sir?   Circus, Bank, Bank!
'Igher up!   'Ullo, Bill, wot a prank!
   If that 'ere old carcase aint shied!
Down 'Ob'n, sir?   Circus, Bank, Bank!
   'Ere's a huproar, my bloomin', hoff side!

SPRING VOICES.

Fine Violets! fresh Violets! come buy!
   Ah, rich man! I would not be you.
All spring-time it haunts me, that cry:—
Fine Violets! fresh Violets! come buy!
Whose loss if she tell me a lie?
   "They're starving; my God, sir, its true."
Fine Violets! fresh Violets! come buy!
   Ah, rich man! I would not be you!

BETWEEN THE LINES.

Cigar lights! yer honour?   Cigar lights?
   May God forget you in your need.
Ay, damn you! if folks get their rights
(Cigar lights! yer honour?—cigar lights)
Their babies shan't starve in the nights
   For wanting the price of your weed—
Cigar lights! yer honour?   Cigar lights!
   May God forget you in your need!

ERNEST RADFORD.

FROM "FIAMETTA.

Since I am her's and she is mine
    We live in Love and fear no change !
For Love is God, so we divine.
Since I am her's and she is mine,
In some fair love-land far and fine,
    Through golden years our feet shall range.
Since I am her's and she is mine,
    We live in Love and fear no change.

Why dost thou look so pale, my Love?
    Why dost thou sigh and say Farewell?
" These myrtles seem a cypress grove."
Why dost thou look so pale, my Love?
" I hear the raven, not the dove,
    And for the marriage-peal, a knell."
Why dost thou look so pale, my Love?
    Why dost thou sigh and say Farewell?

" Since I can never come again,
    When I am dead and gone from here,
Grieve not for me ; all grief's in vain,
Since I can never come again ;
But let no thought of me remain.
    With my last kiss give thy last tear,
Since I can never come again,
    When I am dead and gone from here."

All the night and all the day
    I think upon her lying dead,
With lips that neither kiss nor pray
All the night nor all the day.
In that dark grave whose only ray
    Of sun or moon's her golden head,
All the night and all the day
    I think upon her lying dead.

Why should I live alone,
    Since Love was all in vain?
My heart to thine is flown—
Why should I live alone?
Dost thou too make thy moan,
    In Paradise complain :
Why should I live alone,
    Since Love was all in vain?

What can heal a broken heart?
    Death alone, I fear me,
Thou that dost true lovers part,
What can heal a broken heart?
Death alone, that made the smart,
    Death, that will not hear me.
What can heal a broken heart?
    Death alone, I fear me.

A. MARY F. ROBINSON.

A SNOWFLAKE IN MAY.

I saw a snowflake in the air
    When smiling May had decked the year,
And then 'twas gone, I knew not where,—
I saw a snowflake in the air,
And thought perchance an angel's prayer
    Had fallen from some starry sphere;
I saw a snowflake in the air
    When smiling May had decked the year.
CLINTON SCOLLARD.

APOLOGY FOR GAZING AT A YOUNG LADY IN CHURCH.

    The sermon was long
And the preacher was prosy.
    Dou you think it was wrong?
    The sermon was long,
    The temptation was strong,
Her cheeks were so rosy.
    The sermon was long
And the preacher was prosy.
The Century Magazine.

A TINY TRIP.

THE BILL OF LADING.

She was cargo and crew,
    She was boatswain and skipper,
She was passenger too
Of the *Nutshell* canoe;
And the eyes were so blue
    Of this sweet tiny tripper!
She was cargo and crew,
    She was boatswain and skipper!

THE PILOT.

How I bawled "Ship, ahoy!"
    Hard by Medmenham Ferry!
And she answered with joy,
She moved like a convoy,
And would love to employ
    A bold pilot so merry.
How I bawled "Ship, ahoy!"
    Hard by Medmenham Ferry!

THE VOYAGE.

Neath the trees gold and red
    In that bright autumn weather,
When our white sails were spread
O'er the waters we sped—
What was it she said?
    When we drifted together!
'Neath the trees gold and red
    In that bright autumn weather!

THE HAVEN.

Ah! the moments flew fast,
    But our trip too soon ended!
When we reached land at last,
And our craft was made fast,
It was six or half-past—
    And Mama looked offended!
Ah! the moments flew fast,
    But our trip too soon ended.

J. ASHBY STERRY.

VESTIGIA.

I.

I saw her shadow on the grass
    That day we walked together.
Across the field where the pond was
I saw her shadow on the grass.
And now I sigh and say, Alas !
    That e'er in summer weather
I saw her shadow on the grass
    That day we walked together !

II.

Hope bowed his head in sleep :
    Ah me and wellaway !
Although I cannot weep,
Hope bowed his head in sleep.
The heavy hours creep :
    When is the break of day ?
Hope bowed his head in sleep,
    Ah me and wellaway !

III.

The sea on the beach
    Flung the foam of its ire.
We watched without speech
The sea on the beach,
And we clung each to each
    As the tempest shrilled higher
And the sea on the beach
    Flung the foam of its ire.

IV.

When Love is once dead
    Who shall awake him ?
Bitter our bread
When Love is once dead
His comforts are fled,
    His favours forsake him.
When Love is once dead
    Who shall awake him ?

V.

Love is a swallow
    Flitting with spring :
Though we would follow,
Love is a swallow,
All his vows hollow :
    Than let us sing,
Love is a swallow
    Flitting with spring.

ARTHUR SYMONS.

A poor cicala, piping shrill,
    I may not ape the Nightingale,
I sit upon the sun-browned hill,
A poor cicala, piping shrill
When summer noon is warm and still,
    Content to chirp my homely tale ;
A poor cicala piping shrill,
    I may not ape the Nightingale.

GRAHAM R. TOMSON.

THREE TRIOLETS.

I.

Love's footsteps shall not fail nor faint,
    He will not leave our hearth again :
So safely lulled his murmuring plaint,
Love's footsteps shall not fail nor faint ;
All clasped and bound in fond constraint,
    And circled with a shining chain,
Love's footsteps shall not fail nor faint,
    He will not leave our hearth again.

II.

Your rose-red bonds are all in vain,
    If bound Love weep for weariness :
His faded eyes are drowned in rain.
Your rose-red bonds are all in vain,
He murmurs low a dull refrain,
    And turns his lips from our caress—
Your rose-red bonds are all in vain
    If bound Love weep for weariness !

III.

That grey, last day we said goodbye
    Makes winter weather in my heart ;
Dull cloud wreaths veiled our summer sky
That grey, last day we said goodbye
And loosed faint love ; I wonder why
    (For *then*, in truth, 'twas well to part)
That grey, last day we said goodbye
    Makes wintry weather in my heart.

GRAHAM R. TOMSON.

TRIOLET.

The roses are dead,
    And swallows are flying :
White, golden, and red,
The roses are dead ;
Yet tenderly tread
    Where their petals are lying.
The roses are dead,
    And swallows are flying.

Graham R. Tomson.

REJECTED.

You've spoken of love,
    And I've answered with laughter ;
You've kissed—my kid glove.
You've spoken of love.
Why ! powers above ?
    Is there more to come after.
You've spoken of love
    And I've answered with laughter.

Her lips were so near
    That—what else could I do ?
You'll be angry, I fear,
Her lips were so near.
Well, I can't make it clear
    Or explain it to you.
Her lips were so near
    That—what else could I do ?

From "The Century."

A PAIR OF GLOVES.

My love of loves—my May,
    In rippling shadows lying,
Was sleeping mid the hay—
My love of loves—my May!
    The ardent sun was trying
To kiss her dreams away!
My love of loves—my May,
    In rippling shadows lying.

I knelt and kissed her lips,
    Sweeter than any flower
The bee for honey sips!
I knelt and kissed her lips,—
    And as her dark eyes' power
Awoke from sleep's eclipse,
I knelt and kissed her lips,
    Sweeter than any flower!

The pair of gloves I won,
    My darling pays in kisses!
Long may the sweet debt run—
The pair of gloves I won!
    Till death our loves dismisses
This feud will ne'er be done—
The pair of gloves I won,
    My darling pays in kisses!

C. H. WARING.

IN THE ORCHARD.

A Trio of Triolets.

O the apples rosy-red !
    O the gnarled trunks grey and brown,
Heavy-branchèd overhead !
O the apples rosy-red !
O the merry laughter sped,
    As the fruit is showered down !
O the apples rosy-red !
    O the gnarled trunks grey and brown !

O the blushes rosy-red !
    O the loving autumn breeze !
O the words so softly said !
O the blushes rosy-red,
While old doubts and fears lie dead,
    Buried 'neath the apple-trees !
O the blushes rosy-red !
    O the loving autumn breeze !

O the years so swiftly fled !
    O twin hearts that beat as one,
With a love time-strengthenèd !
O the years so swiftly fled !
O the apples rosy-red,
    That still ripen in the sun !
O the years so swiftly fled !
    O twin hearts that beat as one !

GEORGE WEATHERLY.

The Villanelle, Virelai, and Virelai Nouveau.

VILLANELLE.

J'ay perdu ma tourterelle :
Est-ce-point elle que i'oy ?*
Je veux aller après elle.

Tu regrettes ta jemelle ;
Hélas ! aussy fay-je moy :
J'ay perdu ma tourterelle.

Si ton amour est fidèle,
Aussy est ferme ma foy ;
Je veux aller après elle.

Ta plainte se renouvelle ?
Toujours plaindre je me doy :
J'ay perdu ma tourterelle.

En ne voyant plus la belle
Plus rien de beau je ne voy :
Je veux aller après elle.

Mort, que tant de fois j'appelle
Prens ce qui se donne à toy :
J'ai perdu ma tourterelle,
Je veux aller après elle.

    * J'entends.

—JEAN PASSERAT.

ROSES.

There are roses white, there are roses red,
    Shyly rosy, tenderly white ;—
Which shall I choose to wreathe my head?

Which shall I cull from the garden-bed
    To greet my love on this very night?
There are roses white, there are roses red.

The red should say what I would have said ;
    Ah ! how they blush in the evening light !
Which shall I choose to wreathe my head ?

The white are pale as the snow new-spread,
    Pure as young eyes and half as bright ;
There are roses white, there are roses red.

Roses white, from the heaven dew-fed,
    Roses red for a passion's plight ;
Which shall I choose to wreathe my head ?

Summer twilight is almost fled,
    Say, dear love ! have I chosen right ?
There are roses white, there are roses red,
All twined together to wreathe my head.

L. S. BEVINGTON.

A VACATION VILLANELLE.

O Halcyon hours of happy holiday,
    When frets of function and of fashion flee,
(Sweet is the sunshine, soft the summer's sway).
Ye whisper ' welcome ' to our wandering way,
    And give a gracious greeting to our glee,
O halcyon hours of happy holiday !

Or pacing prairies in pursuit of prey,
    Or sailing silent on a southern sea,
(Sweet is the sunshine, soft the summer's sway),
Or gliding giddy down some glacier gray,
    Or joining in a German jubilee,
O halcyon hours of happy holiday !

We breathe such buoyant bliss that we betray
    Our sportive spirits strangely—*sans souci*
Sweet is the sunshine, soft the summer's sway,
And dear the dreaming of these days *distraits*
    We find we ye, so *fainéants* and free,
O halcyon hours of happy holiday !

Cotsford Dick.

"TU NE QUAESIERIS."

Seek not, O maid, to know
 (Alas ! unblest the trying !)
When thou and I must go.

No lore of stars can show.
 What shall be, vainly prying,
Seek not, O maid, to know.

Will Jove long years bestow ?—
 Or is't with this one dying,
That thou and I must go ;

Now,—when the great winds blow
 And waves the reef are plying ? . . .
Seek not, O maid, to know.

Rather let clear wine flow,
 On no vain hope relying ;
When thou and I must go

Lies dark ; then be it so.
 Now,—*now*, churl Time is flying ;
Seek not, O maid, to know
When thou and I must go.

Austin Dobson.

WHEN I SAW YOU LAST, ROSE.

When I saw you last, Rose,
    You were only so high ;—
How fast the time goes !

Like a bud ere it blows,
    You just peeped at the sky,
When I saw you last, Rose !

Now your petals unclose,
    Now your May-time is nigh ;—
How fast the time goes !

And a life,—how it grows !
    You were scarcely so shy,
When I saw you last, Rose !

In your bosom it shows
    There's a guest on the sly ;
How fast the time goes !

Is it Cupid?   Who knows !
    Yet you used not to sigh,
When I saw you last, Rose ;—
How fast the time goes !

AUSTIN DOBSON.

FOR A COPY OF THEOCRITUS.

O singer of the field and fold,
    THEOCRITUS ! Pan's pipe was thine,—
Thine was the happier Age of Gold.

For thee the scent of new-turned mould,
    The bee-hives, and the murmuring pine,
O singer of the field and fold !

Thou sang'st the simple feasts of old,—
    The beechen bowl made glad with wine. . .
Thine was the happier Age of Gold !

Thou bad'st the rustic loves be told,—
    Thou bad'st the tuneful reeds combine,
O singer of the field and fold !

And round thee, ever laughing, rolled
    The blithe and blue Sicilian brine . .
Thine was the happier Age of Gold.

Alas for us ! our songs are cold ;
    Our northern suns too sadly shine :—
O singer of the field and fold,
Thine was the happier Age of Gold.

AUSTIN DOBSON.

ON A NANKIN PLATE.

" Ah me, but it might have been !
    Was there ever so dismal a fate?"—
Quoth the little blue mandarin.

" Such a maid as was never seen !
    She passed, though I cried to her ' Wait,'—
Ah me, but it might have been !

" I cried, ' O my Flower, my Queen,
    Be mine !'   'Twas precipitate,"—
Quoth the little blue mandarin,—

" But then . . she was just sixteen,—
    Long-eyed,—as a lily straight,—
Ah me, but it might have been !

" As it was, from her palankeen,
    She laughed—' you're a week too late ! ' "
(Quoth the little blue mandarin.)

" That is why, in a mist of spleen,
    I mourn on this Nankin Plate.
Ah me, but it might have been !"
Quoth the little blue mandarin.

Austin Dobson.

VILLANELLE.

Wouldst thou not be content to die
    When low-hung fruit is hardly clinging
And golden autumn passes by?

Beneath this delicate rose-gray sky,
    While sunset bells are faintly ringing,
Wouldst thou not be content to die?

For wintry webs of mist on high
    Out of the muffled earth are springing,
And golden Autumn passes by.

O now when pleasures fade and fly,
    And Hope her southward flight is winging,
Wouldst thou not be content to die?

Lest Winter come, with wailing cry
    His cruel icy bondage bringing,
When golden Autumn hath passed by;

And thou with many a tear and sigh,
    While life her wasted hands is wringing,
Shall pray in vain for leave to die
When golden Autumn hath passed by.

EDMUND GOSSE.

VILLANELLE.

Little mistress mine, good-bye !
    I have been your sparrow true;
Dig my grave, for I must die.

Waste no tear and heave no sigh,
    Life should still be blithe for you,
Little mistress mine, good-bye !

In your garden let me lie;
    Underneath the pointed yew
Dig my grave, for I must die.

We have loved the quiet sky
    With its tender arch of blue ;
Little mistress mine, good-bye !

That I still may feel you nigh,
    In your virgin bosom, too,
Dig my grave, for I must die.

Let our garden-friends that fly
    Be the mourners, fit and few.
Little mistress mine, good-bye !
Dig my grave, for I must die.

EDMUND GOSSE.

VILLANELLE.

Where's the use of sighing?
    Sorrow as you may,
Time is always flying—

Flying !—and defying
    Men to say him nay . . .
Where's the use of sighing?

Look ! To-day is dying
    After yesterday.
Time is always flying.

Flying—and when crying
    Cannot make him stay,
Where's the use of sighing?

Men with by-and-bying,
    Fritter life away.
Time is always flying,

Flying !—O, from prying
    Cease, and go to play.
Where's the use of sighing,
" Time is always flying ? "

W. E. HENLEY.

VILLANELLE.

A dainty thing's the Villanelle.
    Sly, musical, a jewel in rhyme,
It serves its purpose passing well.

A double-clappered silver bell
    That must be made to clink in chime,
A dainty thing's the Villanelle ;

And if you wish to flute a spell,
    Or ask a meeting 'neath the lime,
It serves its purpose passing well.

You must not ask of it the swell
    Of organs grandiose and sublime—
A dainty thing's the Villanelle ;

And, filled with sweetness, as a shell
    Is filled with sound, and launched in
        time,
It serves its purpose passing well.

Still fair to see and good to smell
    As in the quaintness of its prime,
A dainty thing's the Villanelle,
It serves its purpose passing well.

W. E. HENLEY.

VILLANELLE.

In the clatter of the train
    Is a promise brisk and bright.
I shall see my love again !

I am tired and fagged and fain ;
    But I feel a still delight
In the clatter of the train,

Hurry-hurrying on amain
    Through the moonshine thin and white—
I shall see my love again !

Many noisy miles remain ;
    But a sympathetic sprite
In the clatter of the train

Hammers cheerful :—that the strain
    Once concluded and the fight,
I shall see my love again.

Yes, the overword is plain,—
    If it's trivial, if it's trite—
In the clatter of the train :
" I shall see my love again."

W. E. HENLEY.

VILLANELLE.

(To M. Joseph Boulmier, Author of " Les Villanelles.")

Villanelle, why art thou mute?
        Hath the singer ceased to sing?
Hath the Master lost his lute?

Many a pipe and scrannel flute
        On the breeze their discords fling;
Villanelle, why art *thou* mute?

Sound of tumult or dispute,
        Noise of war the echoes bring;
Hath the Master lost his lute?

Once he sang of bud and shoot
        In the season of the Spring;
Villanelle, why art thou mute?

Fading leaf and falling fruit
        Say, " The year is on the wing,
Hath the Master lost his lute?"

Ere the axe lies at the root,
        Ere the winter comes as king,
Villanelle, why art thou mute?
Hath the Master lost his lute!

ANDREW LANG.

VILLANELLE.

(To the Nightingale in September.)

Child of the muses and the moon,
    O nightingale, return and sing,
Thy song is over all too soon.

Let not night's quire yield place to noon,
    To this red breast thy tawny wing,
Child of the muses and the moon.

Sing us once more the same sad tune
    Pandion heard when he was king,
Thy song is over all too soon.

Night after night thro' leafy June
    The stars were hush'd and listening,
Child of the muses and the moon.

Now new moons grow to plenilune
    And wane, but no new music bring ;
Thy song is over all too soon.

Ah, thou art weary ! well, sleep on,
    Sleep till the sun brings back the spring.
Thy song is over all too soon,
Child of the muses and the moon.

" Love in Idleness."

VILLANELLE.

Beautiful, distracting Hetty,
    This was how it came to be
As we strolled upon the jetty.

I had danced three times with Netty,
    She had flirted with Dobree,
Beautiful, distracting Hetty.

I was humming Donizetti,
    Hurt was I, and angry she,
As we strolled upon the jetty.

As she levelled her Negretti
    With provoking nicety,
Beautiful, distracting Hetty,

Suddenly she flashed a pretty,
    Half-defiant glance at me,
As we strolled upon the jetty.

And our quarrel seemed so petty
    By the grandeur of the sea !
Beautiful, distracting Hetty,
As we strolled upon the jetty.

Cosmo Monkhouse.

VILLANELLE.

Life, thou art vaguely strangely sweet,
   Thy gladness fills our throbbing veins,
But Death comes on with footsteps fleet.

With rapture men each morning greet,
   And spite of losses, cares and pains.
Life, thou art vaguely strangely sweet.

We, while with health our pulses beat,
   Heed not the falling hour glass grains,
But Death comes in with footsteps fleet.

Our lips may say " Life is a cheat,"
   But 'tis of Death our heart complains ;
Life, thou art vaguely strangely sweet.

For one hour more do men entreat,
   As life within them quickly wanes,
But Death comes on with footsteps fleet.

Many we miss, but him we meet,
   He is a guest whom nought detains ;
Life, thou art vaguely strangely sweet,
But Death comes on with footsteps fleet.

James Ashcroft Noble.

VILLANELLE.

The air is white with snow-flakes clinging ;
    Between the gusts that come and go
Methinks I hear the woodlark singing.

Methinks I see the primrose springing
    On many a bank and hedge, although
The air is white with snow-flakes clinging.

Surely the hands of spring are flinging
    Woodscents to all the winds that blow.
Methinks I hear the woodlark singing ;

Methinks I see the swallow winging
    Across the woodlands sad with snow ;
The air is white with snow-flakes clinging.

Was that the cuckoo's wood-chime swinging ?
    Was that the linnet fluting low ?
Methinks I hear the woodlark singing.

Or can it be the breeze is bringing
    The breath of violets ?—Ah no !
The air is white with snow-flakes clinging.

It is my lady's voice that's stringing
    Its beads of gold to song ; and so
Methinks I hear the woodlark singing.

The violets I see upspringing
    Are in my lady's eyes, I trow ;
The air is white with snow-flakes clinging.

Dear, when thy tender tones are ringing,
    Even whilst amid the winter's woe
The air is white with snow-flakes clinging,
Methinks I hear the woodlark singing.

JOHN PAYNE.

BONNIE BELLE.

Just to please my Bonnie Belle
    With her winsome eyes of blue,
Lo, I sing a villanelle.

List the merry music swell !
    Haste, ye rhymes, in measure true,
Just to please my Bonnie Belle.

Have a care to foot it well,
    Tripping like a fairy crew,
Lo, I sing a villanelle.

Come from where the Pixies dwell,
    Dance with sandals dipped in dew,
Just to please my Bonnie Belle.

In her ear, the tiny shell
    Let my peerless passion sue ;
Lo, I sing a villanelle.

Will she listen ?   Who can tell ?
    Does she love me ?   Would I knew !
Just to please my Bonnie Belle
Lo, I sing a villanelle.

Samuel Minturn Peck.

IF SOME TRUE MAIDEN'S LOVE WERE MINE.

All worldly dreams I would resign,
    Nor ever long for hidden lore,
If some true maiden's love were mine.

If but two eyes of blue divine
    Could meet my glance forevermore,
All worldly dreams I would resign.

The clouds would show a silver line
    And rainbow tints would hue them o'er,
If some true maiden's love were mine.

A jasmine tree should droop and twine
    And peep within our cottage door,
All worldly dreams I would resign.

Our gems should be the dewdrop's shine,
    Our music float from larks that soar,
If some true maiden's love were mine.

Where is she now ?   She gives no sign,
    That loyal heart, leal to the core !
All worldly dreams I would resign
If some true maiden's love were mine.

SAMUEL MINTURN PECK.

WHEN THE BROW OF JUNE.

When the brow of June is crowned by the rose
    And the air is fain and faint with her breath,
Then the Earth hath rest from her long birth-throes ;--

The Earth hath rest and forgetteth her woes
    As she watcheth the cradle of Love and Death,
When the brow of June is crowned by the rose.

O Love and Death who are counted for foes,
    She sees you twins of one mind and faith—
The Earth at rest from her long birth-throes.

You are twins to the mother who sees and knows ;
    (Let them strive and thrive together) she saith—
When the brow of June is crowned by the rose.

They strive, and Love his brother outgrows,
    But for strength and beauty he travaileth
On the Earth at rest from her long birth-throes.

And still when his passionate heart o'erflows,
    Death winds about him a bridal wreath—
As the brow of June is crowned by the rose !

So the bands of death true lovers enclose,
    For Love and Death are as Sword and Sheath
When the Earth hath rest from her long birth-throes.

They are Sword and Sheath, they are Life and its Shows
    Which lovers have grace to see beneath,
When the brow of June is crowned by the rose
And the Earth hath rest from her long birth-throes.

EMILY PFEIFFER.

O SUMMER-TIME SO PASSING SWEET.

O Summer-time so passing sweet,
    But heavy with the breath of flowers,
But languid with the fervent heat.

They chide amiss who call thee fleet,—
    Thee, with thy weight of daylight hours,
O Summer-time so passing sweet !

Young Summer thou art too replete,
    Too rich in choice of joys and powers,
But languid with the fervent heat.

Adieu ! my face is set to meet
    Bleak Winter, with his pallid showers,
O Summer-time so passing sweet !

Old winter steps with swifter feet,
    He lingers not in wayside bowers,
He is not languid with the heat ;

His rounded day, a pearl complete,
    Gleams on the unknown night that lowers ;
O Summer-time so passing sweet,
But languid with the fervent heat !

EMILY PFEIFFER.

VILLANELLE.

In every sound, I think I hear her feet—
    And still I wend my altered way alone,
And still I say, "To-morrow we shall meet."

I watch the shadows in the crowded street—
    Each passing face I follow one by one—
In every sound I think I hear her feet.

And months go by—bleak March and May-day heat—
    Harvest is over—winter well-nigh done—
And still I say, "To-morrow we shall meet."

Among the city square when flowers are sweet,
    With every breath a sound of her seems blown—
In every sound I think I hear her feet.

Belfry and clock the unending hours repeat
    From twelve to twelve—and still she comes in
        none—
And still I say, "To-morrow we shall meet."

Oh, long delayed to-morrow !—hearts that beat
    Measure the length of every minute gone—
In every sound I think I hear her feet.

Ever the suns rise tardily or fleet,
    And light the letters on a churchyard stone,—
And still I say, "To-morrow we shall meet."

And still from out her unknown far retreat
    She haunts me with her tender undertone—
In every sound I think I hear her feet,
And still I say, "To-morrow we shall meet."

MAY PROBYN.

VILLANELLE.

The daffodils are on the lea—
    Come out, sweetheart, and bless the sun !
The birds are glad, and so are we.

This morn a throstle piped to me,
    " 'Tis time that mates were wooed and won—
The daffodils are on the lea."

Come out, sweetheart, their gold to see,
    And building of the nests begun—
The birds are glad, and so are we.

You said,—bethink you !—" It shall be
    When, yellow smocked, and winter done,
The daffodils are on the lea."

Yet, an' you will, to change be free !
    How sigh you ?—" Changes need we none—
The birds are glad—*and so are we ?* "

Come out, sweetheart ! the signs agree,
    The marriage tokens March has spun—
The daffodils are on the lea ;
The birds are glad—and so are we !

MAY PROBYN.

TO HELEN.

Man's very voice is stilled on Troas' shore,
    Sweet Xanthus and Simois both are mute,
Thus have the gods ordained forevermore !

Springs the rank weed where bloomed the rose before,
    Unplucked on Ida hangs the purple fruit,
Man's very voice is stilled on Troas' shore.

When heavenly walls towered proud and high of yore,
    Unharmed now strays abroad the savage brute,
Thus have the gods ordained forevermore !

And they, the wronged, that wasting sorrow bore,
    Alas ! their tree hath withered to the root,
Man's very voice is stilled on Troas' shore.

In Lacedæmon, loved of heroes hoar,
    No trumpet sounds, but piping shepherd's flute,
Thus have the gods ordained forevermore !

And thou, the cause, through Aphrodites lore, .
    Unblamed, art praised on poet's lyre and lute—
Man's very voice is stilled on Troas' shore.
Thus have the gods ordained forevermore !

CLINTON SCOLLARD.

TO THE DAFFODIL.

O daffodil, flower saffron-gowned,
    Effulgent with the Sun-god's gold,
Thou bring'st the joyous season round !

While yet the earth is blanched and browned,
    Thou dost thy amber leaves unfold,
O daffodil, flower saffron-gowned.

We see thee by yon mossy mound,
    Wave from thy stalks each pennon bold,—
Thou bring'st the joyous season round !

Fair child of April, promise-crowned,
    We longed for thee when winds were cold,
O daffodil, flower saffron-gowned.

Again we hear the merry sound
    Of sweet birds singing love-songs old,—
Thou bring'st the joyous season round !

Again we feel our hearts rebound
    With pleasures by thy birth foretold,—
O daffodil, flower saffron-gowned,
    Thou bring'st the joyous season round !

CLINTON SCOLLARD.

SPRING KNOCKS AT WINTER'S FROSTY DOOR.

Spring knocks at winter's frosty door :
    In boughs by wild March breezes swayed
The bonnie bluebirds sing once more.

The brooks have burst their fetters hoar,
    And greet with noisy glee the glade ;
Spring knocks at winter's frosty door.

The swallow soon will northward soar,
    The rush uplift its gleaming blade,
The bonnie bluebirds sing once more.

Soon sunny skies their gold will pour
    O'er meads that breezy maples shade ;
Spring knocks at winter's frosty door.

Along the reedy river's shore,
    Fleet fauns will frolic unafraid,
The bonnie bluebirds sing once more.

And Love, the Love we lost of yore,
    Will come to twine the myrtle braid ;
Spring knocks at winter's frosty door,
The bonnie bluebirds sing once more.

CLINTON SCOLLARD.

DOT.

O, had I but a fairy yacht,
    I know quite well what I would do—
I soon would sail away with Dot!

I'd quickly weave a cunning plot,
    Had I but fairies for my crew—
O, had I but a fairy yacht!

I'd soon be off just like a shot,
    Far, far across the ocean blue;
I soon would sail away with Dot!

What happiness would be my lot,
    With nought to do all day but woo—
O, had I but a fairy yacht.

To some sweet unfrequented spot—
    If I but thought that hearts were true—
I soon would sail away with Dot.

I'd sail away, not minding what,
    My friends approve, or foes pooh-pooh—
O, had I but a fairy yacht!

For name or fame care not a jot,
    I'd leave behind no trace or clue—
I soon would sail away with Dot!

Forgetting all, by all forgot,
    I'd live and love the whole day through—
O, had I but a fairy yacht !

In distant lands I'd build a cot,
    And live alone with I know who—
I soon would sail away with Dot !

I'd start at once—O, would I not ?
    If I were only twenty-two—
O, had I but a fairy yacht,
I soon would sail away with Dot.

J. ASHBY STERRY.

ACROSS THE WORLD I SPEAK TO THEE.

Across the world I speak to thee ;
    Where'er thou art (I know not where),
Send thou a messenger to me !

I here remain, who would be free,
    To seek thee out through foul or fair,
Across the world I speak to thee.

Whether beneath the tropic tree,
    The cooling night wind fans thy hair,—
Send thou a messenger to me !

Whether upon the rushing sea,
    A foamy track thy keel doth wear,—
Across the world I speak to thee.

Whether in yonder star thou be,
    A spirit loosed in purple air,—
Send thou a messenger to me !

Hath Heaven not left thee memory
    Of what was well in mortal's share ?
Across the world I speak to thee ;
Send thou a messenger to me !

EDITH M. THOMAS.

WHERE ARE THE SPRINGS OF LONG AGO?

Come near, O sun—O south wind, blow,
    And be the winter's captives freed ;
Where are the springs of long ago ?

Drive under ground the lingering snow,
    And up the greensward legions lead ;
Come near, O sun—O south wind, blow !

Are these the skies we used to know,
    The budding wood, the fresh-blown mead ?
Where are the springs of long ago ?

The breathing furrow will we sow,
    And patient wait the patient seed ;
Come near, O sun—O south wind, blow !

The grain of vanished years will grow,
    But not the vanished years, indeed !
Where are the springs of long ago ?

With sodden leafage, lying low,
    They for remembrance faintly plead !
Come near, O sun—O south wind, blow !
Where are the springs of long ago ?

EDITH M. THOMAS.

VILLANELLE.

(To Hesperus, after Bion.)

O jewel of the deep blue night !
    Too soon, to-day, the moon arose,
I pray thee, lend thy lovely light.

Than any other star more bright
    An hundred-fold, thy beauty glows,
O jewel of the deep blue night.

Too soon Selene gained the height,
    And now no more her glory shows ;
I pray thee, lend *thy* lovely light.

Anon our revel of delight
    Towards the shepherd's dwelling goes,
O jewel of the deep blue night !

And I must lead the dance aright,
    Yea—even I—for me they chose :
I pray thee, lend thy lovely light.

No thief am I, nor evil wight,
    Nor numbered with the traveller's foes,
O jewel of the deep blue night !

None would I spoil, nor e'en affright,
    Mine are the Lover's joys and woes ;
I pray thee, lend thy lovely light.

For good it is, in all men's sight
    (Thou knowest well) to favour those,
O jewel of the deep blue night !

Thy golden lamp hath turned to white
    The silver of the olive-close ;
O jewel of the deep blue night !
I pray thee, lend thy lovely light.

GRAHAM R. TOMSON.

VILLANELLE.

"I did not dream that Love would stay.
    I deemed him but a passing guest,
Yet here he lingers many a day.

I said young Love will flee with May
    And leave forlorn the hearth he blest,"
I did not dream that Love would stay.

My envious neighbour mocks me, "Nay,
    Love lies not long in any nest."
Yet here he lingers many a day.

And though I did his will alway,
    And gave him even of my best,
I did not dream that Love would stay.

I have no skill to bid him stay,
    Of tripping tongue or cunning jest,
Yet here he lingers many a day.

Beneath his ivory feet I lay
    Pale plumage of the ringdove's breast,
I did not dream that Love would stay.

Will Love be flown ?   I ofttimes say,
    Home turning for the noonday rest,
Yet here he lingers many a day.

His gold curls gleam, his lips are gay,
    His eyes through tears smile loveliest ;
I did not dream that Love would stay.

He sometimes sighs, when far away
    The low red sun makes fair the west,
Yet here he lingers many a day.

Thrice blest of all men am I ! yea,
    Although of all unworthiest ;
I did not dream that Love would stay,
Yet here he lingers many a day.

GRAHAM R. TOMSON.

274

VILLANELLE.

Come ! to the woods, love, let us go !
    Let us go pluck the purple flowers,
And rest where rosy blossoms blow.

'Twixt glade and shade the sun shall throw
    A halo round the laughing hours ;—
Come ! to the woods, love, let us go !

There are dim nooks the Dryads know,
    And we can hide in hawthorn-bowers,
And rest where rosy blossoms blow.

Shall not the fairies passing strow
    On us the dainty petal-showers?
Come ! to the woods, love, let us go.

And we will roam by rills that flow
    'Neath skies from which no tempest lowers ;
We'll rest where rosy blossoms blow.

Come, heart ! Come, sweetheart, even so
    Life's holiest rapture shall be ours ;—
Come ! to the woods, love, let us go,
And rest where rosy blossoms blow.

SAMUEL WADDINGTON.

THEOCRITUS.

O Singer of Persephone !
   In the dim meadows desolate,
Dost thou remember Sicily ?

Still through the ivy flits the bee
   Where Amaryllis lies in state ;
O Singer of Persephone !

Simætha calls on Hecate,
   And hears the wild dogs at the gate ;
Dost thou remember Sicily ?

Still by the light and laughing sea
   Poor Polypheme bemoans his fate ;
O Singer of Persephone !

And still in boyish rivalry
   Young Daphnis challenges his mate ;
Dost thou remember Sicily ?

Slim Lacon keeps a goat for thee ;
   For thee the jocund shepherds wait ;
O Singer of Persephone !
Dost thou remember Sicily ?

OSCAR WILDE.

SPRING SADNESS.

(Virelai.)

As I sat sorrowing,
Love came and bade me sing
    A joyous song and meet,
For see (said he) each thing
Is merry for the Spring,
    And every bird doth greet
The break of blossoming,
That all the woodlands ring
    Unto the young hours' feet.

Wherefore put off defeat
And rouse thee to repeat
    The chimes of merles that go,
With flutings shrill and sweet,
In every green retreat,
    The tune of streams that flow
And mark the fair hours' beat,
With running ripples fleet
    And breezes soft and low.

For who should have, I trow,
Such joyance in the glow
    And gladness of the May,—
In all sweet bells that blow,
In death of winter's woe
    And birth of Springtide gay,
When in woodwalk and row
Hand-linked the lovers go,—
    As he to whom alway

God giveth day by day
To set to roundelay
    Life's sad and sunny hours,—
To weave into a lay
Life's golden years and grey,
    Its sweet and bitter flowers,—
To sweep with hands that stray
In many a devious way
    Its harp of sun and showers?

Nor in this life of ours,
Whereon the sky oft lowers,
    Is any lovelier thing
Than in the wild wood bowers
The cloud of green that towers,
    The blithe birds welcoming
The vivid vernal hours
Among the painted flowers
    And all the pomp of Spring.

True, life is on the wing,
And all the birds that sing,
    And all the flowers that be
Amid the glow and ring,
The pomp and glittering
    Of Spring's sweet pageantry,
Have here small sojourning,
And all our bright hours bring
    Death nearer, as they flee.

Yet this thing learn of me ;
The sweet hours fair and free
    That we have had of yore,
The fair things we did see
The linkéd melody
    Of waves upon the shore
That rippled in their glee,
Are not lost utterly,
    Though they return no more.

But in the true heart's core
Thought treasures evermore
    The tune of birds and breeze :
And there the slow years store
The flowers our dead Springs wore
    And scent of blossomed leas :
There murmurs o'er and o'er
The sound of woodlands hoar
    With newly burgeoned trees.

So for the sad soul's ease
Remembrance treasures these
    Against Time's harvesting,
That so, when mild Death frees
The soul from Life's disease
    Of strife and sorrowing,
In glass of memories
The new hope looks and sees
    Through Death a brighter Spring.

JOHN PAYNE.

JULY.

(VIRELAI NOUVEAU.)

Good-bye to the Town !—good-bye !
Hurrah ! for the sea and the sky !

In the street the flower-girls cry ;
In the street the water-carts ply ;
And a fluter, with features a-wry,
Plays fitfully, " Scots, wha hae "—
And the throat of that fluter is dry ;
Good-bye to the Town !—good-bye !

And over the roof-tops nigh
Comes a waft like a dream of the May ;
And a lady-bird lit on my tie ;
And a cock-chafer came with the tray ;
And a butterfly (no one knows why)
Mistook my Aunt's cap for a spray ;
And " next door " and " over the way "
The neighbours take wing and fly :
Hurrah ! for the sea and the sky !

To Buxton, the waters to try,—
To Buxton goes old Mrs. Bligh ;
And the Captain to Homburg and play
Will carry his cane and his eye ;
And even Miss Morgan Lefay
Is flitting—to far Peckham Rye ;
And my Grocer has gone—in a " Shay,"
And my Tailor has gone—in a " Fly ;"—
Good-bye to the Town !—good-bye !

And it's O for the sea and the sky !
And it's O for the boat and the bay !
For the white foam whirling by,
And the sharp, salt edge of the spray !
For the wharf where the black nets fry,
And the wrack and the oarweed sway !
For the stroll when the moon is high
To the nook by the Flag-house gray !
For the *risus ab angulo* shy
From the Some-one we designate "Di !"
For the moment of silence,—the sigh !
" How I *dote* on a Moon !" "So do I !"
For the token we snatch on the sly
(With nobody there to say Fie !)
Hurrah ! for the sea and the sky !

So Phillis, the fawn-footed, hie
For a bansom.   Ere close of the day
Between us a " world " must lie,—
Good-bye to the Town !—GOOD-BYE !
Hurrah ! for the sea and the sky !

AUSTIN DOBSON.

Burlesques, Pasquinades, etc.,
in Ballade, Chant Royal, Rondeau,
and Villanelle forms.

If an apology seem needful for the presence of this section,
this quotation will explain why it was included :—

*" We maintain that far from converting virtue into a paradox,
and degrading truth by ridicule, Parody will only strike at what
is chimerical and false; it is not a piece of buffoonery so much
as a critical exposition."*

ISAAC D'ISRAELI.

THE BALLADE OF THE SUMMER-BOARDER.

Let all men living on earth take heed,
    For their own souls' sake, to a rhyme well meant ;
Writ so that he who runs may read—
    We are the folk that a-summering went.
    Who while the year was young were bent—
Yea, bent on doing this self-same thing
    Which we have done unto some extent.
This is the end of our summering.

We are the folk who would fain be freed
    From wasteful burdens of rate and rent—
From the vampire agents' ravening breed—
    We are the folk that a-summering went.
    We hied us forth when the summer was blent
With the fresh faint sweetness of dying spring,
    A-seeking the meadows dew-besprent
This is the end of our summering.

For O the waiters that must be fee'd,
    And our meat-time neighbour, the travelling "gent; "
And the youth next door with the ophicleide !
    We are the folk that a-summering went !
    Who from small bare rooms wherein we were pent,
While birds their way to the southward wing,
    Come back, our money for no good spent—
This is the end of our summering.

Envoy.

Citizens ! list to our sore lament—
    While the landlord's hands to our raiment cling—
We are the folk that a-summering went :
    This is the end of our summering.

H. C. Bunner.

A YOUNG POET'S ADVICE.

(A Ballade.)

You should study the bards of to-day
    Who in England are now all the rage ;
You should try to be piquant and gay :
    Your lines are too solemn and sage.
    You should try to fill only a page,
Or two at the most with your lay ;
    And revive the quaint verse of an age
That is fading forgotten away.

Study Lang, Gosse, and Dobson, I pray—
    That their rhymes and their fancies engage
Your thought to be witty as they.
    You must stand on the popular stage.
    In the bars of an old fashioned cage
We must prison the birds of our May,
    To carol the notes of an age
That is fading forgotten away.

Now this is a ' Ballade '—I say,
    So one stanza more to our page,
But the " Vers de Société,'
    If you can are the best for your ' wage.'
    Though the purists may fall in a rage
That two rhymes go thrice in one lay,
    You may passably echo an age
That is fading forgotten away.

Envoy.

Bard—heed not the seer and the sage,
    ' Afflatus ' and Nature don't pay ;
But stick to the forms of an age
    That is fading forgotten away.

C. P. CRANCH.

A BALLAD OF OLD METRES.

When, in the merry realm of France,
    Bluff Francis ruled and loved and laughed,
Now held the lists with knightly lance,
    Anon the knightly beaker quaffed ;
    Where wit could wing his keenest shaft
With Villon's verse or Montaigne's prose,
    Then poets exercised their craft
In ballades, triolets, rondeaux.

O quaint old times ! O fitting chants !
    With fluttering banners fore and aft,
With mirth of minstrelsy and dance,
    Sped Poesy's enchanted craft ;
    The odorous gale was blowing abaft
Her silken sails, as on she goes,
    Doth still to us faint echoes waft
Of ballades, triolets, rondeaux.

But tell me with what countenance
    Ye seek on modern rhymes to graft
Those tender shoots of old Romance—
    Romance that now is only chaffed ?
    O iron days ! O idle raft
Of rhymesters ! they are ' *peu de chose*,'
    What Scott would call supremely " saft "
Your ballades, triolets, rondeaux.

Envoy.

Bards, in whose vein the maddening draught
    Of Hippocrene so wildly glows,
Forbear, and do not drive us daft
    With ballades, triolets, rondeaux.

The Century.

BALLADE OF CRICKET.

(To T. W. Lang.)

The burden of hard hitting : slog away !
    Here shalt thou make a " five " and there a " four,"
And then upon thy bat shalt lean and say,
    That thou art in for an uncommon score.
    Yea, the loud ring applauding thee shall roar,
And thou to rival THORNTON shalt aspire,
    When low, the Umpire gives thee " leg before,"—
" This is the end of every man's desire ! "

The burden of much bowling, when the stay
    Of all thy team is " collared," swift or slower,
When " bailers " break not in their wonted way,
    And " yorkers " come not off as heretofore.
    When length balls shoot no more, ah never more,
When all deliveries lose their former fire,
    When bats seem broader than the broad barn-door,—
" This is the end of every man's desire ! "

The burden of long fielding, when the clay
    Clings to thy shoon in sudden showers downpour,
And running still thou stumblest, or the ray
    Of blazing suns doth bite and burn thee sore,
    And blind thee till, forgetful of thy lore,
Thou dost most mournfully misjudge a " skyer '
    And lose a match the Fates cannot restore,—
" This is the end of every man's desire ! "

Envoy.

    Alas, yet liefer on youth's hither shore
Would I be some poor Player on scant hire
    Than king among the old who play no more,—
" *This* is the end of every man's desire !

ANDREW LANG.

THE PRODIGALS.

(Dedicated to Mr. Chaplin, M.P., and Mr. Richard Power, M.P.
and 223 who followed them.)

Ministers !—you, most serious,
    Critics and statesmen of all degrees,
Hearken awhile to the motion of us,—
    Senators keen for the Epsom breeze !
    Nothing we ask of posts or fees ;
Worry us not with objections pray !
    Lo,—for the speakers wig we seize—
Give us—ah ! give us—the Derby Day.

Scots most prudent, penurious !
    Irishmen busy as humblebees !
Hearken awhile to the motion of us,—
    Senators keen for the Epsom breeze !
    For Sir Joseph's sake, and his owner's, please !
(Solomon raced like fun, they say)
    Lo for we beg on our bended knees,—
Give us—ah ! give us—the Derby Day.

Campbell—Asheton be generous !   [cheese)
    (But they voted such things were not the
Sullivan, hear us, magnanimous !
    (But Sullivan thought with their enemies.)
    And shortly they got both of help and ease
For a mad majority crowded to say—
    " Debate we've drunk to the dregs and lees ;
Give us—ah ! give us—the Derby Day."

Envoi.

Prince, most just was the motion of these
    And many were seen by the dusty way,
Shouting glad to the Epsom breeze
    Give us—ah ! give us—the Derby Day.
        ANONYMOUS *(after Austin Dobson).*

VILLON'S STRAIGHT TIP TO ALL CROSS COVES.

"Tout aux tavernes et aux filles."

Suppose you screeve? or go cheap-jack?
  Or fake the broads? or fig a nag?
Or thimble-rig? or knap a yack?
  Or pitch a snide? or smash a rag?
  Suppose you duff? or nose and lag?
Or get the straight, and land your pot?
  How do you melt the multy swag?
Booze and the blowens cop the lot.

Fiddle, or fence, or mace, or mack;
  Or moskeneer, or flash the drag;
Dead-lurk a crib, or do a crack;
  Pad with a slang, or chuck a fag;
  Bonnet, or tout, or mump and gag;
Rattle the tats, or mark the spot;
  You can not bank a single stag;
Booze and the blowens cop the lot.

Suppose you try a different tack,
  And on the square you flash your flag?
At penny-a-lining make your whack,
  Or with the mummers mug and gag?
  For nix, for nix the dibbs you bag!
At any graft, no matter what,
  Your merry goblins soon stravag:
Booze and the blowens cop the lot.

THE MORAL.

It's up the spout and Charley Wag
With wipes and tickers and what not.
  Until the squeezer nips your scrag,
Booze and the blowens cop the lot.

W. E. HENLEY.

A BALLADE OF BALLADE-MONGERS.

(After the manner of Master FRANCOIS VILLON of Paris.)

In *Ballades* things always contrive to get lost,
  And Echo is constantly asking where
Are last year's roses and last year's frost?
  And where are the fashions we used to wear?
  And what is a " gentleman," what is a " player?"
Irrelevant questions I like to ask :
  Can you reap the *tret* as well as the *tare?*
And who was the Man in the Iron Mask?

What has become of the ring I tossed
  In the lap of my mistress, false and fair?
Her grave is green and her tombstone mossed ;
  But who is to be the next Lord Mayor,
  And where is King William of Leicester Square?
And who has emptied my hunting flask?
  And who is possessed of Stella's hair?
And who was the Man in the Iron Mask?

And what has become of the knee I crossed,
  And the rod, and the child they would not spare?
And what will a dozen herring cost
  When herring are sold at threehalfpence a pair?
  And what in the world is the Golden Stair?
Did Diogenes die in a tub or a cask,
  Like Clarence for love of liquor there?
And who was the Man in the Iron Mask?

Envoy.

Poets, your readers have much to bear,
  For *Ballade*-making is no great task.
If you do not remember, I don't much care
  Who was the Man in the Iron Mask.

281   AUGUSTUS M. MOORE.

ON NEWPORT BEACH.
(Rondeau.)

On Newport beach there ran right merrily,
In dainty navy blue clothed to the knee,
  Thence to the foot in white *au naturel*,
  A little maid. Fair was she, truth to tell,
As Oceanus' child Callirrhoë.
In the soft sand lay one small shell, its wee
Keen scallops tinct with faint hues, such as be
  In girlish cheeks. In some old storm it fell
    On Newport Beach.

There was a bather of the species *he*,
Who saw the little maid go toward the sea ;
  Rushing to help her through the billowy swell,
  He set his sole upon the little shell,
And heaped profanely phraséd obloquy
    On Newport Beach.

     H. C. BUNNER.

CULTURE IN THE SLUMS.
(Inscribed to an Intense Poet.)
I. RONDEAU.

" O crikey, Bill !" she ses to me, she ses.
  "Look sharp," ses she, " with them there sossiges.
Yea ! sharp with them there bags of mysteree !
For lo !" she ses, "for lo ! old pal," ses she,
  " I'm blooming peckish, neither more nor less."

Was it not prime—I leave you all to guess
How prime !——to have a jude in love's distress
  Come spooning round, and murmuring balmilee,
    " O crikey, Bill !"

For in such rorty wise doth Love express
His blooming views, and asks for your address,
  And makes it right, and does the gay and free.
  I kissed her—I did so ! And her and me
Was pals. And if that ain't good business,
    O crikey, Bill !

II. VILLANELLE.

Now ain't they utterly too-too
 (She ses, my Missus mine,* ses she),
Them flymy little bits of Blue.

Joe, just you kool 'em—nice and skew
 Upon our old meogginee,
Now ain't they utterly too-too?

They're better than a pot'n' a screw,
 They're equal to a Sunday spree,
Them flymy little bits of Blue!

Suppose I put 'em up the flue,
 And booze the profits, Joe?   Not me.
Now ain't they utterly too-too?

I do the 'Igh Art fake, I do.
 Joe, I'm consummate; and I *see*
Them flymy little bits of Blue.

Which, Joe, is why I ses te you—
 Æsthetic-like, and limp, and free—
Now *ain't* they utterly too-too,
Them flymy little bits of Blue?

* An adaptation of " Madonna mia."

III. BALLADE.

I often does a quiet read
    At Booty Shelly's* poetry ;
I thinks that Swinburne at a screed
    Is really almost too-too fly ;
    At Signor Vagna's† harmony
I likes a merry little flutter ;
    I've had at Pater many a shy ;
In fact, my form's the Bloomin' Utter.

My mark's a tidy little feed,
    And 'Enery Irving's gallery,
To see old 'Amlick do a bleed,
    And Ellen Terry on the die,
    Or Franky's ghostes at hi-spy,‡
And parties carried on a shutter.§
    Them vulgar Coupeaus is my eye !
In fact, my form's the Bloomin' Utter.

The Grosvenor's nuts—it is, indeed !
    I goes for 'Olman 'Unt like pie.
It's equal to a friendly lead
    To see B. Jones's judes go by.
    Stanhope he makes me fit to cry.
Whistler he makes me melt like butter.
    Strudwick he makes me flash my cly—
In fact, my form's the Bloomin' Utter.

Envoy.

    I'm on for any Art that's 'Igh ;
I talks as quite as I can splutter ;
    I keeps a Dado on the sly ;
In fact, my form's the Bloomin' Utter !

W. E. HENLEY.

* Probably Botticelli.
† Wagner (?)
‡ This seems to be a reference to *The Corsican Brothers.*
§ *Richard III.* (?)

THE STREET SINGER.

(Villanelle from my window.)

He stands at the kerb and sings.
    'Tis a doleful tune and slow,
Ah me, if I had but wings !

He bends to the coin one flings,
    But he never attempts to go,—
He stands at the kerb and sings.

The conjurer comes with his rings,
    And the Punch-and-Judy show.
Ah me, if I had but wings !

They pass like all fugitive things—
    They fade and they pass, but lo !
He stands at the kerb and sings.

All the magic that Music brings
    Is lost when he mangles it so—
Ah me, if I had but wings !

But the worst is a thought that stings !
    There is nothing at hand to throw !
He stands at the kerb and sings—
Ah me, if I had but wings !

AUSTIN DOBSON.

MALAPROPOS.

(Rondeau.)

Imitated from the French of Count Anthony Hamilton.

Malàpropos do English wits revive
    The Rondeau, which our beauties hear with scorn ;
Hide in an extinct form a heart alive,
And woo bright lasses, whom they wish to wive,
    Malàpropos, with Gaulish verse outworn.

    More fondly would these rosebuds of the morn
Unfold to airs—gay, playful, amative—
Even Astrophel five phrases would contrive—
                Malàpropos.

O dazzling youth, to fashion's follies sworn,
Would you their breasts with love's sweet pains were
    torn ?
Rondeau and Ballade to the Devil drive ;
Use honest English when for them you strive,
Since never to their hearts would thus arrive—
                Malàpropos.

            G. H. (*In " The Lute."*)

BEHOLD THE DEEDS !

(Chant Royal.)

[Being the Plaint of Adolphe Culpepper Ferguson, Salesman
of Fancy Notions, held in durance of his Landlady for a failure
to connect on Saturday night.]

I.

I would that all men my hard case might know ;
    How grievously I suffer for no sin :
I, Adolphe Culpepper Ferguson, for lo !
    I, of my landlady am lockéd in,

For being short on this sad Saturday,
Nor having shekels of silver wherewith to pay;
   She has turned and is departed with my key;
   Wherefore, not even as other boarders free,
      I sing (as prisoners to their dungeon stones
   When for ten days they expiate a spree):
      Behold the deeds that are done of Mrs. Jones!

II.

   One night and one day have I wept my woe;
      Nor wot I when the morrow doth begin,
   If I shall have to write to Briggs & Co.,
      To pray them to advance the requisite tin
For ransom of their salesman, that he may
Go forth as other boarders go alway——
   As those I hear now flocking from their tea,
   Led by the daughter of my landlady
      Piano-ward.   This day for all my moans,
   Dry bread and water have been servéd me.
      Behold the deeds that are done of Mrs. Jones!

III.

   Miss Amabel Jones is musical, and so
      The heart of the young he-boardér doth win,
Playing " The Maiden's Prayer," *adagio*—
      That fetcheth him, as fetcheth the banco skin
The innocent rustic.   For my part, I pray:
That Badarjewska maid may wait for aye
   Ere sits she with a lover, as did we
   Once sit together, Amabel! Can it be
      That all that arduous wooing not atones
   For Saturday shortness of trade dollars three?
      Behold the deeds that are done of Mrs. Jones!

IV.

Yea! she forgets the arm was wont to go
    Around her waist.   She wears a buckle whose
      pin
Galleth the crook of the young man's elbów;
    I forget not, for I that youth have been.
Smith was aforetime the Lothario gay.
Yet once, I mind me, Smith was forced to stay
    Close in his room.   Not calm, as I, was he;
    But his noise brought no pleasaunce, verily.
      Small ease he gat of playing on the bones,
Or hammering on his stove-pipe, that I see.
      Behold the deeds that are done of Mrs. Jones!

V.

Thou, for whose fear the figurative crow
    I eat, accursed be thou and all thy kin!
Thee will I show up—yea, up will I shew
    Thy too thick buckwheats, and thy tea too thin.
Ay! here I dare thee, ready for the fray!
Thou dost *not* " keep a first-class house," I say!
    It does not with the advertisements agree.
    Thou lodgest a Briton with a puggaree,
      And thou hast harboured Jacobses and Cohns,
Also a Mulligan.   Thus denounce I thee!
      Behold the deeds that are done of Mrs. Jones!

Envoy.

Boarders! the worst I have not told to ye:
She hath stolen my trousers, that I may not flee
    Privily by the window.   Hence these groans,
There is no fleeing in a *robe de nuit.*
      Behold the deeds that are done of Mrs. Jones!

H. C. Bunner.

THE CANTERBURY POETS.

EDITED BY WILLIAM SHARP.   1/- VOLS., SQUARE 8VO.
PHOTOGRAVURE EDITION, 2/-.

Christian Year.
Coleridge.
Longfellow.
Campbell.
Shelley.
Wordsworth.
Blake.
Whittier.
Poe.
Chatterton.
Burns. Poems.
Burns. Songs.
Marlowe.
Keats.
Herbert.
Victor Hugo.
Cowper.
Shakespeare: Songs, etc.
Emerson.
Sonnets of this Century.
Whitman.
Scott. Marmion, etc.
Scott. Lady of the Lake, etc.
Praed.
Hogg.
Goldsmith.
Mackay's Love Letters.
Spenser.
Children of the Poets.
Ben Jonson.
Byron (2 Vols.).
Sonnets of Europe.
Allan Ramsay.
Sydney Dobell.
Pope.
Heine.
Beaumont and Fletcher.
Bowles, Lamb, etc.
Sea Music.
Early English Poetry.
Herrick.
Ballades and Rondeaus.

Irish Minstrelsy.
Milton's Paradise Lost.
Jacobite Ballads.
Australian Ballads.
Moore's Poems.
Border Ballads.
Song-Tide.
Odes of Horace.
Ossian.
Fairy Music.
Southey.
Chaucer.
Golden Treasury.
Poems of Wild Life.
Paradise Regained.
Crabbe.
Dora Greenwell.
Goethe's Faust.
American Sonnets.
Landor's Poems.
Greek Anthology.
Hunt and Hood.
Humorous Poems.
Lytton's Plays.
Great Odes.
Owen Meredith's Poems.
Imitation of Christ.
Toby's Birthday Book.
Painter-Poets.
Women-Poets.
Love Lyrics.
American Humor. Verse.
Scottish Minor Poets.
Cavalier Lyrists.
German Ballads.
Songs of Beranger.
Poems by Roden Noel.
Songs of Freedom.
Canadian Poems.
Modern Scottish Poets.
Poems of Nature.
Cradle Songs.

London : WALTER SCOTT, LIMITED, Paternoster Square.

THE SCOTT LIBRARY.

Cloth, uncut edges, gilt top.   Price 1/6 per volume.

ALREADY ISSUED.

Romance of King Arthur.

Thoreau's Walden.

Thoreau's Week.

Thoreau's Essays.

Confessions of an English
Opium-Eater.

Landor's Conversations.

Plutarch's Lives.

Browne's Religio Medici.

Essays and Letters of
P. B. Shelley.

Prose Writings of Swift.

My Study Windows.

Lowell's Essays on the
English Poets.

The Biglow Papers.

Great English Painters.

Lord Byron's Letters.

Essays by Leigh Hunt.

Longfellow's Prose.

Great Musical Composers

Marcus Aurelius.

Epictetus.

Seneca's Morals.

Whitman's Specimen
Days in America.

Whitman's Democratic
Vistas.

White's Natural History.

Captain Singleton.

Essays by Mazzini.

Prose Writings of Heine.

Reynolds' Discourses.

The Lover: Papers of
Steele and Addison.

Burns's Letters.

Volsunga Saga.

Sartor Resartus.

Writings of Emerson.

Life of Lord Herbert.

English Prose.
The Pillars of Society.
Fairy and Folk Tales.
Essays of Dr. Johnson.
Essays of Wm. Hazlitt.
Landor's Pentameron, &c.
Poe's Tales and Essays
Vicar of Wakefield.
Political Orations.
Holmes's Autocrat.
Holmes's Poet.
Holmes's Professor.
Chesterfield's Letters.
Stories from Carleton.
Jane Eyre.
Elizabethan England.
Davis's Writings.
Spence's Anecdotes.
More's Utopia.
Sadi's Gulistan.
English Folk Tales.
Northern Studies.
Famous Reviews.
Aristotle's Ethics.
Landor's Aspasia.
Tacitus.
Essays of Elia.
Balzac.
De Musset's Comedies.
Darwin's Coral-Reefs.

Sheridan's Plays.
Our Village.
Humphrey's Clock, &c.
Tales from Wonderland.
Douglas Jerrold.
Rights of Woman.
Athenian Oracle.
Essays of Sainte-Beuve.
Selections from Plato.
Heine's Travel Sketches.
Maid of Orleans.
Sydney Smith.
The New Spirit.
Marvellous Adventures.
  (From he Morte d'Arthur.)
Helps's Essays.
Montaigne's Essays.
Luck of Barry Lyndon.
William Tell.
Carlyle's German Essays.
Lamb's Essays.
Wordsworth's Prose.
Leopardi's Dialogues.
Inspector-General (Gogol)
Bacon's Essays.
Prose of Milton.
Plato's Republic.
Passages from Froissart.
Prose of Coleridge.
Heine in Art and Letters.
Essays of De Quincey.

LIBRARY OF HUMOUR.

Cloth Elegant, Large Crown 8vo.   Price 3/6 each.

VOLUMES ALREADY ISSUED.

THE HUMOUR OF FRANCE. Translated, with an Introduction and Notes, by Elizabeth Lee. With numerous Illustrations by Paul Frénzeny.

THE HUMOUR OF GERMANY. Translated, with an Introduction and Notes, by Hans Müller-Casenov. With numerous Illustrations by C. E. Brock.

THE HUMOUR OF ITALY. Translated, with an Introduction and Notes, by A. Werner. With 50 Illustrations by Arturo Faldi.

THE HUMOUR OF AMERICA. Edited, with an Introduction and Notes, by J. Barr (of the *Detroit Free Press*). With numerous Illustrations by C. E. Brock.

THE HUMOUR OF HOLLAND. Translated, with an Introduction and Notes, by A. Werner. With numerous Illustrations by Dudley Hardy.

THE HUMOUR OF IRELAND. Selected by D. J. O'Donoghue. With numerous Illustrations by Oliver Paque.

THE HUMOUR OF SPAIN. Translated, with an Introduction and Notes, by S. Taylor. With numerous Illustrations by H. R. Millar.

THE HUMOUR OF RUSSIA. Translated, with Notes, by E. L. Boole, and an Introduction by Stepniak. With 50 Illustrations by Paul Frénzeny.

IN PREPARATION.

THE HUMOUR OF JAPAN. Translated, with an Introduction, by A. M. With Illustrations by George Bigot (from Drawings made in Japan).

London: WALTER SCOTT, LIMITED, Paternoster Square.

BOOKS OF FAIRY TALES.

Crown 8vo, Cloth Elegant, Price 3s. 6d. per vol.

ENGLISH FAIRY AND OTHER FOLK TALES.

Selected and Edited, with an Introduction,
By EDWIN SIDNEY HARTLAND.

With 12 Full-Page Illustrations by CHARLES E. BROCK.

SCOTTISH FAIRY AND FOLK TALES.

Selected and Edited, with an Introduction,
By SIR GEORGE DOUGLAS, BART.

With 12 Full-Page Illustrations by JAMES TORRANCE.

IRISH FAIRY AND FOLK TALES.

Selected and Edited, with an Introduction,
By W. B. YEATS.

With 12 Full-Page Illustrations by JAMES TORRANCE.

London: WALTER SCOTT, LIMITED, Paternoster Square.